Advance praise for INTERROGATING (HI)STORIES

"This brilliantly constructed historiographical study of the middle grades is as much an intellectual tour de force as a deeply committed moral and political call for action. Adolescents in the middle grades are in a critical period of transition between childhood and adulthood. Our dominant culture tends to ignore or deny matters of spirit within the context of adolescent development. It may 'tolerate' childhood spiritual sensibilities of awe and wonder, tenderness, wholeheartedness, reverie, and 'unruly' imagination that roams freely in the largeness of the world and cosmos; but not for long. The usual assumption seems to be that children have to be weaned off these 'childish' experiences as soon as possible so that they can take up the adult-sized responsibility of entering the industrial workforce. The result is the current culture of massive alienation, isolation, and anomie. The young folks become—and we collectively have become—existentially wounded at our core, and profoundly insecure. Audrey Lingley's book is both a critical guide to understanding the neglect of spirit in the middle grades and a call for political action that centrally involves educational reform in North America in order to restore humanity. As Lingley puts it incisively, 'oppressive political systems depend upon participants who are not aware of each other's essential humanity. An education that explicitly addresses student (and teacher) spirituality is not as much an ethical issue, therefore, as it is a political one.' Palms together to Lingley in gratitude and solidarity!"

—Heesoon Bai, Professor, Philosophy of Education, Simon Fraser University;
Co-editor, *Contemplative Learning and Inquiry Across Disciplines*

"This pioneering volume brings to light for examination and understanding the domain of spiritual development that has, regrettably, been overlooked in formulating developmentally responsive education, particularly the middle school concept. Bypassing this dimension of learning is undoubtedly a major reason why public education has come to serve the mind, in its narrowest sense, almost exclusively while rarely serving the heart and soul. Every serious professional middle level educator should read, reflect on, and, indeed, study this fascinating, scholarly, and significantly important research-based work."

—John H. Lounsbury, Dean Emeritus, John H. Lounsbury College of Education,
Georgia College; Author, *A Curriculum for the Middle School Years*

"Research dealing with spirituality, as opposed to religion, is disturbingly absent from the teacher education literature. The spiritual development of students is too important to be dispensed out of existence like a tissue dropped in the principal's wastepaper basket; it needs to be taken seriously in any discussion of student development and learning. Audrey Lingley's keen scholarship reveals that there is much to be gained in utilizing historiography as a mode of inquiry into spiritual development since it illuminates how power is productively deployed through the process of knowledge creation in varied and entangled contexts. Lingley makes a convincing case for the creation of meaning as both a hermeneutic and spiritual engagement, and that to antiseptically cleave spiritual development from discussions of intelligibility is to do so at our own peril. Written in the venerable tradition of holistic education, *Interrogating (Hi)stories* offers a vibrant new lens through which the needs, interests, and abilities of students can be met."

—Peter McLaren, Distinguished Professor in Critical Studies,
Chapman University; Author, *Life in Schools*

"*Interrogating (Hi)stories* is a timely and important work in which Audrey Lingley articulates the relevance of spiritual development in the middle grades. She utilizes hermeneutics to explore this underdeveloped area with the goal of establishing a critical framework for a spiritually responsive pedagogy. Such a framework will not only enhance the student's learning experience but, most importantly, will ground teaching and learning in caring relationships. With its focus on the centrality of spirituality in human development, this is a book that should be read by anyone involved in education at any level."

—Deborah Orr, Associate Professor, Humanities Department, York University;
Founder and Editor, Mindfulness and Contemplative Education
virtual commons, www.contemplativeeducation.ca

"Audrey Lingley's vision for a new conceptual landscape of middle grades education is deeply provocative! In establishing the centrality of spiritual/holistic development in adolescence she unearths a clear path to meaningful inquiry. Lingley's relentless advocacy for critical historiography as an important method unveils a host of intellectual borders now made porous and inviting for interdisciplinary work. *Interrogating (Hi)stories* is a must-read for any student of qualitative research. It is meticulously researched and engagingly written. Lingley walks you through her passion for history, knowledge production, and commitment to critical pedagogy, making no apologies, towards creating a sense of belonging for youth."

—Leila E. Villaverde, Associate Professor, Department of Educational Leadership
and Cultural Foundations, The University of North Carolina, Greensboro;
Editor, *The International Journal of Critical Pedagogy*

INTERROGATING
(HI)STORIES

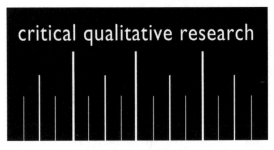

critical qualitative research

CRITICAL ISSUES FOR LEARNING AND TEACHING

Shirley R. Steinberg and Gaile S. Cannella
General Editors

Vol. 12

The Critical Qualitative Research series
is part of the Peter Lang Education list.
Every volume is peer reviewed and meets
the highest quality standards for content and production.

PETER LANG
New York • Washington, D.C./Baltimore • Bern
Frankfurt • Berlin • Brussels • Vienna • Oxford

Audrey Lingley

INTERROGATING (HI)STORIES

Establishing the Educational Relevance of Spiritual Development Through Critical Historiography

PETER LANG
New York • Washington, D.C./Baltimore • Bern
Frankfurt • Berlin • Brussels • Vienna • Oxford

Library of Congress Cataloging-in-Publication Data
Lingley, Audrey.
Interrogating (hi)stories: establishing the educational relevance of
spiritual development through critical historiography / Audrey Lingley.
pages cm. — (Critical qualitative research; vol. 12)
Includes bibliographical references.
1. Education—Research—Methodology. 2. Middle school education—Research.
3. Historiography. 4. Holistic education. 5. Critical pedagogy. I. Title.
LB1028.L48 370.72—dc23 2014000837
ISBN 978-1-4331-2523-2 (hardcover)
ISBN 978-1-4331-2522-5 (paperback)
ISBN 978-1-4539-1310-9 (e-book)
ISSN 1947-5993

Bibliographic information published by **Die Deutsche Nationalbibliothek**.
Die Deutsche Nationalbibliothek lists this publication in the "Deutsche
Nationalbibliografie"; detailed bibliographic data is available
on the Internet at http://dnb.d-nb.de/.

The paper in this book meets the guidelines for permanence and durability
of the Committee on Production Guidelines for Book Longevity
of the Council of Library Resources.

© 2014 Peter Lang Publishing, Inc., New York
29 Broadway, 18th floor, New York, NY 10006
www.peterlang.com

Printed in the United States of America

Dedicated to

Dr. Karen Noordhoff,
*who models embodied scholarship
and courage in the world.*

Table of Contents

Foreword

Once an event, an utterance, a flutter of a bird's wing happens.... It's gone.

As the avatars modernist education molds us to be, we've been schooled to be consumers and proclaimers of history, philosophy, culture, and truth. Some of the education we were programed with is pretty good. And we become moderately educated individuals. In fact, we become professors, scholars, recorders, and writers of more history, philosophy, culture, and truth. I contend that while many of us are often taught "critical" thinking, inventive ways to *think deeper,* sometimes even to *deconstruct,* our learning (how we are educated) skirts the surface. I don't know what type of statistic I would need to triangulate my observation, but I'd be glad to wager my first born (with his agreement, of course) that the notion of informed research fails to investigate the etymology, the essence, the historiographical essence of an event, an utterance, nor a flutter of a bird's wing. We are often historiographically ignorant, spiritually devoid of the depth to which any incident, consequence, or breath takes place. Indeed, it is the interrogation of *taking place* which historiography interrogates...taking place—the occurrence, and investigating how the taking place came to be, and...asking: Who recorded it? Why was it recorded? How was it recorded? What is the relevance? What structures were in place to enact the recording (Kincheloe, 1991)?

Audrey Lingley's uniquely crafted volume, *Interrogating (Hi)stories: Establishing the Educational Relevance of Spiritual Development Through Critical Historiography* challenges scholars and students to revisit the construction of their knowledges and to create a personal paradigm with which to humanize, understand the taking of place, and to interrogate the spiritual relevance of a critical historiography. Other than the latter sentence being wordy, possibly run-on, it is the crux on which the point of this book hangs: Critical Historiography is a time-travel, which *takes the researcher, the knowledge seeker to the time **before** an occurrence.* This journey is filled with an agenda to textually fill in the gaps of the knowledge, which precedes the actual artifact/event. And this agenda is intellectual, it is political, and it is spiritual.

Without going into philosophical esoteric speak, I'll mention one of my favorite historiographical/spiritual anecdotes, avoiding the obligatory citations; as we all know, one can check it out on *Wikipedia,* the ultimate a-historiographical "reference" tool in a simulacra-contrived research barren, dare I say, postmodern world. Sometime in the first century after what is known as the Christian Era, a Jew, a historian, Josephus, was commissioned by Titus, the son of the Roman emperor, to write a history of the Jews. Josephus devoted his life to his commission. In fact, two millennia later, the history(ies) of the Jewish people are often drawn from Josephus' voluminous works. When we search the books for the history and life of the man called Jesus, we find only 16 lines out of this 8-volume tome. The life of Jesus is historicized by the royal court's historian in these 16 lines. More space was given to discussing the life of a man called James, the brother of Jesus. Josephus eventually was granted Roman citizenship for his services (Steinberg, 2008).

So what critical historiographical layers are smoldering under near-vanished historical ashes? This short reference to Jesus in Josephus' *history* of the Jews is a sobering realization of just how "accurate" anything called *history* can be. My research persona relates to the personal first, even when involved in scholarship. One must consider that the words, deeds, and history attributed to this being, Jesus, converted, occupied, manipulated, conquered, murdered, and molded much of an entire planet for over two thousand years, and the effects, the *history* of this being, are imprinted in a metaphorical *History of the Earth*. What could explain a fervor so fierce that billions of humans have devoted their lives to these 16 lines from an 8-volume set of books, written surely, by an informed historian, devoted to speaking *the truth?*

Historiography insists that we interrogate not the event, but the recording of the event, who recorded it, how, and why. Critical historiography pushes us further to the ever-suspicious questioning of how power served in the creation of the history. In the case of Josephus, we must ask: Why did Titus want a "history" of the Jews? Why was Josephus selected? How was Josephus instructed?

What was *left out* of this history? Why were references to Jesus so brief, as compared to the rest of the history? Why would Josephus, a Jew, take this commission? Why would he accept Roman citizenship? What powers were behind this entire undertaking?

Critical historiography reminds us that there are no certainties, guarantees, witnesses, nor accuracies in the retelling of a possible historical event. Indeed, questioning whether or not the event ever occurred underpins the criticality of our investigation (Kincheloe, 2001). This doesn't discount the importance of attempts to record the past, but creates a healthy tentativeness, which informs our understanding of *how knowledge is created, how people learn, and how "truths" are born* (Kincheloe & Steinberg, 1993). Critical interrogation and suspicion should not be taken as cynical, but as rigorous research. Audrey Lingley accomplishes just that in this compelling and unique book.

Shirley R. Steinberg

References

Kincheloe, J. L. (1991). Educational historiographical meta-analysis: Rethinking methodology in the 1990s. *Qualitative Studies in Education, 4*(3), 231–245.

Kincheloe, J. L. (2001). Describing the Bricolage: Conceptualizing a new rigor in qualitative research. *Qualitative Inquiry, 7*(6), 679–692.

Kincheloe, J. L., & Steinberg, S. R. (1993). A tentative description of post-formal thinking: The critical confrontation with cognitive theory. *Harvard Educational Review, 63*(3), 296–321.

Steinberg, S. R. (2008). *Christotainment: Selling Jesus through popular culture.* Boulder, CO: Westview Press.

Shirley R. Steinberg is Research Chair and Professor of Youth Studies, and Director of The Werklund Foundation Centre for Youth Studies Education at the University of Calgary, Alberta, Canada.

Acknowledgments

In the spring of 2013, I was browsing the Peter Lang booth at AERA in San Francisco when I saw on the counter a business card for Shirley Steinberg. Her name had been on my mind, as I had recently completed a major research project that, in design and spirit, was an homage to her late partner, Joe Kincheloe. During my research design process, I had looked up Kincheloe, a scholar whose work I was increasingly falling in love with the more I read. I discovered he had died a few years before, and read an obituary that described what a vibrant and joyful presence he had been in his various communities of practice. He was sorely missed by many after his unexpected passing. I intended to write Shirley, as Joe's proxy, a note of acknowledgment of and gratitude for his life and work. I delayed contact, however, out of a combination of shyness and the pressing nature of the daily demands borne of parenting, teaching, writing, and self-care.

Standing at the Peter Lang booth on that April afternoon, I asked the young man behind the counter if Shirley Steinberg was present. He pointed to a table a few feet away, and for a moment, I was stunned to realize I had the opportunity to thank her in person. When I tentatively approached her, I inquired, "Excuse me, but are you the Shirley Steinberg who was married to Joe Kincheloe?" She straightened right up, growing a full foot in the process, and pronounced, "I AM married to Joe Kincheloe." And I knew in that moment my shy hesitation was unwarranted; she would understand why I wanted to convey my deep appreciation for the man who mentored me, in spirit, through a complex and transformative research process.

Thank you Joe Kincheloe, for leaving behind such a rich and authentic body of scholarship for those of us who seek to promote educational experiences grounded in compassion, justice, love, and empowerment for all students. Consider this work a deep bow in your memory. Thank you Shirley Steinberg for encouraging me to make my own contribution through this book and for offering me the most powerful endorsement I could hope for by including *Interrogating (Hi)stories* in the Critical Qualitative Research Series.

Sophie Appel, Stephen Mazur, and Chris Myers at Peter Lang offered generous guidance during the production process, and I am indebted to them for their kindness and clarity. Amy Botula read an early draft of the manuscript, and offered essential feedback from her experiences as a high school English teacher, journalism advisor, writer, and advocate for adolescent learners.

I am incredibly fortunate to be part of an academic community of peers with whom I share intellectual intimacy. The hearts and minds of Bernd Ferner, Sarah Lundy, Edgar Solares, Katie Toppel, and Jennifer Wells are present in this work, and I am grateful to them for their steadfast support and confidence. This book grew from my dissertation research at Portland State University. I wish to acknowledge the important contributions of the members of my committee—Micki M. Caskey, Samuel Henry, Yves Labissiere, Dot McElhone, and Karen Noordhoff (chair)—who provided me with extensive feedback and wisdom during my time as a doctoral student. I am grateful for their leadership and for shepherding a process that was imbued with trust, respect, and joy. I am especially in debt to Karen Noordhoff, to whom this book is dedicated, for her academic career as a scholar of spiritual integrity. Olivia Murray and Dilafruz Williams offer friendship and compassionate solidarity, and I am grateful for their presence in my life at PSU.

Finally, I thank my husband, Jon Emens, and our daughters, Lucy and Maya, for our life together as a family. My work has integrity because of the strong bonds of our family.

Audrey Lingley
January, 2014

Introduction

Different images of the same landscape enable us to see different possibilities, different relationships, and perhaps enable us to imagine new phenomena in that educational landscape. A new image must be articulated or described so others can move within the landscape as they did in the past, but with greater freedom and new awareness of their choices and limitations. (Huebner, 1999, p. 404)

Critical historiography in educational research is a unique and highly effective methodology for interrogating beliefs, assumptions, and values treated as normal or natural as a means of challenging dominant pedagogy and opening up space for new visions of educational practice. One of the empowering aspects of critical constructivism—the researcher paradigm that guides critical historiography—is its commitment to theory explicitly situated in classroom practice. Critical historiography offers an authentic and transformative methodology for exploring and discussing theory and practice in ways that serve both academics and practitioners. By blurring the hierarchical lines between scholars and teachers while still maintaining rigorous standards for research, critical historiography is an exemplar of critical research.

However, as a research methodology in education, critical historiography is neither common nor well-understood. Doctoral programs in the fields of education (e.g., curriculum and instruction, leadership, and policy) typically categorize research methods courses into two camps: quantitative and qualitative. Historiographical techniques may draw from those two categories, but as a method of scholarly inquiry, it is distinct in terms of purpose, design, and results. One of the challenges of advocating for critical historiography in educational research is use of the term *critical historiography* does not make things clearer for (most) audiences, certainly in education. That is one of the main purposes of this book: to offer greater clarity to the principles and the suggested techniques of critical historiography.

To demonstrate the method in action, I offer a research project on the relevance of spiritual development in middle grades reform. Issues of purpose, design, and results are addressed in descriptive language and through the example of critical historiographical research into the landscape of middle grades reform. The project used to illustrate the opportunities and challenges facing critical historiography in education was conducted as dissertation research for a doctoral degree in Educational Leadership at a public university in the Pacific Northwest region of the United States. The chapters within serve as a guide for emerging and established scholars who are using or curious about using critical research methodology.

While one of the book's purposes is to serve as an instructional reference for educational researchers, the depth and complexity of critical historiography is revealed through a thick description of my research on the relevance of young adolescent spiritual development in middle grades education. Middle grades education is frequently overshadowed in the larger field of K–12 education. The academic needs, interests, and abilities of young adolescents are often not adequately addressed through policies, instruction, and school organization that view middle school students as either older elementary students or "junior" high school students. In the United States, a glaring example of the inconspicuousness of middle grades students and educators is reflected in the title of the federal legislation that funds public education: the Elementary and Secondary Education Act (ESEA). Over the last 50 years, middle grades advocates in the United States have called for education that is developmentally responsive to *young adolescence* as a distinct period of human development. Because of its potential to strengthen aspects of the reform recommendations that promote belonging for young adolescents in their school context, the research described in this book is useful for middle grades scholars and advocates, holistic educators, and educational psychologists.

In the following chapters, I describe in detail the principles and strategies for critical historiography in educational research. The first chapter unpacks critical constructivism through an analysis of how I rendered the politics of the relevance of spiritual development in education, a reconstruction of the pathways to choosing critical historiography as a methodology, and a summary of the principles of critical constructivism as they relate to critical historiography. Chapters Two and Three provide background and further discussion on the problem I identified in the field of middle grades reform: the absence of explicit pedagogical knowledge of the spiritual domain of human development. For readers interested more in the topic of my research than the methodology, those two chapters supply a framing of the topic through a review of the main perspectives of middle grades educators, developmental psychologists, and holistic educators. In keeping with the deeply interdisciplinary nature of this research, I present the perspectives within a conceptual framework of significant interrelationships amongst the fields.

For readers more interested in the specifics of critical historiography, I suggest skimming Chapters Two and Three in order to have sufficient background with which to contextualize my discussion of the research process and results in Chapters Four, Five, Six, and Seven. Chapter Eight offers implications of the results for practice in middle grades education and educational research. These conclusions and implications would be of interest to readers of all backgrounds and roles in the fields of middle grades education and educational research. I conclude this book with a call for a new framework for scholars and K–12 practitioners: spiritually responsive pedagogy.

Huebner's (1999) vision of the importance of "different images" cited at the beginning of this introduction reflects my main metaphor for critical historiographical research. In this work, I am not merely deconstructing the canon of middle grades reform philosophy for the sake of pointing out its political, cultural, and social deficiencies as seen through a critical analysis. Deconstruction through a de-centering of the subject has its place in educational research, but from my perspective as a classroom teacher and administrator, what good is a stack of criticisms as I prepare my colleagues and myself to serve the needs, interests, and abilities of our middle grades students? What most energizes me about critical historiography is its role in facilitating knowledge creation accessible for classroom practice. The beloved idea of developmentally responsive middle grades education, a.k.a. the same landscape, is re-created in the form of a different image.

Chapter One

Critical Constructivist Research in Education

Perceiving the Politics of Spirituality in Education

THE historical exclusion of the spiritual dimension of learning and human growth from dominant pedagogy in many Western, State-sponsored educational systems is rooted in the maintenance of political, economic, and social worldviews that allow for the continued oppression of marginalized populations. A pedagogy that renders spirituality and spiritual growth as irrelevant to the learning process requires that both teachers and students cultivate images of Self and Other as fragmented, therefore facilitating the self-suppression of compassion, wonder, tolerance for ambiguity, and a sense of interconnection. Oppressive political systems depend upon participants who are not aware of each other's essential humanity. An education that explicitly addresses student (and teacher) spirituality is not as much an ethical issue, therefore, as it is a political one.

My purpose in the research described in this text is to articulate the educational relevance of the spiritual development of middle grades students as a curriculum and instruction issue as a counter-narrative to the secularization of public school education in the United States. Relevance implies legitimacy; in this research, I establish a clear understanding about the legitimacy of addressing student spiritual development in the context of public schooling. Advocates of middle grades reform in the United States argue that curriculum and instruction—as well as leadership, organization, and community relationships—should be informed by knowledge of the developmental characteristics of 10- to 15-year-olds within physical, social, emotional, psychological, cognitive, and moral domains. Noticeably absent from their conception of human development are spiritual developmental characteristics of young adolescents.

In the West, explicit incorporation of spirituality enjoys relative acceptance in private, parochial, and homeschool settings (Benami, 2006; Revell, 2008); therefore, I situate my work within the public school context in the United States. Also, given the ways in which I perceive the absence of spiritual development from the authoritative literature on middle grades education, my target audience for this research is educators and advocates who directly reach a wider swath of young adolescents; namely, public school educators.

Given my perspective that the inconspicuous absence was an intentional oversight with political undertones, I chose critical historiography (Villaverde, Kincheloe, & Helyar, 2006) to investigate the absence of spiritual development from the middle grades education. In the design of my research, I was guided by the work of Kincheloe on critical constructivism (2008) and interdisciplinary research (2001, 2005) as well as Popkewitz's (1991) theory of social epistemologies. I used a guiding question, What is the educational relevance of spiritual development in middle grades education? I also employed two subquestions to focus my analysis strategies:

1. What prevalent paradigms underlie the academic discourse on spirituality as a developmental domain, the middle grades concept, and holistic education?
2. What are the inter-textual and inter-discursive relationships within the convergence of the paradigms of the three fields?

In Chapters Four and Five, I describe in detail key features of critical historiography as a method and in this research. For now, my discussion centers on how one's research purpose is related to critical historiography as a methodology in educational research.

My overarching research purpose was to understand more explicitly the educational relevance of spiritual development, specifically as a curriculum and instructional issue in the middle grades. I was also motivated by the following purposes: (a) to understand how the inclusion of spirituality as a domain in early adolescent developmental theory manifests in teacher practice; (b) to situate spirituality as a developmental domain within a developmentally responsive pedagogical framework; and (c) to understand how practicing teachers perceive the educational relevance of spirituality. I used a review of the relevant academic literature to assimilate the theoretical perspectives about spiritual development in education and to determine how educational researchers and developmental psychologists researched questions analogous to my research purposes.

The lack of research literature on the educational relevance of spiritual development in education in general, and regarding spiritual development at the middle grades in particular, is well-documented (Roehlkepartain et al., 2006). In addition to cultural and political resistance for locating spirituality within education, another contributing factor is the challenge associated with using established research methodologies to study spirituality in education (Benson, 2004, 2006; Borgman, 2006). Benson articulated the central quandary experienced by developmental psychologists: "As a developmental concept, what part of human development are we addressing with the adjective spiritual?" (p. 485). An additional methodological challenge is designing research that is culturally-sensitive to take into account the socio-cultural effects on spiritual development (Nicholas & DeSilva, 2008). Despite these challenges, a growing body of empirical literature on spirituality in education exists (e.g., Warren, Lerner, & Phelps, 2012; Stoyles, Stanford, Caputi, Keating, & Hyde, 2012). In the spiritual development research literature I read from the developmental sciences, the following principles are reflected: (a) spiritual development research should be conducted in collaboration with practitioners; (b) quantitative methodologies are preferred over qualitative ones; (c) operationalizing what is meant by spiritual development is a challenge; and (d) spiritual development research methodology must be culturally responsive. While there is a growing body of research on spiritual development in non-Christian contexts (e.g., Sallquist, Eisenberg, French, Purwono, & Suryanti, 2010) historically, the theory and research base has been within Christian contexts.

In a review of the research conducted on spirituality and education, the issue of relevance is foregrounded in introductory and concluding remarks with an explicit defense of spirituality's inclusion in the field. Spiritual development's standing as a legitimate area of research centered around three rationale: (a) improving teacher practice and effectiveness (Benami, 2006; Fraser, 2007); by (b) reducing students' experience of alienation and personal fragmentation (Long, 2008; Pearmain, 2005; Revell, 2008); and (c) increasing access points to the academic curriculum (Belousa, 2006; Cottingham, 2005; Deakin Crick & Jelfs, 2011; Leopold & Juniu, 2008). The research literature on spirituality as a developmental domain and spirituality in an educational context highlights the definitional, measurement, and validity challenges of empirical research in these two areas. This literature also illustrates the need for additional research as a means of more skillfully situating spirituality as an educational concern.

The findings of this review of the body of work on spiritual development as an educational issue suggested that teachers and students are aware of its relevance. The results also suggested that the aspects of spiritual development found particularly relevant by teachers and students are: cultivating a sense of interconnectedness; developing coping strategies; relating to something greater than self (transcendence); and exploring personal ways of making meaning. For example, in Revell (2008), the participants (28 teachers and principals) viewed responding to the spiritual development of their students as a form of "counter-narrative" (p. 111) to the alienating aspects of being a young person in the United States. In other words, the educators in this study frame the relevance question as one that is situated in a particular social, political, and economic context—and in that specific context, they view spirituality as a critical component of formal schooling.

In contemplating the body of research conducted within the related fields, I detected an absence of a rigorous interrogation of the interrelationship between human development theories, middle grades education, and spirituality/spiritual development. I read literature that addressed each of those three fields independently, but none that explored (theoretically or empirically) the conceptual space between and among the three academic fields.

Noting the absence of such literature, I became curious along critical (McLaren, 2009) lines of inquiry. I explored my curiosity by posing hunch-inspired questions that led, eventually, to my research questions. I wondered: What social and/or political factors contribute to this absence in the literature? Who benefits from a developmentally-based model of middle grades education that neglects the spiritual domain of development? Who benefits from a model of human development that does not include spirituality? Who is harmed through this omission in theory and practice? Historically, what has led to this absence? What has led me to imagine a middle grades concept that explicitly incorporates the spiritual domain?

While exploring these questions, I reflected upon how my cultural identity influences my choice of research questions and methodology. As an upper/middle class White female teacher, I am an insider in the field of education. I take for granted many practices in education, such as the dominance of critical rational epistemologies and positivist research methodologies, because they align with the values, perspectives, and assumptions of my cultural and economic background. These practices are invisible to me, and I am less likely to interrogate them because they seem natural and normal. Yet, as Rury (2006) argued, new interpretive stances in educational research are important because they offer different ways of thinking about and practicing education.

Pathways to Research Design

In the course of designing this research, I was influenced by my review of the literature, as well as preparations for a teacher training I volunteered to conduct in Nepal. In this section, I describe how both experiences influenced my research design, and conclude by connecting my professional/personal background with my decision to use critical historiography.

During the months I was reviewing the literature, I discerned research methods that reflected academic approval in the field of education such as statistical analysis (e.g., Muijs, 2011), case study (e.g., Yin, 2009), and ethnography (e.g., Wolcott, 2008). I read histories of spirituality as an educational concern (e.g., Miller, 1997), but none of the educational researchers I reviewed had employed historiography as a method for studying the relevance of spiritual development in education.

Although I did not encounter Kincheloe's (2008) *Critical Constructivism* until I began to read more deeply on critical historiography as a research methodology, this quotation from his chapter on research describes my stance during the literature review: "Critical constructivism openly attempts to subvert the researcher's perception of her stable location in the web of reality" (p. 120). As an attempt to subvert my perception, I volunteered as a teacher trainer in Nepal during the summer of 2011. I partnered with an NGO run by Nepali teachers and administrators. My hope was that being an outsider in another country's educational system would allow me to become aware of new approaches to conceptualizing and researching spirituality in U.S. education. I chose Nepal intentionally, a nation without the same kind of cultural distinctions between secular and spiritual human activities that are made in the United States.

The initial stages of my turn from field-based research methods (such as grounded theory and case study) toward a conceptual methodology of research began during my preparations for Nepal. As I sought to co-construct professional development curriculum that would be relevant and desirable to the Nepali teachers, I used historical (e.g., Lohani, Singh, & Lohani, 2010) and historiographical literature (e.g., Carney & Bista, 2009) on educational reform in Nepal to inform the curriculum design and instructional strategies. The literature was helpful not only in terms of providing historical background, but also in terms of identifying prominent paradigms that influenced educational policy and practice in Nepal. Knowing more about guiding paradigms proved essential to my professional work as an educator in Nepal because that knowledge equipped me with some keys to understanding unfamiliar interactional dynamics. For example, during the teacher training I experienced confusing interactions with my male co-facilitator and with male workshop participants. Knowledge of prevalent paradigms influencing the importance of male authority in Hindu

Nepali families and the related concept of teacher as guru, or spiritual guide, helped me negotiate those interactions.

Returning to my doctoral work, I wrestled with imposing field-based research methods on my research purposes. I recalled the utility of historiographical approaches to inquiry as a means of providing me with the kind of clarity that contributed to the effectiveness of my professional interactions in Nepal. Encountering Popkewitz's (1997) metaphor of scaffolding as a means of conducting historiography helped me to understand the potential of conceptual research methods for this study:

> My traveling among different sets of ideas is to think of them as part of a scaffolding, to think of them as a grid or overlay of historically formed ideas, whose pattern gives intelligibility to today's debates. (p.18)

My "different sets of ideas" is the gathering of holistic education, spiritual development, and the middle grades concept. I was looking for any pattern that is created when I laid their historiographies over each other in the hopes that doing so would "give intelligibility to today's debates."

The work represented in this research is a result of almost 20 years of reflective practice as a classroom teacher, administrator, and emergent scholar. Five years into my teaching career, I began to notice how a personal mindfulness meditation practice was having a positive effect on my professional practice. I observed in myself more ease, more joy, and an increased ability to respond effectively to the challenges of working with young adolescent learners. Because I conceive of meditation as a spiritual practice, I became curious about how the spiritual development of a teacher affects her professional performance. Later in my career as an administrator in a middle grades school, I also became interested in the study of how a teacher's knowledge of adolescent developmental issues affects student learning. As I saw less distinction between my personal and professional identities, my work as an educator came from a less fragmented orientation, and my students and colleagues seemed the better for it. The works of hooks (1994, 2003), Palmer (1998), Bateson (1994), Mezirow (2000), Miller (2007), and Kessler (2000) shaped and informed how I conceptualize the relationship between spirituality as a developmental domain and the implementation of the middle grades concept.

The connection between how the personal experiences of teachers are woven into the fabric of their professional pedagogy is one that has been explored before (Palmer, 1998). My work differs from Palmer's (1998) in that I situate human developmental theory within the dynamic between the personal and professional aspects of teaching. My positionality is well-expressed by Nakkula and Toshalis (2006), whose work on the middle grades concept includes a rare reference to students' inner lives:

> A constructionist perspective argues that people work with one another in creating development...development is conceived of as fundamentally relational. [This approach] is intended to help educators recognize how their own development, professional and personal, is affected by their relationships with students....From this perspective, the core meaning of adolescent development lies fundamentally in the interpretations adolescents make of themselves and their worlds. It argues that the meaning they make of their experience is theirs, and that we as educators can play key roles in the meaning youth make of their lives, just as they can play that role in the meaning we make of ours. (pp. x–xi)

I have an earned respect for the courage, confusion, and curiosity of students who are 10 to 15 years old. My hope is that this research offers both an increased awareness of the inner resources students have always possessed and a direction for middle grades teachers who understand and value the inner life.

My experiences as a student and as an educator supported my use of critical historiography as a dissertation research method. In fact, my professional and academic backgrounds were essential for my success in designing a dissertation research project that used unconventional methods. I faced the challenge of convincing a trusting yet skeptical dissertation committee that my status as an emergent researcher would not handicap the outcome of my research. There was no one on my committee who had extensive experience with critical historiography in educational research.

Critical historiography complements my own positionality regarding the social construction of written history. As someone who was educated in history and historical methods in the poststructural era of the 1980s and 1990s and who has taught middle and high school level history classes since 1994, I approach the study of history as a highly complex, socially mediated endeavor regulated by power relations. Also, my approach aligns with the critical historiographical privileging of the interrelationship between past, present, and future. I agree wholeheartedly that a critical knowledge of the past can empower and mobilize transformative action for a more just and equitable future (Villaverde, Kincheloe, & Helyar, 2006). My support of such a position has been one of the motivating forces for my work as an educator with adolescents, a group I have found to be delightfully ambitious in their quest for justice and fairness.

I have long believed that how people understand current challenges and victories strongly shapes how history is constructed and transmitted (e.g., Henry, 2006). Perhaps this is especially true in education (e.g., Rury, 2006), where contemporary policy discussions reframe or ignore past reform movements in an effort to persuade the public of the necessity of the most current reform policy. Kaestle (1997) argued for the connection between contemporary perspectives and historical writing in his historiography of education history. Although Kaestle is not writing from a critical perspective, his conclusion about the value of historiography as a method in educational research affirms my researcher's goal of transformative collective and individual empowerment.

And so, I chose critical historiography as a result of the alignment between the method and: (a) the purpose of my research; (b) the conclusion drawn from a review of the related literature; (c) a positive experience with applying historiographical knowledge with teaching practice; and (d) my academic background.

Principles of Critical Constructivism

Critical historiography embodies the conceptual credo of critical constructivism, an epistemological and ontological framework for re-envisioning teaching and learning in school contexts (Kincheloe, 2008). Drawing from constructivism and critical theory, critical constructivism supports a self-reflective pathway to emancipatory teaching and learning. Critical constructivist reflection involves a rigorous interrogation of the assumptions and worldviews that determine our interpretations of knowledge, curriculum, learners, and the purpose of school. A hearty tolerance for ambiguity; a fierce commitment to the voices of marginalized students, families, and educators; and an appreciation for the complex dynamics of teaching and learning in schools are core qualities of critical constructivist educators.

Therefore, I characterize my researcher paradigm as critical constructivist. The central concepts of critical constructivism drive some of the main characteristics of critical historiography. Kincheloe (2008)—whose text *Critical Constructivism* is a useful primer for scholars, teacher educators, and K–12 teachers—summarizes the critical constructivist research process in the following passage:

> When it comes to analysis of the construction of self or the nature of texts, critical constructivists are aware of the discursive practices in which self or text is embedded and the context in which self or text operates. Whether one is attempting to make sense of a novelist, an interviewee or a historical manuscript, discourse and context are central dimensions of the act of knowledge construction. (p. 148)

By "discursive practices," Kincheloe (2008) is referring to the rules, typically tacit, which regulate all aspects of knowledge production and replication in schools: whose knowledge is considered legitimate, who must be listened to, and who must listen (p. 36). Becoming aware of these rules is a necessary process for developing a critical consciousness as an educator.

Kincheloe's (2008) work on critical constructivism expands constructivist learning theory to include critical theory. By merging critical theory with constructivism, Kincheloe articulates a bridge between a teacher's knowledge of learning theory and her *praxis* (Freire, 1993). Guba's (1990) description of the critical theory paradigm in relation to research practice is germane here, as my application of critical historiography used paradigms as units of analysis:

Because they are human constructions, paradigms reflect the values of their human constructors (p. 23)....If values *do* enter into every inquiry, then the question immediately arises as to what values and whose values shall govern. If the findings of studies can vary depending on the values chosen, then the choice of a *particular* value system tends to empower and enfranchise certain persons while disempowering and disenfranchising others. (p. 24)

By viewing paradigms as reflective of values, critical researchers interpret the ways certain values are privileged over others. My hunch, as I designed a research project that investigated the absence of spiritual development in middle grades literature, was that this absence had political and social roots. The roots manifested as discursive practices regulating the supposed inappropriateness of tending to spirituality in public schools in the United States.

I chose a critical constructivist lens to explore this conjecture because it is an interpretive lens that foregrounds deployment of power and knowledge. An implication of a critical constructivist lens, as suggested by Guba (1990) and Kincheloe (2008), is that the *findings* of any study depend upon the values privileged by the researcher's interpretive lens. I embraced the term findings to describe the results of my research on the critical historiography of the relevance of spiritual development in developmentally responsive middle grades education, but my usage reflects Guba's subjectivist meaning as opposed to a positivist connotation of the term. I do not use the term findings to suggest that, as a result of this research, I have found something that existed before I gave expression to its existence. The results of this work are very much a construction of knowledge rendered from systematic, trustworthy inquiry. The results also reflect the historical and cultural contexts within which I framed an initial research, designed a course of study, and re-presented my findings. Results of a critical historiography are recognized as one vantage point among many potential and actual perspectives. The position of research results vis-à-vis the field of educational research depends on their relation to the historical and political contexts within which they are produced and disseminated.

Hermeneutics is a key component of the critical constructivist researcher paradigm, as well as of historiographical inquiry. In keeping with the subjectivist notion that results are not "found" as if they existed disengaged from the seeker, the act of interpretation is ongoing through the critical historiographical research process. In my description of my specific research methods, I outline in more detail how I applied hermeneutics as a research technique through, for example, constant-comparative analysis and memo-writing.

The constructivist aspect of the critical constructivist researcher paradigm, as described by Guba (1990), is reflected by the belief that any specific knowledge is one possible outcome of a multiplicity of interactions, grounded in tacit or explicit epistemological and ontological assumptions. In research that reflects a constructivist paradigm, Guba (1990) counsels, "The constructivist proceeds in ways that aim to identify the variety of constructions that exist..." (p. 26). Critical historiography epitomizes the constructivist process by denaturalizing the assumptions or paradigms scaffolding knowledge in schools, then weaving in critical theory to call out the ways in which such knowledge is trapped within a web of historical and political forces. For critical constructivists, the way in which a story is told is as relevant as the story itself. Critical historiography offers critical researchers a methodology for interrogating how the stories are told.

Contrasting critical constructivist methods with positivist ones, Kincheloe (2008) highlighted the main deficiencies of positivist research:

> Here, knowledge production is reduced to a notion of rigor that relies exclusively on fidelity to the scientific method. Thus, knowledge production is no longer an act of insight, contextual analysis, intuition and creative brilliances as much as it is a procedure. Critical constructivists demand something more. (p. 102)

The "more" that Kincheloe referred to is a powerful personal practice of re-engaging one's whole self with the processes of research, teaching, and learning. In the act of choosing to stay fully present with the discomfort of challenging hegemonic (and often subtle) rules of educational research and classroom practice, as well as facing one's own privilege and oppression, the critical constructivist scholar brings forth a wellspring of hope, passion, joy, and peace available to herself and those in her communities of practice.

Critical Historiography in Educational Research

Within the humanities, historiography is the study of the writing of history and written histories. It is distinguished from the actual writing of history in most of the definitional literature (e.g., Burke, 2001). However, in some cases, a secondary definition involves historiography as the writing of history as well (*Oxford Dictionary of English*, 2011). The blending of the two activities is a reflection of the 'new' history of the last half of the 20th century, a perspective on historical inquiry that incorporates techniques previously associated with historiography such as cultural relativism (Burke, 2001).

The distinction between studying the writing of history and the act of writing history is relevant to an accurate understanding of critical historiography. For example, in my research, I was not attempting to construct a history of spiritual development as a curricular and instructional issue in the middle grades. My research purpose was to better understand the educational relevance of spiritual development as it relates to the core principles of the middle grades concept of developmentally responsive education. And so, one of the focal activities was a critical analysis of *how* the (hi)stories of the related fields, middle grades education, spirituality as a developmental domain, and holistic education *were told*, rather than an descriptive analysis of the content of the histories of the three fields. A historiographical approach allows the researcher to interpret and interrogate the ways in which academic fields have been constructed. I refer to these constructions as *(hi)stories*.

The focus of a historiographical analysis is ideas, assumptions, values, beliefs, and worldviews of the historian-author, although precise definitions of historiography are influenced by academic discipline. For example, sociologists describe studying historiography as studying "the methodological (including epistemological) questions raised by the writing of historical accounts" (Scott & Marshall, 2009). Critical theorists emphasize the constructed, socially and politically mediated nature of the writing of history; for them, historiography "refers to the interpretation and articulation of those events" (Buchanan, 2010). In both examples, however, the writing of history is viewed from a hermeneutic perspective in which the subject of historical accounts is de-centered (Foucault, 1973; Kuhn, 1996). The interpretive process of de-centering the subject in an educational context shifts the act of data analysis from the knowledge (i.e., the curriculum, developmental theories, pedagogical perspectives) to the formation of that knowledge. From a critical constructivist perspective, de-centering the subject is especially important in education, where power and knowledge work together to protect hegemonic interests (Popkewitz & Brennan, 1998).

So, historiography as a research method reflects a constructivist epistemology (subjectivist) and ontology (relativist). Critical historiography is distinct as a type of historiography characterized by its stance of inquiry as a political act (Villaverde, Kincheloe, & Helyar, 2006). Similar to Foucault's genealogy, a critical historiography explores "[academic] discipline as a discursive system within arbitrary and exclusive boundaries" (Kincheloe, 2001, p. 684).

To illustrate the practice of historiography, we can look at a historiography of cuisine (Smith, 2003). Such an account examines: (a) the ways in which food preparation has been recorded through out time (from recipes to thematic cookbooks to scholarly journals); (b) the various research methodologies (content analysis, recipe re-enactment); and (c) the evolution of research purposes (from inventorying cookbooks to studying how food reflects socioeconomic relationships). In a historiographical inquiry, questions of methodological rigor and researcher trustworthiness arise. For example, in the first half of the 20th century, the Americans used imprecise and informal strategies for researching cuisine, whereas, the British established a variety of conceptual frameworks and methodologies within which to study food and drink. A historiographical account of the history of cuisine ends by situating the study of cuisine as its own field of academic inquiry as well as its inclusion in other more established fields such as global history and sociology. A historiography is an interpretation of what was problematized, the types of research questions asked, the kinds of methods used to investigate the problems, and the worldview(s) reflected in the conclusions drawn. In the previous example, cuisine is not the subject of the historiography; the subject of inquiry is the (constructed) *history* of cuisine, with its attendant researchers and methodologies.

Kaestle's (1997) historiographical account of the history of education in the United States is also a useful example to explore, for his account models some of the key techniques of critical historiography. He begins by justifying his use of this method: "beliefs about the historical role of schooling in America are encountered everyday as arguments for educational policies" (Kaestle, 1997, p. 75). He identifies and interprets paradigms (Kuhn, 1996) that guided the writing of the history of education in the United States. He searched for indirect evidence of the paradigms by interpreting the assumptions (his term; they could also be characterized as values) held by historians, and categorizing those assumptions.

He used analytical categories to describe different historical stances. Applying a genealogical analysis (Foucault, 1973) to Kaestle's (1997) work, his categorization of historical stances generated a discursive construct of ideas about education, as illustrated by the labels Kaestle chose for the analytical categories. Kaestle divided the history of education into two analytical categories: traditional education history, a period he locates in the first half of the 20th century, and revisionist educational history, which took hold in the 1960s. With the literature/data in my research on the relevance of spirituality in middle grades education, I used the same kind of historiographical approach Kaestle used with his analytical categorization. I view categorization as both a communication strategy and a productive deployment of power (Popkewitz & Brennan, 1998): "a political as well as an intellectual strategy for disrupting that knowledge/power relation through making visible and open to resistance the systems of ideas that construct the subject" (p. 20). This description of the research design is not the place to critique the binary implied by Kaestle's (1997) analytical categories of "traditional" and "revisionist." My point is to call attention to the effects of and the intentionality behind analytical categories in historiographical study.

Kaestle (1997) interpreted categories of the assumptions/values held by educational histories. He used those categories as indirect evidence of paradigms (beliefs) that guided educational policies, practices, and research. In Kaestle's analysis, "traditional" educational historians wrote from the following assumptions/values: (a) education is public, formal schooling; (b) education promotes democracy and freedom; (c) more education is better; and (d) historical evidence comes from educational leaders and institutions, not practitioners and students. Kaestle interpreted two strands of "revisionism" in the writing of education history. One strand expands upon the activities and forms included in the term education. A second strand critiques the previously unquestioned assumption that educational leaders acted as promoters of freedom and democracy. In his historiographical approach, Kaestle interrogated *how* the history of education has been written and constructed a narrative of his findings. In doing so, he identified the positionality of the historians, the types of sources used in the creation of written histories, the socio-political contexts in which history is constructed, and the worldviews privileged in those (hi)stories.

For the critical constructivist researcher, the goals of historiography align with key underlying ideas of critical constructivism: (a) knowledge is created by people in historical and social contexts embedded in multilayered interactions; (b) claims for legitimate or relevant knowledge in education mislead practitioners and policymakers by veiling the deeply cultural-historical (i.e., subjective) process of knowledge construction; and (c) educational research must reflect/reveal the complexity and diversity of the teaching-learning processes through an unveiling of ways in which teachers-learners co-construct shared knowledge within educational systems that privilege some and marginalize others (Kincheloe, 2008). Critical historiography, as a research methodology in educational research, has great potential for critical researchers. This potential can perhaps be realized through a more explicit understanding of the principles and techniques of the method. The aim of this text is to provide a deeper understanding, through a transparent account of a critical historiographical study of the educational relevance of spiritual development.

Chapter Two

Caring as Advocacy in the Middle Grades

IN the field of middle grades education, pedagogical emphasis has been on designing and implementing practices referred to as developmentally appropriate for students between the ages of 10 and 15 years (e.g., Alexander, Williams, Compton, Hines, & Prescott, 1968). This emphasis is known as the *middle grades concept.* Among other recommendations, caring relationships that provide support and foster belonging are valued as developmentally responsive. In the most prestigious literature on the middle grades reform efforts, caring is linked with the terminology of advocacy, as in, middle grades teachers advocate for their young adolescent students through a culture of caring (NMSA, 2010).

In aligning specific practices with early adolescent developmental theory, much of the literature describes the characteristic developmental traits for the cognitive, social, emotional, psychological, physical, and moral domains (e.g., Caskey & Anfara, 2007; Roeser, Eccles, & Sameroff, 2000; Van Hoose, Strahan, & L'Esperance, 2001). In the middle grades literature, the spiritual domain of human development is not referenced. An implication of this absence is that middle grades teachers and administrators are less prepared than they could be to holistically respond to the needs, interests, and abilities of young adolescents. Given the primacy of caring as a developmentally responsive practice with middle grades students, this absence of a central affective developmental domain is striking. From a critical constructivist perspective, the omission suggests the relationship between power and knowledge construction within the field of middle grades education.

Making the connection between power and knowledge production part of how I frame the problem for my research had implications for the methodology I chose to investigate the problem of this omission of spiritual development from the middle grades concept. The background information presented in this chapter and the next is useful for the reader's understanding of the context within which a critical historiography was chosen. In this chapter, I describe the academic context (i.e., the main literature in the field of middle grades reform) in which I designed a critical historiographical study, including the significance of the problem I identified. This description of middle grades reform is not meant to be an exhaustive review of the literature on middle grades education. Rather, I use it to introduce and explain how human development theories have influenced and informed what is considered to be exemplary middle school practice—the middle grades concept of developmentally appropriate education.

Value of Including the Spiritual Domain

Before portraying the features of middle grades reform efforts in the late 20th century, I describe the potential for a more holistic vision of a developmentally responsive education for young adolescents. This is an appropriate place for me to also explain how I define spirituality and spiritual development, in the context of this research.

Defining spirituality and spiritual development. In the United States, the Establishment Clause of the federal Constitution prohibits public institutions from supporting religious activities. So, for many in the United States, questions of legitimacy immediately arise when faced with the notion of spirituality as a matter of educational relevance. As constructs, spirituality and religion may overlap, but they are not identical.

Defining spirituality is a task fraught with complexity, nuance, and diplomacy. It is one thing to describe the typical physical characteristics of early adolescent development, although the characteristics may be confusing at the time one goes through them. The physiological shifts of the human body are accepted within academia as something knowable, and by implication, describable, in empirical terms (e.g., Lerner, 2006). Situating spirituality within an academic context, however, is much more controversial. The literature describes why this is so: a fear of invoking resistance (DeBlasio, 2011; Kessler, 2000); the difficulty of describing spirituality in developmental terms (Nakkula & Toshalis, 2006); and the perception that spirituality involves indoctrination of religious dogma (Tacey, 2006), among others.

In his dissertation on the relationships between spirituality and English Language Learner pedagogy, Bradley (2011) used Palmer's (1998) rationale for the importance of having a definition of spirituality, even one that is imprecise: "...it performs a key function of any good definition by giving us a place from which to launch an exploration" (Palmer, 1998, p. 377). My exploration attempts to respond to Kessler's (2000) epochal question: "The most important challenge has always been not *whether* we can address spiritual development in secular schools but *how*" (p. ix, author's emphasis). Part of the how is clarifying what is meant by the terms *spirituality* and *spiritual development* in an educational context.

I reviewed theoretical, empirical, and historical literature about spirituality and spiritual development for definitional guidance. (A more detailed review of this literature also follows in the next chapter.) I immediately ran into a problem: the terms "spirituality" and "spiritual development" were often used interchangeably (e.g., Wintersgill, 2008). This transposition became problematic for me as I sought definitional clarity in the literature. Initially I used them interchangeably myself; however, further review of the literature yielded a more precise distinction between the two.

Spirituality is an embedded, universal human quality that reflects how the self relates with and is concerned with matters of the spirit: a sense of awe and wonder, a sense of being connected with something greater than oneself, a sense of reverence and mystery (Miller, 2007). Identifying or describing a person's spirituality is examining that person's orientation toward issues of transcendence, ultimate concerns, and intimate beliefs. Theoretical models of spirituality can involve factors such as the essence of (self) awareness; interconnectedness with humanity, nature, and the cosmos; and a relationship with an Ultimate Other (Hamilton & Jackson, 1998).

Spiritual development is a dynamic process of human development. This process involves an evolution of knowing one's purpose, experiencing interconnectedness, and discovering meaning. The study of spiritual development is within the jurisdiction of the science of human development. Spiritual development has been conceptualized as a stage-structural theory (e.g., Fowler, 1981) and as a developmental systems theory (e.g., Lerner, 2006).

Many authors made an explicit distinction between spirituality and religion (e.g., Hay, Reich, & Utsch, 2006; Johnson, 2008; King & Benson, 2006; King & Roeser, 2009; Orr, 2005; Revell, 2008; Scott, 2006). Tacey (2006) conceptualized spirituality as a bridge to religion, after frequently observing his college-level students specify that they were spiritual, but not religious. Tacey argued that a definition of spirituality emphasizing critical thought, self-reflection, and direct experiences of the sacred belongs in educational contexts. He explained the rise of interest in spirituality in secular venues along similar lines of logic that Kessler (2000) and Palmer (1998) used: spirituality is there all the time whether we name it or not and will make itself known. As Tacey wrote, speaking of a Western cultural context: "Secular society alienates people from traditional religious forms, but it cannot entirely alienate people from their souls" (p. 204).

That said, the overlap between religion and spirituality as theoretical constructs has practical considerations in the United States and therefore for my research. According to the Pew Forum on Religion and Public Life (2008), approximately 80% of the adult population in the U.S. identifies as a member of a religion. The First Amendment of the U.S. Constitution prohibits the state from establishing any religion. The Establishment Clause has been applied to public education in several key Supreme Court decisions in the later half of the 20th century (e.g., *Everson v. Board of Education*, 1947; *McCullom v. Board of Education*, 1948). Parents can be sensitive to even the historical associations of contemporary practices, such as yoga. In 2013, the school district of Encinitas, California was sued for violating the Establishment Clause by teaching yoga as part of its physical education program. Some parents were concerned that yoga promotes Hindu religious beliefs. Because of the legal issues and cultural biases at stake, clarity is crucial in terms of a distinction between religiosity/religious development and spirituality/spiritual development.

King and Roeser (2009) observed "debate over the substantive and functional distinctions between *religiousness* and *spirituality* is one of a number of central challenges...that bears centrally on developmental science theories of religious and spiritual development" (p. 440, authors' emphasis). In their review of the literature on the distinctions between the two constructs, they advocated for an approach used by Koenig, McCullough, and Larson (2001): to research religion at the societal level and to research spirituality at the individual level. As such, individuals can have a spirituality that is "moored" to specific religion or a spirituality that is "unmoored" to a specific religion (p. 18). But to study spirituality does not automatically mean to study religion. The point is that religion and spirituality are overlapping but not synonymous constructs, and I do not treat them as synonymous in my research of the educational relevance of spiritual development as a curriculum and instruction issue.

Given the data about religious affiliations in the U.S., the Establishment Clause of the Constitution, and the complexity of distinguishing between religion and spirituality in a Western cultural context, I see the definitional issue as inexorably linked to the education relevance issue. How can middle grades teachers apply their knowledge of young adolescent spiritual development— if desirable—if they are unclear about what is meant by spirituality and/or spiritual development? While the empirical and theoretical literature suggests a nascent consensus on an operational definition of spirituality and spiritual development in the fields of psychology (e.g., Benson, 2006) and nursing (e.g., de Jager Meezenbroek, Garssen, van den Berg, Tuytel, van Dierendonck, Visser, & Schaufeli, 2012), the literature on middle grades education does not reflect the same level of understanding and acceptance.

Potential for more holistic vision of young adolescent development. The cognitive, affective, physical, moral, and psychological domains of human development are defined, by their explicit inclusion, as the relevant—or legitimate—domains to address in middle grades education. A core foundational element of the field of middle grades reform is that educational experiences address the needs, interests, and abilities of young adolescents (ages 10–15) as a distinct developmental group (NMSA, 2010). I have no significant challenge to this stance. What I question is the wisdom of excluding spiritual development, a developmental domain that I see as equally foundational in terms of academic achievement and student engagement.

In framing the problem in this way, I seek to advance the claim made by Nakkula and Toshalis (2006), whose work represents the only mainstream literature on middle grades education that explicitly addresses the spiritualty of young adolescents as an educational issue:

> When we speak of faith as the dynamic and symbolic frame of orientation or the ultimate concern to which a person is committed and from which one derives purpose in life, it is clear how critical it is that we prepare ourselves to work with adolescents as they develop in this domain. (p. 222)

Nakkula and Toshalis' call for teacher preparation that includes knowledge of student spiritual development reflects an important distinction that I make as well. In this research, I distinguish between teaching spirituality in schools and leveraging knowledge of spirituality in schools—I am focusing on the latter, not the former. The middle grades concept is not about teaching young adolescents about their developmental stage, even though at times explicit reference to experiences common to young adolescents, such as feeling unique, may be useful. It is about purposefully teaching with those developmental traits in mind. What I suggest is the explicit inclusion of the spiritual domain when teaching with developmental characteristics in mind.

I take this position to enhance instruction and curriculum in the same ways that leveraging knowledge of the characteristics of the other, more commonly referenced domains of development enhances instruction and curriculum. In this work, I posit that it can be just as hazardous (Felner, Seitsinger, Brand, Burns, & Bolton, 2007) for teachers to disregard or be ignorant of the spiritual development as it can be to ignore the intellectual, socio-emotional, psychological, moral, and biological needs, interests, and abilities of young adolescents.

I contend that effective teachers acknowledge that students do not leave parts of themselves at the door when they enter a classroom. I argue it is not healthy to expect learners to compartmentalize essential parts of themselves during the messy, confusing, exhilarating process of learning. Indeed, the process of learning is when students need all of their human resources. To help young adolescents navigate the many developmental challenges experienced during middle school, teachers can draw upon a more holistic educational perspective. Because the field of holistic education distinguishes itself from other attempts to address affective qualities of students by its explicit inclusion of spirituality and spiritual development (Miller, 2007), my hope for this work is that it offers a rationale and a language for a more holistic middle grades concept.

The Field of Middle Grades Education

The education of young adolescents, youth who are between 10 and 15 years old, in the United States has only relatively recently been considered worthy of special distinction and attention. The field of middle grades education emerged with its own identity in the 1960s, with an increased understanding of the unique developmental characteristics of young adolescents (Lounsbury & Vars, 2003) and dissatisfaction with the junior high program (Smith & McEwin, 2011). Evidence abounds of the field's emergence as an authority on curriculum and instruction, teacher education, teacher certification, school organization, and building and district leadership. For example, 46 U.S. states and the District of Columbia offer licensure or endorsement for the middle grades as a level distinct from elementary and secondary education (McEwin, 2013). The movement to recognize the middle grades as distinct from elementary and secondary education emerged from a combination of leadership from the field of higher education and the day-to-day experiences of middle school principals and classroom teachers (Erb, 2006). George (2009) described the rise of the middle grades concept as a grassroots movement, with a national leadership evolving out of a need for greater coordination of regional efforts to improve middle grades schools. In the years since 1963, when William Alexander first called for the term middle school to be used as a replacement for junior high school (Alexander, 1963; Lounsbury & Vars, 2003), several national organizations, such as the Association for Middle Level Educators (AMLE, formerly known as the National Middle School Association) and the National Forum to Accelerate Middle Grades Reform, have provided professional networks for administrators, practitioners, and researchers. National organizations have also tried to influence policy at federal, state, and local levels, with some success in the 1970s and 1980s (Toepfer, 2011). These efforts have had mixed long-term results, with many of the central components of the middle grades movement (e.g., common planning time for teamed teacher cohorts) jeopardized by technocratic federal and state educational policies (e.g., No Child Left Behind). Also, the U.S. Department of Education, despite lobbying efforts by the AMLE, still only recognizes two levels of K–12 education—elementary and secondary. One major advocacy organization, the National Association for Secondary School Principals, recognized the middle level distinction by issuing a position paper about leadership practice as it relates to the middle grades (NASSP, 2006). To date there is not a national principals' organization for the middle grades although the AMLE has an inclusive membership of administrators, teachers, researchers, and teacher educators.

The field of middle grades education is an example of a reform movement in education. The reform goal was to improve leadership, organization, and instruction for middle grades students by advocating for developmentally appropriate practices (Carnegie Council on Adolescent Development, 1989). The movement's main criticism of education for young adolescents in the first half of the 20th century was that it did not address the unique developmental needs, interests, and abilities of students between 10 and 15 years old as a critical period of development. In their position papers, four of the major middle level advocacy groups make frequent references to the developmental characteristics of young adolescents. In this way, middle grades advocates have formed an interdisciplinary partnership with developmental psychologists, to whom they rely upon for authoritative knowledge about young adolescence.

Challenges to implementation. While the wisdom of using developmental theory as a foundation for the middle grades concept is not challenged by the field, I found evidence of ways in which implementation of the model is challenged in the United States today (Erb, 2000; Felner et al., 2007; Hamm et al., 2010; Woolley & Bowen, 2007). Some of the challenges to implementation of developmentally appropriate practices can be addressed by a more explicit incorporation of spiritual development in teacher professional development. In my reading of the literature on implementation of the middle grades concept, I see three main ways in which it is impeded.

First, the recommendations are implemented piecemeal, as if the presence of one or two is sufficient (Erb, 2000; Lounsbury & Vars, 2003). The problem with a piecemeal approach is that it constructs the students' needs and abilities as checklists. If we have an advisory period, we've got the social and emotion needs met— Check! If we have rigorous expectations we've got the cognitive needs met—Check! The field of applied developmental theory, as I review in more detail in the next chapter, suggests that human development does not work that way. While different domains of development are identified, their distinction does not imply that the domains exist in a vacuum. The developmental domains are viewed as interrelated (Caskey & Anfara, 2007; NMSA, 2010). Instead of picturing the domains as independent silos, a more accurate metaphor would be the domains, and the practices that address them in a school context, as threads in a spider web (Jewett, 2009). In a web metaphor, the whole hangs together based on the integrity of the individual strands, the strands themselves stick to each other, and there is a mysterious and luminous quality to the genius of its engineering. I see the spiritual domain as being distinct from other domains while also being interrelated. Inclusion of this domain in teacher preparation and professional development programs may help teachers and administrators envision more ways in which the domains interact with each other, especially because, as I describe in the literature on spiritual development and holistic education, one of the defining traits of spirituality is being aware of the interconnectedness in life.

Second, educational reform is often seen as a structural or organizational issue (Felner et al., 2007), not as a professional development issue (Hamm et al., 2010; Jackson & Davis, 2000). While organizational health (Roney, Coleman, & Schlichting, 2007) and good leadership (Leithwood, Louis, Anderson, & Wahlstrom, 2004) are important, the effect of teacher—student relationships on young adolescents cannot be disregarded (Osterman, 2000). Simply altering structural elements of a school without also tending to the knowledge, skills, and dispositions of the teachers is insufficient. An example of this problem is how teaming—a highly recommended practice in middle grades schools—is implemented. When teachers are placed in teams without also being given the necessary resources (e.g., professional development training in the co-teaching models), the efficacy of teaming is compromised (Erb, 2000; Parker, Allen, Alvarez McHatton, & Rosa, 2010). As Juvoven (2007) reported, "Students may continue to feel isolated or disconnected even in schools that rely on teaming practices and advisory programs" (p. 198). Middle grades teachers must be supported through ongoing professional education as they connect responsive practices with young adolescent developmental traits.

Last, the increasing emphasis on standards-based accountability has jeopardized many of the affective aspects of the recommended practices (Juvoven, 2007; Woolley & Bowen, 2007). Greene and associates (2008) found that in Oregon, middle grades teachers felt challenged to implement many of the elements of the middle school concept because of the pressures put on them to prepare students for high-stakes, standardized testing, even when they knew how valuable the recommended practices were in terms of academic achievement and student engagement. This last area of implementation challenge gives the inclusion of the spiritual domain a delicate, yet powerful, opportunity for application. Leveraging knowledge of young adolescent spiritual development may create openings for more holistic assessment practices as well as a new understanding of what it means to be accountable to middle grades students.

Translating Developmental Theory Into Educational Practice

Human development theory informs and guides practice with young adolescent students. For example, one of the key social developmental needs and interests of young adolescents is interpersonal engagement (Eccles & Roeser, 2009). An implication for practice within the classroom is the incorporation of learning activities that involve a high degree of peer collaboration (Caskey & Anfara, 2007). An implication for school organization is a regular advisory program in which student gatherings are guided and supported by teachers who are knowledgeable about young adolescents (NASSP, 2006; NMSA, 2010). An implication for building-level leadership is principals who engage directly with students in frequent, informal, and collegial ways (Gentilucci & Muto, 2007).

Eccles and Roeser (2009) framed the relationship between developmental theory and educational practice within the stage-environment fit theory (Eccles & Midgley, 1989). They posited that a good match, or fit, must exist between the learner and his or her social environment to facilitate academic motivation, engagement, and growth. A significant implication of this theory, as middle level advocates have argued for decades, is that a poor fit between young adolescents and their school context has disastrous consequences in the short and long term (Eccles et al., 1993). Mental health problems, adjustment difficulties, and problem behaviors faced later on as older adolescents and young adults have their roots in young adolescence (Eccles et al., 1993).

The field of middle grades education in the last 60 years has reflected the following set of positions: (a) young adolescents, between ages 10 and 15 years old, have developmental characteristics that are distinct from those of young children and older adolescents; (b) educational practices should be tailored to developmental theory; and (c) middle grades schools should, therefore, be developmentally appropriate in terms of instruction, curriculum, organization, leadership, and school climate (George, 2009; Jackson & Davis, 2000; NASSP, 2006; National Forum to Accelerate Middle Grades Reform, n.d.; NMSA, 2010). Advocates of the middle grades concept believe that middle grades teachers should be knowledgeable about the developmental characteristics associated with young adolescents, and should teach with that knowledge in mind. This section describes these characteristics and their corresponding applications in middle grades education.

In aligning specific practices with young adolescent developmental theory, much of the literature describes the characteristic developmental traits for the cognitive, social, emotional, psychological, physical, and moral domains (Caskey & Anfara, 2007; Roeser et al., 2000; Van Hoose et al., 2001). The characteristic markers for young adolescents are categorized by developmental domain in the list below (Caskey & Anfara, 2007):

Physical Development
- Refinement of fine and gross motor skills
- Rapid physical growth
- Biological maturity

Intellectual Development
- Increased capacity for abstract, conceptual thought patterns and problem-solving
- Builds upon prior knowledge and experiences to develop broader conceptualization of the world
- New artistic, recreational, and academic interests emerge frequently and can change rapidly

Moral Development
- Developing ability to make choices based on an emerging consciousness of personal values, principles, and ethics
- Moving from being mostly self-centered to an awareness of the needs and perspectives of others
- Interest in wrestling with moral dilemmas
- Beginning recognition of cause and effect in personal behaviors

Emotional/Social Development
- Increasing need to experience an authentic sense of belonging to a group, usually a peer group

- Adult authority (especially parental) is challenged in immature ways; at the same time affirmation, approval, and/or recognition from significant adult figures (such as teachers) is sought

Psychological Development
- Self-centered without much perspective: sensitive to criticism, lack self-esteem, believe personal experiences and feelings are unique
- Erratic moods and inconsistent behavior
- Exploring independence from parents and conceptualizing their own potential adult identity

An example of how developmental theory is connected to practice is the pedagogical implications of the physical developmental characteristic of rapid bone growth. Bone growth during young adolescence is not always matched by equally rapid growth in the muscular tissues, resulting in what is colloquially referred to as growing pains. The aches and pains resulting from this kind of growth can leave middle grades students feeling restless and uncomfortable as well as making it physically painful to remain seated in hard chairs. A developmentally responsive approach to classroom instruction, especially in 80-minute block classes, would be to incorporate movement or kinesthetic learning activities. One science teacher with whom I used to work created a series of dance movements that symbolized the steps of the water evaporation cycle. The eighth-grade students were introduced to the content through more physically passive activities, such as reading and listening to a lecture, then invited to stand and jump around making certain shapes with their bodies that represented the water cycle along with a rhythmic chant.

The main idea behind developmentally appropriate education is that students are more likely to be academically successful and possess positive perceptions of their school climate if middle grades leaders and teachers are knowledgeable about and are able to address developmental needs, interests, and abilities (Hamm et al., 2010). A "qualified" middle grades teacher, in the context of the middle grades concept, means teachers who are knowledgeable not only about their content and mandated standards, but also about the developmental readiness and interests of young adolescents.

The practices advocated by leaders in the field of middle grades education (Jackson & Davis, 2000; NASSP, 2006; NFAMGR, n.d.; NMSA, 2010) are related to appropriate developmental characteristics. For example, advocates recommend that middle grades curriculum is challenging, relevant, integrative, and rigorous. Courses that are designated as "extra"-curricular should be deeply embedded within all curricula. A variety of continuous and authentic assessments (summative and formative) are recommended to promote quality learning. These recommendations about curriculum are intended to be responsive to a young adolescent's increased capacity for conceptual thought patterns and interest in building upon prior knowledge. With young adolescent learners, new academic, cultural, and athletic interests emerge frequently.

Another example of the relationship between knowledge of developmental theory and educational practice is in the area of school community. Middle grades reform philosophy stipulates that the school community should be organized to cultivate safe, supportive, caring, healthy relationships based on mutual respect, shared purpose, and intellectual development. Adults should offer advocacy and guidance via small learning communities. Families and the greater community should be actively involved as partners and resources for learning. These recommendations about community and climate respond to the typical early adolescent trait of emotional sensitivity, especially to perceived criticism and to an orientation of self-centeredness that lacks greater perspective.

Within the two general examples mentioned earlier, each specific recommendation can be linked back to a specific developmental characteristic (or a specific combination of characteristics). For example, a differentiated instructional approach allows for the diversity in rates of developmental growth within and across the domains. Such differentiation is crucial in the middle grades, when a potential consequence of asking a student to attempt an assessment (formative or summative) that is beyond his or her cognitive development can damage the student's positive self-identity as a learner. In the next section, I argue for why a more holistic understanding (i.e., one that explicitly includes the spiritual domain of development) of young adolescents can address a significant educational problem for middle grades students.

Alienation in the Middle Grades

There are many good reasons for educational researchers to focus on the middle grades. The middle grades are seen as a critical and transformational period (e.g., NASSP, 2006). Outcomes impacted by the middle grades experience include college readiness and success (Balfanz, 2009); later opportunities to meet grade-level standards, especially for low-income and minority students (Bondy & Ross, 2008); and integration of health-promoting behaviors (Feldman, 2008).

A current problem in the middle grades is the alienation of students. Middle grades students experience a deep perception of disconnection within the context of their formal education in public schools in the United States. The alienation of many young adolescents in middle grades schools as a phenomenon has been well-documented (Beachum, Dentith, McCray, & Boyle, 2008; Daniels, 2005; Juvonen, 2007; Lee & Smith, 1993; Osterman, 2000). Reasons for their alienation range from instructional strategies that do not provide opportunities for dialogue and discourse (Juvoven, 2007) to organizational practices such as "ability-based" tracking and departmentalization (Osterman, 2000).

In my analysis of the literature on young adolescents and their need for belonging in their school context, I identified the causes and conditions of belonging and its near enemy, alienation. From that analysis, I came to the conclusion that the absence of the spiritual development of middle grades students within the foundational literature on middle grades education is problematic. I made this connection between alienation and spiritual development through analyzing the specific recommendations for promoting a sense of belonging (e.g., NMSA, 2010). These recommendations, such as using strong relationships to foster and promote a culture of learning, were justified by invoking students' developmental needs. Each specific recommendation was strengthened when teachers and administrators were addressing the developmental domains as a holistic entity. Using the same logic as middle grades advocates, the impact of the developmental model could be strengthened with the inclusion of the spiritual needs, interests, and abilities of young adolescents. I saw that potential most clearly when studying belonging.

I highlight some of the ways in which alienation manifests as well as some of the reasons for this problem. This review is not meant to be an exhaustive summary of the problem. I have limited my scope to the aspects of alienation that are most directly benefited by a middle grades concept that explicitly includes the spiritual domain.

In the developmental sciences, spiritual development is considered a component of human psychology (Roehlkepartain, Benson, King, & Wagener, 2006). The psychological health of middle grades students is threatened by the phenomenon of alienation. As the second leading cause of death amongst adolescents, suicide is one of the most threatening consequences of alienation; the link between alienation and "various forms of emotional distress including loneliness, violence, and suicide" (Osterman, 2000, p. 343) is established in the literature (Nichols, 2008). A lack of belonging is associated with other at-risk behaviors such as drug and alcohol abuse, nicotine use, absenteeism, cheating, and/or associations with negative peer groups (Nichols, 2008; Osterman, 2000; Roeser et al., 2000). In her review of the literature, Nichols (2008) found that "the consistent finding that belonging is inversely related to negative belief systems...suggests that belonging may be a critical variable that contributes to students' capacities to adapt to school cultures in psychologically positive ways" (p. 148).

Middle grades students are aware of their own experiences of alienation and the importance of their perception of belonging in their school context. Doda and Knowles (2008) analyzed more than 2,700 middle grades student free-write essays on their school experience, collected from 30 different middle level schools in the United States and Canada. Doda and Knowles identified two patterns, in terms of student expectations about their education, from their analysis of the data: middle grades students want supportive and rewarding healthy relationships with teachers and other students as well as learning experiences that are personally relevant and challenging. However, Doda and Knowles (2008) found that the relationships the young adolescents aspired to "are the exception rather than the norm" (p. 27) and "according to the data represented here, teachers too often underestimate...the capacities of young adolescents, and, at times, use the perils of puberty to dismiss student disengagement," (p. 29).

Interpreting student disengagement as an indication of a student's personal failings (i.e., lack of effort, poor moral fiber, bad upbringing) is one frame through which to develop strategies for increasing engagement. From the perspectives of the students in Doda and Knowles' (2008) study, it is a lens through which student behavior is commonly viewed. Osterman (2000) offered an alternative: what if student disengagement and alienation were indicators of the failure of the *schools* to provide for the basic psychological needs of, in this case, young adolescents? This shift in perspective is a crucial one to explore in terms of the problem of alienation of middle grades students, as many in the literature (Juvoven, 2007; Lee & Smith, 1993; Osterman, 2000) strongly argued for middle level schools as the best place to focus on how students experience belonging.

Another way in which alienation is negatively affecting young adolescents relates to their academic achievement. In her review of the literature on student belonging at all three levels of K–12 education, Nichols (2008) found that "although it is not always evident, some researchers found that belonging beliefs relate significantly to achievement in middle school settings" (p. 148). Academic achievement is impacted by student perceptions about their academic life. While the literature does not indicate a direct relationship between belonging and academic achievement, it does suggest that alienation inhibits motivation for academic pursuits (Nichols, 2008; Osterman, 2000; Roeser et al., 2000).

A sense of connection to teachers has a stronger relationship with academic achievement than a sense of connection with peers or family (Osterman, 2000): "How students feel about school and their coursework is in large measure determined by the quality of their relationship with their teachers in specific classes" (p. 344). Palmer (1997) also found that when he asks people to describe good teachers, responses vary in terms of the techniques teachers used, "but all of them describe people who have some sort of *connective* capacity, who connect themselves to their students, their students to each other, and everyone to the subject being studied" (p. 27, author's emphasis). Palmer's observation, made in the context of his larger work on the spirituality of teachers, invokes one of the three elements of spirituality—a sense of interconnectedness with humanity.

For middle grades students, experiencing belonging is a developmental need that contributes to their psychological health, their level of engagement in school, and their academic achievement. While addressing the social, emotional, psychological, and moral developmental domains when designing curriculum and instruction can go a long way toward decreasing alienation and increasing belonging (Durlak, Weissberg, Dymnicki, Taylor, & Schellinger, 2011; Jewett, 2009; Juvoven, 2007; Van Hoose et al., 2001), I argue that the exclusion of the spiritual domain is a failure to take full advantage of the middle grades reform concept of a developmentally responsive education.

Domain of spiritual development is missing. I see the exclusion of the spiritual domain of human development from the middle grades concept of developmentally responsive education as related to the problem of alienation. A more holistic approach to developmentally responsive middle grades education—one that explicitly includes spiritual development—could be a way to reduce student experiences of alienation. In framing this problem in the field of middle grades education, I conceive of spirituality as a developmental resource (Nakkula & Toshalis, 2006) and see the middle grades concept as reflective of the stage-environment fit component (Eccles & Midgley, 1989) of developmental systems theory.

The question about including the domain of spiritual development as a curriculum and instruction issue reflects epistemological debates about how students learn, as well as the regulatory relationship between power and knowledge production (Kincheloe, 2008; Popkewitz, 1991). Believing only two ways of knowing count in a classroom—empirical and rational—discounts the immense value of instruction that address what Hart (2004) called, the "third" way of knowing: how learners draw upon intuition, emotion, creativity, and sensation. Hart categorized this third way of knowing as contemplative or spiritual. In other words, middle grades instruction looks one way if teachers are only targeting empirical and rational ways of knowing, and looks another way if they are leveraging students' spiritual ways of learning. I argue that a holistic consideration of the middle grades concept can increase the ability of middle grades students to fulfill their potential as human beings through academic achievement and student engagement.

Today, the field of middle grades education, like the students it serves, needs to use all of its resources to face significant obstacles. Perhaps the most daunting challenge to the middle level concept, with its emphasis on meaningful relationships, is the federal emphasis on accountability as measured by standardized, high-stakes assessments (Greene et al., 2008; Juvoven, 2007). Another barrier comes from the field of teacher education. Many schools of education reflect state licensing policies and offer their students a choice between an elementary program and a secondary program, with few electives that focus on the middle grades (Caskey, 2003). Organizing teacher preparation programs in this way impedes the cultivation of a middle grades teaching force that values young adolescents and is specifically prepared to do so (NMSA, 2010). Successful implementation of developmentally appropriate practices is defied on many fronts: emotionally distant adults, outdated fidelity to 42-minute class periods, punitive restrictions on lunchtime behaviors, and limited opportunities for public celebration of success (Van Hoose et al., 2001). In my view, it is crucial that middle grades educators explore and embrace a more holistic developmental theory that can address these challenges.

The Middle Grades Concept Through the Lens of Critical Constructivism

In my years of experience with middle grades students, their families, and their teachers, I observed the developmental distinctness of young adolescents from either children or older (i.e., high school) adolescents. When formally introduced to the middle grades concept of an education that is developmentally responsive, the recommendations resonated with me. I felt as if I had been creating curriculum, designing instructional strategies and assessment practices, and demonstrating administrative leadership in ways that were powerfully guided by my knowledge in practice of the needs, interests, and abilities of young adolescents long before I read the National Middle School Association's (2010) *This We Believe*.

Despite my enthusiasm for the middle grades concept, as a critical constructivist educator and emergent scholar, I have two main critiques of it. My first critique is the premise for this research: the absence of information about the spiritual domain of human development in the literature influencing teacher and school practice for middle grades students. This absence is a lost opportunity to address a significant problem, the experience of alienation by young adolescents in their school context. If caring is truly embraced as an act of advocacy for young adolescent learners, then I believe middle grades educators should be equipped with more tools, such as a culturally respectful language for adolescent spiritual development—with which to create classrooms of mutual care, respect, and creativity.

My second critique, however, is more complicated because it jeopardizes the foundation of my research. I take issue with the assumption made by developmental psychologists and educators influenced by that field that *it is possible* to make declarative statements about typical adolescent development. The linearity of stage theory seems in conflict with what I know of human growth and learning—my own, my children's, and my students (both adolescent and adult). When studies were conducted to ascertain the "typical" characteristics of young adolescents, who was included from the studies? Who was excluded? Fortunately, the field of developmental psychology, as I will delve into in the following chapter, has expanded beyond stage-based theories of human growth to incorporate a systems-based perspective, in keeping with the general shift in both natural and social sciences to a metaphor of ecology over industry.

A tension in how I have framed the problem lies in my second critique of the middle grades concept: If I (or anyone else) cannot trust knowledge produced by developmental psychologists, what is the value of trying to improve the model of developmentally responsive middle grades education through an articulation of the relevance of the spiritual domain of development? This is a tension I have not fully resolved for myself in this work. Suffice it to write here that as a practitioner and as a scholar, I find sufficient credibility in the notion that people aged 10 to 15 years old have distinct needs, interests, and abilities that, if ignored, cripple their educational experience. From my critical constructivist perspective though, I am wary of positivist statements generated by quantitative research about the 'nature' of human growth. With that disclaimer in mind, I turn now to a deeper investigation of the theories about human growth, including within the spiritual domain.

Chapter Three

Excluding the Spiritual Dimension From Developmentally Responsive Education

HUMAN development theory informs and guides recommended practices with young adolescent students. Developmental theory is not necessarily of more importance in the middle grades than it might be in other grades. From the perspective of middle grades advocates, the danger lies in not distinguishing between children, young adolescents, and older adolescents when considering pedagogy. For example, Nakkula and Ravich (1998) used the term *applied developmentalists* as a means of emphasizing how successful middle grades teachers approach their professional practice. When applying human development theory to middle grades education, the typical characteristics of intellectual, social, emotional, psychological, moral, and physical changes are used to inform school-related practices such as assessment, curriculum, instruction, leadership, and organization. In sum, if middle grades education and developmental psychology were represented visually as two overlapping circles, the overlapping space in between would represent the middle grades concept of developmentally responsive education:

Figure 3.1

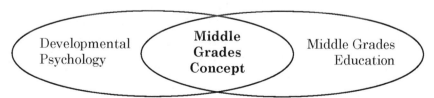

The interrelationship between the fields of developmental psychology and middle grades education is only one of three significant disciplinary interrelationships I see as part of the issue of the educational relevance of spiritual development in middle grades education. The critical constructivist worldview supports framing complex educational issues as interdisciplinary. The boundaries of academic disciplines, as human constructs formed in historicized contexts, are not the rigid and clear lines advocated by post-positivist academics. Choosing to "see" the subjectivity and interdependence of an academic field's ideas, constructs, and rules is a critical constructivist strategy to create space for alternative visions in educational practice. The other two interrelationships that bear careful examination in this research are holistic education, as a product of spirituality and education, and spiritual development, as a product of spirituality and developmental psychology.

Taken together, the ways in which I have organized the significant relationships amongst the related literatures looks like this:

Figure 3.2

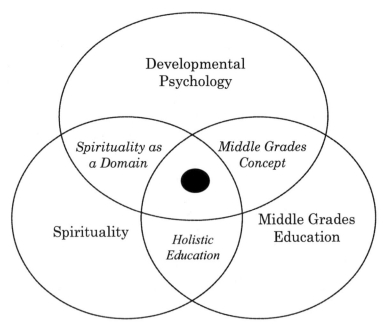

In this chapter, I delve deeply into a review of how these inter-relationships are described in the related literature. I begin with the pedagogical relationships between developmental theory and middle grades education. A greater understanding of the ways in which middle grades advocates draw from the field of developmental psychology reinforces the purpose of my critical historiographical research: to articulate the educational relevance of the spiritual domain of human development in middle grades concept of developmentally responsive pedagogy. With the interrelationship between developmental psychology and middle grades pedagogy as a starting point, I provide a survey of the current thinking on the content, processes, and boundaries of spirituality as a developmental domain. In that account, I emphasize various theoretical models of spiritual development, while also attending to issues related to the challenges of research in this area of developmental psychology. Finally, I address the third significant interrelationship, the field of holistic education, which explicitly conceptualizes student and teacher spirituality as relevant to education.

Middle Grades Connection to the Field of Developmental Psychology

The concept of developmental appropriateness in an educational context has connections to developmental stage theory (e.g., Piaget, 1967) and developmental systems theory (e.g., Eccles & Midgley, 1989; King & Benson, 2006; Lerner, 2006; Search Institute, 2011b). To identify the middle grades as a distinct period of human development reflects the works of Piaget (1967), Erikson (1968), and Kohlberg (1981), each of whom articulated a stage theory of human development. The metaphor of a stage theory implies that human beings have distinct periods during which certain tasks must be resolved or accomplished to successfully progress to the next stage of development. Middle grades advocates argue that the middle grades should be treated differently from the elementary and secondary programs to facilitate successful navigation of the developmental tasks characteristic for young adolescents.

In the field of psychology, stage theory has been augmented in recent years by developmental systems theories, which emphasize the dynamic between the individual and the environment (Lerner, 2006). In this section, I summarize key aspects of developmental systems theory and the related constructs of stage-environment fit theory (Eccles & Midgley, 1989) and of developmental assets (Search Institute, 2011b). Later, I return to the stage theory model of human development in my account of the past and current theoretical work on spirituality as a developmental domain. The developmental systems framework is helpful in terms of understanding some of the short- and long-term implications of failing to implement the middle school concept. Some authors in the field of middle grades education have even gone as far as to describe middle grades schools that are not sensitive to the distinct abilities and needs of young adolescents as systems that are "developmentally hazardous" (Felner et al., 2007; Juvoven, 2007).

Developmental systems theory. Developmental systems theory hinges on the adaptive nature of the relationship between an individual and the community (Lerner, 2006). Adaptive, in this context, is described as health-promoting or beneficial. The ideal goal of this theoretical framework, in an adolescent context, is what is referred to as positive youth development (Lerner, 2006). King and Benson (2006) identified thriving as an outcome of positive youth development. King and Benson defined thriving as "more than positive functioning....A thriving young person not only grows and flourishes as an individual but also contributes to family, community, and/or society" (p. 385). The theory is that an individual adapts to his or her environment, and the environment (community, context, society, and so on) adapts based on the behavior of the individual, for the mutual benefit (and detriment) of both. As a classroom teacher, and as a student, this idea makes perfect sense to me. Students make adaptations to fit into a teacher's classroom all the time, and teachers make adaptations to their classrooms in response to the students.

Lerner, Roeser, and Phelps (2008) characterized this reciprocal relationship between self and society as one of mutual commitment: the individual commits to making positive contributions to his or her context, and the community commits to fostering an environment that is healthy for all individuals. In King and Benson's work (2006), the outcome of growth, in the developmental systems framework, is contingent upon the values of the developing subject's environment: "Youth whose interactions with their contexts are adaptive commit to a sense of identity that yields fidelity to an ideology that promotes reciprocity with their family, community, and society" (p. 386). In short, a developmental systems theory situates an individual's developmental integrity within a larger framework of integrity within a community, for the mutual benefit of both.

Using this framework to understand the recommendations of middle grades advocates, the recommended practices become the manifestations of the community's commitment to positive youth development. The middle grades concept emerged as a reaction against educational practices that were not adaptive enough to the needs of young adolescents. In a developmental systems framework, mutuality is a key principle. According to the middle grades advocates, for middle schools to be successful, the needs of the students and the needs of the school/community must be considered simultaneously. Their claim, along the lines of developmental systems theory, is that a developmentally responsive middle grades school will inspire students to be willing to contribute to the greater good of their communities.

Stage-environment fit theory. The stage-environment fit theory (Eccles & Midgley, 1989)—as an example of a systems theory—frames schools as social contexts within which development takes place. The implications of this theory are (a) that schools as organizations and those who work in them must be mindful of how the developmental needs of students change from elementary to middle to high school, and (b) that if policy-makers, administrators, and classroom teachers are not mindful of providing a developmentally-appropriate academic environment, students will respond in self-protective ways that inhibit or prevent full access to educational opportunities and resources (Eccles & Roeser, 2009; Loukas & Murphy, 2007; Mulhall, 2007). For example, an extreme self-protective response is dropping out of school. The connection between a developmentally inappropriate practice (i.e., ability-based tracking) and a self-protective response is described by Mulhall (2007): "the images, perceptions, and interactions of lower tracked students compared to the upper tracked students...may create deeper and profound feelings of superiority, resentment, and even racism...given the sensitive nature and vulnerable feelings of young adolescents" (p. 12).

Hamm and associates (2010) tested this hypothesis using a quantitative study in a rural school with a professional development intervention. They concluded that "helping teachers to develop a more developmentally oriented perception of their students, and strategies to interact with students in ways aligned with students' developmental needs and level, are necessary to interventions that aim to support early adolescent school adjustment" (p. 346). Hamm and associates identified statistically significant gains in school adjustment and student perception of the school's social and academic climate for both Native American and White students when teachers engaged in professional development. However, gaps between Native American and White students were reduced more for the students whose teachers were subject to the intervention. Additionally, gains were higher for Native American students than for White students, confirming results elsewhere (e.g., Felner et al., 2007; Mertens & Flowers, 2003; Woolley & Bowen, 2007) about how minority students seem to benefit more than majority students from the middle school concept.

As Balfanz (2009) and others (Bondy & Ross, 2008; Gutman & Eccles, 2007; Juvoven, 2007; Osterman, 2000) have argued, experiences, both positive and negative, during the middle grade years serve as jumping off points for longitudinal outcomes. So, a poor fit between a middle grades student and his/her school can contribute to the emergence of serious problems further along the trajectory of his or her lifetime.

Developmental assets theory. A related extension of the stage-environment fit theory is the developmental assets framework developed by the Search Institute (King & Benson, 2006; Scales, Benson, Leffert, & Blyth, 2000; Search Institute, 2011b).

Developmental assets are resources that facilitate positive behavioral outcomes during developmental transition periods. The Search Institute (2011b), which has been working on its developmental assets framework since 1990, identified eight resources that are valuable during developmental growth. Four are *external* resources: support, empowerment, boundaries and expectations, and constructive use of time. Four are considered *internal* resources: commitment to learning, positive values, social competencies, and positive identity. An implied assumption of the developmental assets framework is that these assets can be cultivated; that these resources are acquired, they are not exclusively intrinsic. The asset metaphor also implies that these traits need to be actively promoted: "The Search Institute has advanced the proposition that healthy youth development requires the investment of all people who care about youth" (Nakkula & Toshalis, 2006, p. 74). The goal of using developmental theories with educational practice—from the perspective of enhancing assets—is to create and sustain middle grades schools that are resource-rich for youth who are in the midst of massive developmental challenges and opportunities (NMSA, 2010).

The developmental assets theory has been tested empirically with positive results. Scales, Benson, Leffert, and Blyth (2000) used regression analysis in a large sample (N = 6,000) to determine the predictor effect of developmental assets on adolescent thriving. Scales and associates asserted that the developmental assets accounted for a large amount of the variance (47%–54% across ethnic groups) in thriving outcomes. They also claimed that some of the assets positively predicted more than one thriving outcome (e.g., school success). Scales and associates (2000) concluded their study with this word of caution: "These findings underscore Benson's (1997) admonition that numerous assets work both directly and in combination to account for positive adolescent development. Each 'molecule' is necessary to ensure that the resulting whole person is more than the sum of his or her deficits and assets" (p. 44). This last point reinforces the argument of other middle grades advocates (Felner et al., 2007; Jackson & Davis, 2000; NMSA, 2010) for the importance of holistic implementation of a developmentally appropriate middle grades experience.

In sum, developmental psychologists seem to be in agreement about the holistic and deeply integrated nature of development. Two major processes of development are the interaction within an individual (Magnusson & Cairns, 1996) and the interaction between the individual and the social context (Eccles & Midgley, 1989; Lerner, 2006). From the perspective of an advocate for the middle grades concept, the lesson to be learned from the work of developmental psychologists is that failure to implement fully and faithfully an educational program that is designed with the needs, interests, and abilities of young adolescents breeds alienation in the short term (Bondy & Ross, 2008), with long-term maladaptations to the demands and expectations of society (Feldman, 2008).

Spirituality as a Developmental Domain

In this survey of the second significant interrelationship related to spiritual development and the middle grades concept, I highlight efforts to craft and refine definitions of spirituality and spiritual development within the context of the scientific study of human development. Such work attempts to identify patterns and describe processes of spiritual development. I explore two developmental frameworks employed in this field: stage-structural theory and developmental systems theory. I describe a call in the literature for spiritual development research and theory that is culturally responsive. Although the majority of my review is of work that considers the entire human life span, given the focus of this research I included a brief section on young adolescent spiritual development.

Definitional literature. Spirituality as a *legitimate* subject of inquiry within the developmental sciences has been a relatively recent phenomenon. In a study of the six most significant journals on human development, no articles on spiritual development during childhood and adolescence were published between 1990 and 2002 (Benson, Roehlkepartain, & Rude, 2003). Using the same methods, similar results were produced in a follow-up study by King and Roeser (2009).

Given the power of language to shape knowledge, I review key definitional literature on spirituality as a developmental domain. How have contemporary developmental psychologists conceptualized and described spiritual development? Much of the literature on spiritual development, in or out of an educational context, begins with a qualification about the challenges of defining spirituality within the academy. This qualification usually precedes a clarification by the author(s) about their definition of spirituality and spiritual development. Entire dissertations have been written just on the search for a common understanding of spirituality within academia (e.g., Niederman, 1999; Van Rooyen, 2007). The consistent pattern of qualification signaled to me that the explicit inclusion of scholarly work on spiritual development represents a challenge to hegemonic academic discourse.

Among the definitions of spirituality I read there was more overlap and similarity than difference; differences usually arose from a shift in the purpose of the text. This initial observation affirmed the critical constructivist perspective on how knowledge is constructed within multiple perspectives, by different individuals in various historicized contents. For this description of the emergent field of spiritual development within developmental psychology, I decided to include authors who have offered frameworks for understanding spiritual development that are particularly rich, clarifying, and/or reflect my overall purposes in this study. I chose to include authors whose work seems to be seminal in this field. This section draws almost exclusively from the developmental sciences. The third section of this chapter includes works that define spirituality in the context of education.

Dynamics of human development. I start with the work of Peter Benson, who is by all accounts one of the founding fathers in the field of spiritual development. Benson defined spiritual development while at the same time attempting to establish its place within the scientific study of human development. His strategy for doing both tasks was to embed a definition within the pre-established context of human development theory. In his review of the previous definitional literature, Benson (2006) advocated for a

definition that reflects the "three dynamics of human development" (p. 485): processes, outcomes, and influences.

To illustrate how Benson viewed these three main processes
manifesting within the domain of spiritual development, I paired
his 2006 work with an earlier piece he co-authored with another
key figure in the field of spiritual development, Eugene
Roehlkepartain (Benson, Roehlkepartain, & Rude, 2003). In the
2003 piece, the aspects of spiritual development that reflected central processes of human development were described as "...growing
the intrinsic capacity for self-transcendence, in which the self is
embedded in something larger than the self, including the sacred"
(p. 205). Benson's second dynamic of human development, developmental   outcomes,   is   captured   as   the   "...search   for
connectedness, meaning, purpose, and contribution" (pp. 205–206).
Benson (2006) characterized a third developmental dynamic as environmental   influences,   or   "...contexts   than   inform   how
developmental processes play themselves out" (p. 485). In Benson,
Roehlkepartain, and Rude (2003), spiritual development is
"...shaped both within and outside of religious traditions, beliefs,
and practices" (p. 206).

Benson (2006) defended his definition of spiritual development
on the grounds that it encapsulates the universality of how humans experience spirituality. By explicitly unlinking a conceptual
construct of spirituality from religion, Benson attempts to offer a
vision of spiritual development that does not necessarily reaffirm
the 21st century positivist dismissal of religion as not relevant for
academic research. He is not invoking the recent refrain of people
asserting they are spiritual but not religious in a way that deval-
ues religion. Benson is not, in other words, trying to privilege
spirituality over religiosity to make spiritual development theory
more palatable for Cartesian advocates. Rather, his distinction between spiritual development and religious affiliation is offered to
emphasize the influence of environmental context (including, possibly but not necessarily, religion) over all human developmental
domain, including the domain of spiritual development.

Expanding upon some of Benson's seminal ideas, Roehlkepartain, Benson, King, and Wagener (2006) edited one of the few
collections of scholarly works on the spiritual development of chil-

dren and adolescents. Roehlkepartain and associates set the boundaries of their collection within a set of assumptions about spiritual development. These four assumptions are repeated here because of their potential value in describing how spiritual development is conceptualized by developmental psychologists:

- Spiritual development is a universal human process
- Spiritual development is a multidimensional, multilayered domain
- Spiritual development is an ongoing, iterative process
- Spirituality is a life-shaping force

These two works (Benson, 2006; Roehlkepartain et al., 2006) reflect the definition of spiritual development I use in this research. I refer to spiritual development as a legitimate domain of human development, therefore subject to the same criteria for establishing human experiences that are developmental. Feldman (2008) offers a rich and illustrative set of criteria for legitimizing spiritualty as a developmental domain that I address later on in this section. I conceptualize spiritual development as a universal process with diverse manifestations and multiple sources of external influence. While my definition is aligned with stage-based, progressive theories of spiritual development, I also conceptualize the developmental process as iterative—more akin to spiral metaphors than linear ones. Finally, I define spiritual development as an essential developmental process for making meaning of one's life, experiencing transcendence from self, constructing an interpretive narrative, and knowing joy, peace, and mystery.

Stage theory. Because of its inclusion of influences, Benson's definition seems closely aligned with the developmental systems perspectives described in this chapter's section on developmental theories (i.e., stage-environment fit theory). However, spiritual development was initially conceived of within the tradition of stage-based theories of human development. A pioneer in developing a stage-based theory for what he termed faith development, James Fowler (1981) worked with Lawrence Kohlberg, Carol Gilligan, and Sharon Parks at Harvard in the 1970s and 1980s in the fields of cognitive, moral, and spiritual development. Fowler, who like Kohlberg was influenced by Jean Piaget's staged developmental theory, proposed a faith development theory based on the progression through sequential stages. Fowler, with Dell (2006) later qualified his theory of stage progression with the caveat that human development in the spiritual domain occurs within a broader context of biological, emotional, and cognitive development and ecological influences, such as family and culturally-based gender expectations. Fowler's work is compelling because he made explicit references to the application of his theory in an educational context.

Fowler used the word *faith* when describing this domain of development; however, others (e.g., Benson, 2006) have referenced him in the context of discussion on spiritual development, as I also do in this research. Like Benson, Roehlkepartain, and Rude (2003), Fowler conceived faith as not necessarily inclusive of religious beliefs and practices. He described faith development as an "unfolding pattern [that] can be characterized in terms of developing emotional, cognitive, and moral interpretations and responses. Our ways of imagining and committing in faith correlate significantly with our ways of knowing and valuing more generally" (Fowler & Dell, 2006, p. 36). Using Benson's (2006) model for the dynamics of human development, key elements of Fowler's definition of faith/spiritual development are described in the list below:

- Central processes (Benson, 2006)
- "An integral, centering process, underlying the formation of beliefs, values, and meanings...relying on that which has the quality of ultimacy in their lives." (Fowler & Dell, 2006, p. 36)
- Developmental outcomes (Benson, 2006)
- "Give[s] coherence and direction to persons' lives....Enables [persons] to face and deal with the challenges of human life and death..." (Fowler & Dell, 2006, p. 36)
- Environmental influences (Benson, 2006)
- "[Faith development] link[s] [persons] in shared trusts and loyalties in a sense of relatedness to a larger frame of reference." (Fowler & Dell, 2006, p. 36)

Fowler (1981) acknowledged that his construct of faith might cause dissent between those who embrace the stages of faith theory on the grounds of its clinical application and those who, for theological reasons, resist this definition on the grounds that it makes faith/spirituality too universal and groundless. In the context of describing this point of contention, Fowler (Fowler & Dell, 2006) made the same case that I make in this book regarding the educational relevance of the spiritual development (in my research, relevance as it pertains to middle grades students in particular):

> The stage theory makes its contribution...by helping to match the competencies of each stage—and the operations of mind and emotion that characterize them—with ways of teaching and with the symbols, practices, and contents of faith at different levels of reflective inquiry and complexity. Educators of this mind-set find faith development theory helpful for preparing persons to teach at different age and stage levels, and to match their methods and communicative practices with the groups' probable state or range of stages. (p. 43)

In this passage, Fowler and Dell (2006) articulated my research interest in the educational relevance of the spiritual domain of human development. In keeping with the overall vision of exemplary middle grades education being responsive to the developmental needs, interests, and abilities of the students, I think that explicit inclusion of the spiritual domain can help teachers design and implement curriculum and instruction that builds upon what teachers already know about human development in the biological, cognitive, and psychological domains.

Advancing Fowler's faith theory, Feldman (2008) used a set of criteria for establishing whether or not a phenomenon is developmental. This distinction is crucial in the context of situating spirituality within the developmental sciences. Feldman used his criteria to identify what he termed *spiritual markers* that established spiritual development as falling within the range of developmental domains. For example, in establishing that developmental processes include change that is positive and qualitative, Feldman referred to intrapersonal reflections "expressed through more mature and better explanations" (p. 187). His remaining criteria for characterizing an aspect of human growth as human development were: changes that are sequential and irreversible, large-scale and/or pervasive, have profound emotional implications, and emerge through intentional efforts.

Feldman (2008) seemed to be interested not only in exploring spirituality as a developmental domain but also in posing suggestions for research strategies and areas of inquiry. For example, when considering the last criteria—intentionality—he suggested qualitative approaches that study "the kinds of questions asked, the kinds of answers sought, and the kinds of structures that form as expressions of intentionality" in regard to spiritual development (Feldman, 2008, p. 189). In the middle grades, collecting qualitative data such as he suggests from students might yield a rich understanding of the markers for young adolescent spiritual development.

I include Feldman's (2008) work here as another example of how the literature on spirituality as a domain of human development conceptualizes the contents and processes of what is meant by spiritual development. Both Feldman (2008) and Fowler (1981) offered theories that embrace progressive growth marked by identifiable stages, such as Feldman's (2008) characterization of questions as increasingly complex. Their work is significant to my research because I, with some qualification, assume it is possible to describe young adolescent spiritual development in similar ways that the other domains are described (e.g., Caskey & Anfara, 2007).

An inclusive framework. The foundational work of Fowler (1981) and others (e.g., Oser, 1991) has been criticized on the grounds that it is exclusive to Western research perspectives and paradigms. A functionalist critique of Fowler and Oser's work is claims for universal theories of spiritual development might not adequately represent all people. A critical constructivist critique would address the potential for oppression when developmental theory does not explicitly integrate multiple perspectives and contexts. Given the additional challenges that young adolescents who are ethnic minorities face in schools (Beachum, Dentith, McCray, & Boyle, 2008; Brown & Leaman, 2007; Bondy & Ross, 2008; Jewett, 2009; Walker & Shuangye, 2007; Woolley & Bowen, 2007), it is important to address spiritual development frameworks that are culturally responsive and reflect research that is not limited to one (Western) perspective. In this section, I address ways in which scholars in applied psychology respond to the question of an inclusive framework for spiritual development.

Mattis, Ahluwalia, Cowie, and Kirkland-Harris (2006) critiqued the field of spiritual development on the grounds that it is infused with Western (White, European) values at the expense of other cultural perspectives. This exclusion is problematic, Mattis and associates argued, because constructs that are central to the field of inquiry—such as selfhood, chronology, and secularism—reflect assumptions that are not universally held. For example, while the Western model may look to the biological beginning of a person's life to track his or her spiritual development (e.g., Oser, 1991), in some African and Caribbean communities a young child may display traits that identify him in his community as an "old soul" (Mattis, Ahluwalia, Cowie, & Kirkland-Harris, 2006, p. 287), with a spiritual development that may have begun long before this particular incarnation appeared. In any cultural context, factors in addition to biological age can exert profound influence on a young person's spiritual development (e.g., life-span transitions, non-parental community members, creative and artistic popular expressions, and local and national policy). Mattis and her associates argued that as such, scholarly research must address those factors when constructing a model for adolescent spiritual development. Juang and Syed (2008) also recommended that future research more deeply investigate the intersection of adolescent ethnic and spiritual identities as well as how ecological context affects identity formation.

The Search Institute's Center for Spiritual Development has put forth a culturally responsive framework for understanding spiritual development. This framework was generated through a collaborative process involving participants from all over the world. Their goal was to develop a construct that could transcend diverse cultures, traditions, disciplines, and worldviews (Search Institute, 2011a). Using literature review, focus groups, and survey data, the Search Institute's investigators constructed a definition of spiritual development that involves three core proc-esses: awakening, belonging, and a way of living. Their framework stipulated that spiritual development is a universal process, but each of the three core processes may manifest in different ways depending upon the cultural context in which human development is occurring. Their framework also emphasized the interconnection between spiritual development and other developmental domains, as well as the significant influence of the interconnection between the individual and the environment.

Young adolescent spiritual development. Thus far I have emphasized spiritual development constructs that address growth across the human lifespan. Given the focus of this research on young adolescent spiritual development, I turn now to a brief de-scription of the work on adolescent spiritual development. In my review of that literature, I found few texts (e.g., Lerner, Roeser, & Phelps, 2008; Roehlkepartain et al., 2006) dedicated to adolescent spiritual development and to the theoretical, programmatic, and empirical work being done in that sub-specialty. More widely read publications, such as the *Handbook of Child Psychology* and the *Journal of Adolescence*, addressed adolescent spiritual develop-ment more explicitly than they have in the past (Roehlkepartain et al., 2006). For example, in 2006, for the first time in its 60-year publication, the editors of the *Handbook on Child Psychology* dedi-cated a chapter to spiritual development (Oser, Scarlett, & Bucher, 2006).

Likewise, in 2009, for the first time in its history of publication, the editors of *The Handbook of Adolescent Psychology* included a chapter on adolescent spiritual development (King & Roeser, 2009). The chapter is mostly a review of the theoretical and em-pirical literature on adolescent spiritual (and religious) development. King and Roeser's review is situated within other factors of adolescent development, such as health, education, and family. King and Roeser reported six ways in which adolescent spiritual development was conceptualized: (a) as a relational sys-tem; (b) as a meaning system; (c) as the creation of cognitive-conceptual schema; (d) as an identity-motivation system; (e) as the experience of various states of transcendent awareness; and (f) as a "dynamic developmental systems perspective in which [spiritual development] is seen in relation to multiple contexts, people, symbol systems, and opportunities and risks" (p. 440). For example, when King and Roeser addressed the cognitive-conceptual strand of literature, they relate the early adolescent emergent capacity for meta-cognition, abstract thought, and reflection to how adolescents during this period are re-examining intuitive spiritual beliefs from childhood.

The interaction between cognitive and spiritual development in adolescence is the central theme of Good and Willoughby's (2008) theoretical paper on adolescent spiritual development. The authors characterized adolescence as "a sensitive period for spiritual development" (p. 32). In other words, from a developmental perspective, there are attributes of adolescents that may leave them more likely or prone to exploring and questioning aspects of their spirituality. Good and Willoughby identified several of these developmental characteristics, e.g., thinking in abstractions, experiencing intense emotional states, and limited impulse control. They contended that some of these traits have been treated in the empirical literature as negative and suggested "that these same characteristics could also make adolescents more likely to engage in spiritual experiences, which may be a positive behavior that promotes well-being for some adolescents" (p. 36). Lerner, Roeser, and Phelps (2008) made a similar case in their introduction to *Positive Youth Development and Spirituality*. They located adolescence as an "ideal portion of the life span within which to seek this new spiritual knowledge" because of the "profound convergence of quantitative and qualitative changes" in the developmental domains (p. 8).

In conclusion to my survey of constructs of spirituality and spiritual development, I re-emphasize that my purpose for reviewing this literature is to contextualize the topic of spirituality and education. Without the work done in the developmental sciences to formulate and refine working definitions and theories of spirituality as a domain of human development, the challenge to situate spiritual development in an educational context is much, much greater. However, even with the growing evidence of the academy's acceptance and the publication of foundational work (e.g., Benson,

2004; King & Roeser, 2009; Oser et al., 2006) my impression is that, within the developmental sciences, there is not consensus on an empirical theory of spiritual development. Perhaps this lack of consensus speaks to the enduring nature of some of the questions that are associated with matters of the spirit. However, in my research I agree with Peter Benson (2006), who stated that while mystery may be part of spiritual development, keeping it a mystery in the academy is "shortsighted and irresponsible" (p. 494). In the context of this research, the lack of definitional clarity about young adolescent spiritual development hinders a teacher's understanding of how to respond holistically to middle grades students.

Holistic Education

The third interrelationship related to educational relevance of spiritual development in middle grades pedagogy is holistic education. Holistic education is a field that describes itself as explicitly inclusive of spirituality (e.g., Miller, 1997; Miller, 2007). As with the previous two major sections in this chapter, my goals are to provide context and background for a more complete understanding of my decision to use critical historiography as a research methodology and to model a critical constructivist framing of the problem in middle grades education: the absence of spiritual development in the (hi)story of the middle grades concept.

Similar to the lack of definitional clarity in the field of spiritual development, literature that addresses spirituality and education falls under differently named fields. All these fields emphasize seeing students' emotional, social, psychological, moral, and spiritual growth as deeply related to learning in schools. Much of the literature I reviewed on spirituality and education referred to human development theory. For example, Kessler (2000) argued that healthy spiritual development supports integration of and healthy development in other domains, such as social development.

In organizing this part of my review, I chose to begin with literature from two clearly defined fields—social-emotional education and holistic education—that have experienced more acceptance in the United States than the concept of spiritual development in the middle grades. I then review what I have identified as relevant literature on spirituality as an issue in education. This literature ranges from practitioner-based theory and program description (e.g., Kessler, 2000) to frameworks for understanding the social justice implications of addressing student spirituality (e.g., Ryoo, Crawford, Moreno, & McLaren, 2009).

In my framing of the significant interrelationships germane to the topic of the relevance of spiritual development within the middle grades concept, the field of holistic education lies between the overlapping circles of the fields of spirituality and (middle grades) education. I have categorized this overlapping conceptual area as holistic education for two reasons: (a) the field of holistic education specifically situates spirituality and spiritual development within education; and (b) the conceptual model of overlapping fields represents my interpretation of the ways in which the ideas relevant for this research are interrelated with each other. As a model specific to this research, I make no definitive claims about holistic education being the only body of literature that could be conceptualized as sharing ideas with spirituality/spiritual development and (middle grades) education. My framing is imperfect, in that the field of holistic education is not specific to the middle grades—it addresses schooling at all levels, from pre-school through adult education (e.g., Miller, 2007). While I include scholarly works not explicitly self-defined as from the field of holistic education (e.g., Hunter & Solomon, 2002), I use holistic education as signifier for literature that sees spirituality as relevant to education.

Socio-emotional education and holistic education. The fields of socio-emotional education (Cohen, 2008) and holistic education (Miller, 2007) are distinct, though similar, responses to the accepted practice of human fragmentation in educational contexts. As ancillaries to what is considered *education* in this country, both fields have experienced a degree of acceptance. What I find interesting about the very existence of fields such as socio-emotional education or holistic education is the implied assumption that when talking about education as a concept, a descriptive qualifier is added if what is meant is education that addresses the affective qualities of being human. In the field of holistic education, a central principle is that human beings of any age cannot be sectioned off into separate parts as a condition of formal learning in school (e.g., Palmer, 1998).

In the context of middle grades education, the affective needs of young adolescents are paramount (Gentilucci & Muto, 2007; Jewett, 2009; Mulhall, 2007; Nichols, 2008; Van Hoose et al., 2001). As reflected in their position papers (Carnegie Council on Adolescent Development, 1989; NASSP, 2006; NFAMGR, n.d.; NMSA, 2010), advocates of the middle level concept called for schools to be organized in ways that promote healthy, supportive, and meaningful interactions between community members—such as students, teachers, administrators, support staff, families, and community partners—to address the affective needs of the students. Addressing affective needs in their school context is a manifestation of the construct of caring as advocacy for young adolescent learners.

Valuing the affective needs of students is not exclusive to the middle grades. Cohen (2008), a leading pioneer in the field of socio-emotional education across the K–12 spectrum, made the case that an education inclusive of social, emotional, moral, ethical, and academic capabilities and needs is a human right. He explicitly addressed this implication of this position: when schools fail to treat students as multi-dimensional beings, an injustice is done to the students and to the greater society. Connecting his case for socio-emotional education to a democratic society, teacher education, and the aims of education, he drew upon a large body of theoretical and empirical literature. He identified the goals of socio-emotional education as "the promotion of social-emotional competencies and ethical dispositions on the one hand, and the creation of a safe climate for learning on the other" (p. 205). He cited a partnership between educators and mental health professionals as critical to more fully conceptualizing and designing effective practices for social emotional learning.

One of Cohen's (2008) points is particularly relevant, especially for readers who are skeptical of the place of spirituality in public schools. Drawing upon one of his earlier works, Cohen stated that one of the strategies characterizing the successful inclusion of socio-emotional education in an academic context was "purposively teaching children to be more socially, emotionally, ethically, and cognitively competent" (p. 209). What I find significant about this description is his use of the word *purposively*. If I apply Cohen's logic to how I have defined the problem in middle grades education (the absence of explicit inclusion of spiritual domain), I see purposive teaching as the intentional incorporation of knowledge of the spiritual developmental characteristics of young adolescents into curriculum and instruction.

In a meta-analysis of the effectiveness of 213 school-based socio-emotional educational programs, Durlak and associates (2011) found that compared to controls, students in the experimental group showed significant gains in social and emotional competencies and in academic achievement. Noting the current political climate in education (i.e., NCLB), they cited the 11% gain in academic performance as good news for teachers who value an education that is more inclusive of affective needs but are told to emphasize academic needs. The Durlak and associates' findings indicated, as Cohen (2008) and others have argued, that academic needs are being met when affective needs are being met as well. The results from Durlak and associates (2011) suggested that academic rigor versus nurture is a false dichotomy and that believing in it has perilous implications for students as well as societal goals.

In the field of holistic education, I identified Ron Miller (1997, 1999) and John P. Miller (2005, 2007) as leading advocates. Nel Noddings (1988, 2005) is also a prominent figure in the field, and in representing the results of my critical historiographical study, I returned to her seminal work on the construct of caring. One helpful distinction between the fields of holistic education and social-emotional education is provided by Miller (2005); in his distinction between educational approaches that are inclusive of more than the domain of intellect (i.e., Cohen, 2008), he stated that holistic education's inclusion of spirituality is what makes it unique from socio-emotional education. Miller (2005) described holistic education as having three core principles. The first—connectedness—references a criticism of the attempts to fragment curriculum and instruction and therefore, teachers and students. Dewey (1902) also critiqued the disconnection between "the unity and completeness" of the student's life and the same student who "goes to school, and various studies divide and fractionalize the world for him" (p. 10). Miller's (2005) second principle—inclusion—refers to the use of multiple and varied instructional and assessment techniques in order to meet the educative needs and abilities of all students. Inclusion also denotes a conceptualization of content as integrated across subjects, a key element of the middle grades concept. Balance—Miller's (2005) third holistic education principle—refers to the "complementary energies" (p. 6) of the rational and the intuitive. Drawing from the Eastern philosophy of Taoism, Miller advocated for balance via a critique of dominant social values: "Generally, our education has been dominated by yang energies such as a focus on rationality and individual competition, and has ignored yin energies such as fostering intuition and cooperative approaches to learning" (pp. 2–3).

Because holistic education is defined by its inclusion of human spirituality, I use the term *holistic education* to refer to an educational approach that addresses spirituality. I now turn to the various sources that explore spirituality as an educational concern, but may not explicitly self-identify as part of the field of holistic education.

Spirituality as an educational concern. Many authors wrote of spiritual development as an under-utilized yet powerful resource for students and teachers (Hunter & Solomon, 2002; Palmer, 1998; Schoonmaker, 2009). Much of the literature on spirituality and education opened with some form of explicit justification for the pairing. This pattern reflects the critical constructive perspective that current scholars, practitioners, and researchers interested in spirituality in education are operating within a greater social, political, and educational context which privileges secularism in the name of postmodern critical rationality. Critiquing public education's response to societal inequities, Purpel (1999) wrote, "What would seem to be required is a pedagogy of moral and spiritual transformation, but instead our profession has fashioned a pedagogy of control and standardization focused on technology, competitiveness, and materialism" (p. 59). This theme of situating the educational relevance of spiritual development within a specific socio-political context led me to choose a research approach—critical historiography—that foregrounds historical context as part of data analysis strategies.

Few works focused on spirituality and middle grades students. One book on middle grades education (Nakkula & Toshalis, 2006) has a chapter on spiritual development. Three additional works (de Souza, 2006; Miller, 2005; Sadowski, 2008) address adolescent spirituality in the context of its relevance in education, but not the middle grades specifically. Therefore, I expanded my area of inquiry beyond the middle grades specifically and looked at the literature on spirituality in K–12 education. While there is a growing body of literature on spirituality in higher education, I chose not to include any of it here (with the exception of Palmer, 1998) because the debate over the educational relevance of spirituality is slightly different in an adult learning context than it is in a young adolescent learning context.

Identifying spirituality as an educational concern is not a new issue. In his review of the historical context of spirituality in education, Miller (2007) cited Plato, Rousseau, and Tolstoy as historical contributors to holistic education. In the 20th century, Gandhi promoted a holistic educational approach that explicitly identified student spirituality in his prolific writing on educational philosophy (e.g., Gandhi, 1953). The foundational assumptions supporting Gandhi's Nai Talim or, "New Education" are: all children can learn; learning happens through one's mind, spirit, and body; the teacher—student relationship is mutual, reciprocal, and grounded in trust; and deep learning happens in community, not just in solitude (Gandhi, 1953). For Gandhi, the traditional "3 R's" were head, heart, and hand. From these core assumptions, a theory of education emerged from him that advocates for equitable practices; strong community and family partnerships; varied modalities for instruction; an integration of intellectual, spiritual, and physical curriculum; adults as intentional role models for character and morality; and service-learning to nurture student growth and development in schools (Gandhi, 1953). When I first encountered Nai Talim, I was struck by some of the parallels between what Gandhi proposed as educational reform in a post-independent India and the reforms for middle grades schools in

the United States. Both emerge from a critique of the current system as overly mechanical, ineffective, and inappropriate to the
point of being demeaning to the students it is supposed to serve.
And, both offer alternatives grounded in compassionate, health-
affirming human relationships, curriculum and instruction that
are integrated and engaging, and a culture of dignity, integrity,
and mutual growth.

Rachael Kessler (2000) has written eloquently about spirituality, and her work is frequently referenced by others working
within the field of holistic education (e.g., Bruce & Cockerham,
2004). Kessler noted that while educators and community members argue over whether or not it is a good idea to bring
spirituality into the schools, children and adolescents are bringing
their spiritualities with them right along with their bodies, hearts,
and minds. In this position she resembles another often-referenced
author in the field of spirituality and education, Palmer (1998).
For Kessler and Palmer, the salient question is *how* do educators
skillfully work with students as they grapple with universal questions, seek transcendent experiences, and discover their own
sacredness, not *if* educators should be doing this.

Kessler (2000) rejected the excuse that schools can blame "per-
sistent violent and self-destructive behavior" on larger societal ills.
She acknowledged the impact of poverty, racism, and neglect but
argued "We cannot really understand or heal from these plagues if
we do not begin to recognize and meet the spiritual needs of our
children. Do we need periodic reminders from sawed-off shotguns
to show us that these young people *feel*?" (p. xii). In fact, Kessler
called for schools to give students tools with which to deal with
poverty, racism, and neglect. Palmer (1998) made a similar case,
although the focus on his work is how teachers can recognize and
meet their own spiritual needs—especially as they work in schools
that are deeply affected by poverty, racism, and neglect—for the
purpose of being able to connect with their students.

Kessler's theoretical framework for addressing the spirituality of
students (which she refers to as their soul) used the metaphor of
passages and pathways. She developed a "passages" program in
California in the mid-1980s that used ritual, symbolic play, community dialogue, and skillful adult facilitation to support adolescents

as they considered the mysteries of the human experience during their times of transition (i.e., adolescence). From that work, and her subsequent experience as an educator in Colorado, she devised a model that identifies seven gateways, or pathways, to addressing the spiritual development of young people in a school context.

In her model, there are overlapping pathways (e.g., creativity, connection) to students finding and experiencing the central pathway to the soul: meaningful relationships with themselves and with other people. In this way, her model for spiritual development parallels the construct of developmental domains described in the fields of middle grades reform and applied developmental psychology; domains are to be treated as overlapping and interactive rather than distinct and independent. Kessler arranged the gateways using circles to illustrate the non-linearity of her model. Teachers can guide students to access their spiritual natures using any of the pathways; some will be more or less attractive to different students based on their temperaments and preferences. Kessler's model appealed to many holistic educators who seek to address the spiritual needs of their students (e.g., Nakkula & Toshalis, 2006). Her model allows for differentiation and honors the iterative process of teaching and learning. In addition, her explanation of how the creative gateway functions reflects a theme in the literature on spirituality: a recommendation to access students' spirituality through creativity (Colalillo Kates, 2005; da Conceição Azevedo & Gil da Costa, 2006; Nakkula & Toshalis, 2006).

Several authors have identified frameworks for understanding the implications of spiritual development within education. Hunter and Solomon (2002), writing for school administrators, argued that educational leaders who do not take into account their own spirituality and the spirituality of their staff miss opportunities to foster the level of motivation and morale that positively impacts pre-K–12 students. They constructed spirituality as part of a person's meaning system that influences ideas of professional and personal roles and responsibilities: "We suggest that it is important for individuals to be aware that drawing upon personal spiritual meaning systems is a valid means of conceptualizing, framing, and approaching work" (p. 38). Hunter and Solomon focused on the interrelationship between school leadership and addressing spirituality. Their ideas—administrators using the frame of spirituality to support the integration of teachers' personal and professional meaning systems—reflect the type of leadership advocated by middle grades leaders (e.g., NMSA, 2010).

Schoonmaker (2009) framed spirituality as something that can be seen in classrooms as an interpretive lens guiding practice. Her metaphor of a lens with which to see spirituality is drawn from Huebner (1985, 1999), who explored spirituality and education in the context of curriculum theory. Schoonmaker (2009) offered a construct that situates spiritual matters squarely in the realm of public education. She made the case that learning is inherently a spiritual endeavor; it is a search for meaning, understanding, and connection occurring within a context that is greater than oneself. Like Kessler (2000), Schoonmaker dismissed the question about whether or not spirituality is in the classroom but instead, offered suggestions for how teachers can intentionally work with the spiritual development of themselves and their students. Her suggestions included having a personal sense of one's own spirituality through practices and fostering recollections of one's own spiritual development. Through personal work, Schoonmaker claimed that teachers would be better positioned to see the sacred in the classroom, experience moment-to-moment awareness, and more deeply understand learning through the perspective of children.

Milojevic (2005) proposed a three-tiered approach to understanding how the inclusion of spirituality can impact education. She argued that inclusion of spirituality locates the educational process within the inner life of a student, expands the structure of education to life-long activities in and out of schools, and brings closer the content of education to the same preoccupations of living. Her work echoes the middle grades recommendations for authentic learning activities that draw from a student's previous sources of knowledge.

De Souza (2006), writing in the context of the Australian educational system, argued that because of the decline in the influence of institutions that have historically ministered to spirituality (e.g., a search for meaning), a need has arisen for other institutions, such as schools, to respond. De Souza (2006) illustrated as clearly as Kessler (2000) the specific teacher practices and student benefits that come from tending to the spiritual development of students. Her work is useful in the hyper-accountability climate of the United States because she used the language of standards-based "learner outcomes" to distinguish between cognitive, affective, and spiritual outcomes in a holistic pedagogy.

In addition, echoing both developmental psychologists (Fowler & Dell, 2006) and middle grades advocates (NMSA, 2010), de Souza (2006) brought forward the claim that since educators have a responsibility to design and sustain learning environments that respond to and address all of the needs of learners, knowledge about the spiritual development of learners can improve a teacher's work. Citing the interdependence of all of the developmental domains as well as different learning modalities, de Souza proposed a model for teachers to consider when designing learning environments. Her theoretical model emphasizes the interplay between inner-reflective and outer-relational activities within and among intellectual, emotional, and spiritual ways of thinking, feeling, and intuiting. In her model, spirituality is at the core (center) of the other two ways of knowing and learning.

Because de Souza's (2006) premise about the potential value of integrating spiritual development in an educational context aligns so closely with my own, I return to it in my discussion of the results. One distinction between her work and my own is that while we are both working within a Western cultural context, I intend for this research to be firmly grounded within the context of public middle grades education in the United States. Her work is highly complementary to my own, but I still see a need for the development of a model that is tailored for middle grades educators working in the public system in the United States.

Holistic Education Through the Lens of Critical Constructivism

As I concluded the previous chapter on the middle grades concept, I also end here with a consideration of the third significant interrelationship—holistic education—through the critical constructivist perspective. Pairing spirituality with critical theory and constructivism occurred to me quickly after revisiting Freire's (1993) *Pedagogy of the Oppressed* a few years ago. Freire's characterization of dialogue as dependent upon love, humility, faith, trust, and hope invoke some of the processes and expressions of spiritual development. I realize I am not alone in seeing human spirituality as deeply intertwined with critical pedagogy (e.g., hooks, 1994). Also, many of the central holistic educators (e.g., Miller, 1997) advocate for a holistic pedagogy on the grounds that in a free, democratic society, it is untenable to allow technocratic schools to politically cripple historically marginalized youth.

A critical constructivist analysis of the field of holistic education merges holistic pedagogy with critical pedagogy as a means of expanding the potential for human liberation in schools. To wit, a potential source of relevance for spiritual development in relation to middle grades education is seeing this developmental resource as one that facilitates critical thinking and reflective action akin to Freire's (1993) concepts of *praxis* and *humanization*. Sometimes referred to as critical spiritual pedagogy, this framework contends that a truly transformative education must stimulate critical inquiry and reflection at the intuitive, non-verbal levels (i.e., spiritual) as well as the intellectual and emotional levels. Orr (2005) claimed: "Antioppressive pedagogy...must involve teaching the whole person. Simply teaching a more acceptable set of ideas to replace discriminatory ones will not suffice if that teaching fails to address the emotional, bodily, behavioral, and spiritual aspects of those ideas in a student's life" (p. 88). Like de Souza's (2006) model, the critical spiritual pedagogical framework reflects an epistemology of interdependent domains of knowing and learning. An implication of critical spiritual pedagogy is a critique of the dominance of positivist epistemology in education in the United States. This critique identifies how certain types of knowing have been privileged over other types in ways that sustain certain sociopolitical economic groups in the U.S.

Ryoo, Crawford, Moreno, and McLaren (2009) distinguished critical spiritual pedagogy from critical pedagogy by grounding critical spiritual pedagogy in spirituality, as a supplement to critical pedagogy's emphasis on humanity and power. Like Orr (2005), Ryoo and associates critiqued critical pedagogy on the grounds that it is incomplete, and therefore, insufficient as a challenge to dominant power paradigms: "To create a revolutionary spiritual pedagogy, educators must move beyond the constructs of critical pedagogy to incorporate an acknowledgement and respect for the spiritual and sacred in teaching and learning" (pp. 136–137).

Explicit inclusion of students' spiritual development can counteract hegemonic practices in schools (Gatto, 1999; hooks, 2003; Ryoo et al., 2009; Sherrod & Spiewak, 2008; Simmer-Brown, 1999). Owen Wilson (2005) offered an alternative way that schools could utilize the metaphor of benchmarks. Instead of applying that metaphor only to academic gains (or physical gains, such as in gym class), Owen Wilson called for the integration of rites of passage rituals that reach the hearts and souls of adolescents. Her rationale is that rites of passage make schooling more personal and meaningful for students by providing an opportunity for an ethnically identified diverse population to see their home culture reflected in their school context. She strongly critiqued the domination of the industrialized Western factory model—what Freire (1993) called the banking system of education—on the grounds that it is impersonal, oppressive, and outdated. Citing Hill (1991), Owen Wilson argued that the stakes are high in a system where "the benefits of custom, ceremonies, faith, and ritual acculturation have been discarded...[and so] we have educated away from ourselves" (p. 68).

Throughout the literature are similar claims that warn of the dangers of psychological fragmentation in a learning context, i.e., schools (de Souza, 2006; Kessler, 2000; Palmer, 1998; Pearmain, 2005; Ryoo et al., 2009). This warning invokes the importance of the problem I propose to study: What is the cost of continuing to separate a student from his or her spirituality? What the literature on holistic education, as reviewed in this section, seems to suggest is such a separation is not an inevitable practice. Collectively, the authors represented in this section suggest that integration of the spiritual domain of human development can happen in many ways: through creativity (Kessler, 2000), as a lens for guiding practice (Schoonmaker, 2009), or as an interplay between inner-reflective and outer-relational learning activities (de Souza, 2006). Once the critical constructivist educator accepts that "...dehumanization, although a concrete historical fact, is *not* a given destiny" (Freire, 1993, p.44), a different image of the landscape of education in the United States can be generated through critical historiography.

Chapter Four

A Research Design for Interrogating the (Hi)stories

History...cannot simply be an act of recognition, of fitting events into fixed patterns, of just seeing the light. It must begin, rather, by apprehending the sources of light and the present objects they shed or illuminate, and follow with an active, incessant engagement in the process of naming and renaming, covering and uncovering, consuming and producing new relations, investigating hierarchies of power and effect: distilling light into sun, moon and fire. (Alcalay, 1993, p. 2)

CRITICAL historiography is an interdisciplinary conceptual research approach that offers investigators data collection and analysis methods used to identify, interpret, and synthesize complex intersections of power and knowledge. In my inquiry area of spiritual development and middle grades education, many disciplinary fields overlapped and interpenetrated each other. In addition to the challenge of keeping track of these theoretical interactions, I was challenged to clearly articulate the social and historical contexts in which the ideas are situated and the ways in which those contexts influence or affect each other. An interdisciplinary research approach can be used to unpack these areas of intersection (and collision) as well as raise to the surface the underlying assumptions and paradigms (Kuhn, 1996) that guide the foundational literature.

To introduce this chapter on the principles and techniques of critical historiography, I briefly address some of the methods I considered using to investigate my research question. This journey is offered here as an example of a path other educational researchers might find themselves on when exploring the fit between their research purposes and a research methodology. It is also offered as additional justification for my unconventional decision to select a research methodology not commonly utilized for a professional doctorate in education.

The literature I read on researching spirituality in education guided me toward choosing qualitative methodologies, such as case study, narrative study, and grounded theory, with which to investigate my guiding research questions. I rejected experimental and non-experimental quantitative research methodologies for my study because I was not comfortable operationalizing spirituality through measurable indicators. That said, I could envision quantitative approaches having potential as a strategic methodology to call upon, given the supremacy of the positivist paradigm in Western society.

In considering a qualitative approach, I found two main reasons from the literature to select a method from that research framework. First, I wanted to articulate an explicit understanding of the educational relevance of spiritual development and one way to do that is by exploring personal perspectives of teachers and students (e.g., Wintersgill, 2008). Qualitative methods such as case study, grounded theory, and phenomenology are better suited in terms of what counts as data and data analysis methods for a study that seeks to more deeply understand a phenomenon in a naturalistic setting (Creswell, 2007; Guba & Lincoln, 2005; Janesick, 2011).

Second, one repeated theme in the literature was the way in which creativity was used to access and address adolescent spirituality. A complementary research approach in the qualitative field is arts-based research (Leavy, 2009). Given the anecdotal strength of the relationship between creativity and spirituality, incorporating an arts-based research approach holds tremendous promise for the purpose of understanding the educational relevance of spiritual development in the middle grades.

Although both of the reasons aforementioned justify grounds for qualitative work that involved collecting data (e.g., interviews, student work, observations) from human subjects, such an approach felt incomplete as well as premature, given the lack of theoretical literature on spirituality in middle grades education. In future research that is guided by the results of this study, researchers could collect and analyze data directly from the field that could offer a glimpse into educators' understanding of the spiritual lives of their students. The results of this research can also be used to design professional development curriculum for middle grades teachers (e.g., Benami, 2006) and test the effectiveness of a specific professional development intervention. But, from my review of the literature, there is a stronger need at this time to establish a clear rationale for situating spirituality in public schools through conceptual work that synthesizes the ways in which competing paradigms shape knowledge about spiritual development as a pedagogical concern.

Zeichner (1999) argued that one of the great benefits of historical research is the conceptual knowledge it contributes to a field that seeks to advocate for its interests and respond strategically to challenges. When deciding to use critical historiography, pondering the challenges of the aspect of education that most interests the researcher can be helpful for clarifying the appropriateness of the method. Do the challenges, as characterized by the researcher, call for a research methodology that yields new conceptual knowledge? From my perspective, today's debates in the middle grades include the following three challenges: (a) how to honor the intent of the middle grades concept in an era of policies that jeopardize its relational aspects; (b) how to be more developmentally responsive in the middle school's organization and leadership; and (c) how to recognize and respond to the whole child in the classroom. When considering the suitability of critical historiography, a key question I raised was: What potential could a more holistic understanding of the developmental needs, interests, and abilities offer to these debates? Based on my review of the research on spiritual development in education, I came to the conclusion that while my question could be addressed in part by empirical, field-based methods, the landscape for this topic was much larger than those methods facilitate inquiry into.

Outline of chapter. For my research, the primary inquiry question was: What is the educational relevance of spiritual development in middle grades education? Two subquestions guided and focused the data analysis: (a) What prevalent paradigms underlie the academic discourse on spirituality as a developmental domain, the middle grades concept, and holistic education? and (b) What are the inter-textual and inter-discursive relationships within the convergence of the paradigms of the three fields? My intention, as Alcalay (1993) wrote in the quotation cited at the beginning of this chapter, was to "apprehend the sources of light and the present objects they shed or illuminate" (p. 2). And, my expectation was that a critical interpretation of the prevalent paradigms that have influenced the shaping of these fields, followed by an interpretation of the paradigms' inter-discursive relationships, would offer definitional clarity to the educational relevance of the domain of spiritual development and implications for practice in the field of middle grades education.

In this chapter, I describe the underlying principles and specific techniques associated with critical historiography. To illustrate these principles and techniques in action, I provide a general overview of my research design. I conclude this chapter by addressing issues related to the integrity of my research.

In the following chapter, I present a more detailed account of the processes used for data collection and analysis in my research on spiritual development and the middle grades concept, addressing validation issues (Creswell, 2007) when appropriate. Embedded within my description of the research methods employed in my project is a rationale for critical historiography as the appropriate research methodology.

Taken together these two chapters present a comprehensive case of and for critical historiography in educational research, even at the doctoral level. Although I faced challenges as an emergent researcher using unconventional research methodology, the fit between my research purposes and the principles of critical historiography provided a strong foundation for scholarly inquiry.

Principles of Critical Historiography

A primary architect of critical historiography in educational research is Kincheloe, who outlines the method in his works on bricolage (2001, 2005) and critical constructivism (2008) as well as his work directly on critical historiography (Villaverde, Kincheloe, & Helyar, 2006). Using Wolcott's (2001) distinction between methodology and method, I describe and justify critical historiography by identifying the underlying principles (methodology), and then, by surveying the specific techniques (methods) associated with critical historiography.

Principles. The principles, or dimensions, underlying critical historiography are criticality, affirmative presentism, bricolage, and multilogicality (Villaverde, Kincheloe, & Helyar, 2006). Criticality refers to the perspective that historical discourses reflect constructed relationships between individuals and societal structures that are influenced by power and privilege; that is, history is not a forward march through pre-determined events with definitive causes. In the context of educational reform, Popkewitz (1991) referred to the principle of criticality as "an approach for considering 'change' as social ruptures in ongoing patterns, rather than as an evolution or a chronology of events that seems inevitably or potentially progressive" (p. 3). In critical historiography, shifting the focus of analysis from the subject of the (hi)story to the worldviews of the author(s) of the (hi)story is a manifestation of the criticality principle.

As a foundational principle, criticality overlaps with the second principle, affirmative presentism. Criticality challenges the linear, one-dimensional notion of time (e.g., Greenblatt, 1998) by expanding it to accommodate overlapping and simultaneous experiences. The relationship between the past, the present, and the future is fluid, multidimensional, and co-constructed through applying affirmative presentism. The present is viewed as a process of transformation between past and present, not simply a static period in time (Novoa & Yariv-Mashal, 2003). This perspective is crucial to my research, as I attempt to interpret the layered effect of situating three previously disparate conceptual fields "as a grid or overlay of historically formed ideas" (Popkewitz, 1997, p. 18).

Affirmative presentism is a response to the charge that good history does not use contemporary values and understandings by which to make assertions about the past. An affirmative presentism acknowledges that present values and understandings shape how we construct our transmission of the past. As with the qualitative researcher who acknowledges her subjectivity (e.g., Janesick, 2011), the value of this acknowledgment—from the perspective of a critical historiographer—is to bring more integrity to the researcher's analysis than that of a researcher who claims pure neutrality and objectivity (Henry, 2006). Also, affirmative presentism reflects my critical constructivist paradigm in terms of my relativist ontology and subjectivist epistemology.

What affirmative presentism does *not* do is substitute fidelity to the data with either cultural relativism or a "rhetoric of blame" (Said, 1993, p. 18). Criteria for establishing rigor and trustworthiness are necessary. For example, Rury (2006) made the distinction between a "sufficient" (p. 330) and a "necessary or definitive explanation" (p. 329) in historical inquiry. Rury wrote, "Often it is necessary to move persistently forward and find new evidence to address questions that arise until there is an interpretive frame and descriptive account that seems satisfactory. It is only at this point that investigation abates" (p. 330). Rury's application of the qualitative principle of saturation (Creswell, 2007) to historical inquiry was reflected in my research through my use of constant-comparative analysis (Charmaz, 2006) during data analysis.

The third principle of critical historiography—bricolage—comes from the French verb *bricoler*; the literal translation is to tinker or fiddle with something. It is also a term used in the context of the visual arts and in humanities research. In both contexts, it means crafting something by using many different resources that are available (Kincheloe, 2001, 2005):

> Drawing on the concept of bricolage, they understand that they must use multiple research tradition and theoretical tools to understand the way these factors influence how we make sense of the world around us. Bricoleurs appreciate that any research that fails to account for these dynamics cannot produce a complex, thick and textured picture of a phenomenon. (Kincheloe, 2008, p. 24)

In the context of critical historiography, bricolage can involve "making connections between apparently disparate ideas" (Villaverde, Kincheloe, & Helyar, 2006, p. 334) through the use of multiple research methods that draw from different disciplines. This principle of critical historiography supported my intention to re-present three apparently disparate fields as an overlapping grid and my use of interdisciplinary research methods to interpret inter-textual and inter-discursive patterns in the nexus of the grid. As a bricoleur, I borrowed data analysis techniques from constructivist grounded theory (Charmaz, 2006) and from literature theory (Said, 1993). When addressing my research design, I describe how I drew from the bricolage principle. I offer these specific examples to bring greater clarity to how a critical researcher would conduct a critical historiographical study.

The fourth principle—multilogicality—refers to the valuing of different perspectives, particularly those of indigenous people who have been historically silenced through marginalization and oppression. One method of valuing under-represented perspectives is to select primary sources of data generated by marginalized people. I did not select this type of data in my research on spiritual development and the middle grades concept. Instead, I selected data from sources recognized as authoritative by the audience I sought to address. Because my primary audience was middle grades advocates in the United States, I used as criteria for my data published texts that are foundational to the fields of middle grades reform, spiritual development, and holistic education. After applying these criteria, I was left with texts that were written by authors primarily from the United States, with one Canadian author (Jack Miller) and two European authors (Anton Bucher and Fritz Oser).

However, I honored the principle of multilogicality by applying the data analysis strategy of contrapuntal reading (Said, 1993). As an analysis technique, contrapuntal reading involves seeing multiple discourses within a text. The technique of contrapuntal reading presumes the existence of a tension between dominant discourse and a discourse of resistance (Said, 1993), and foregrounds that tension. Through a critical interpretation of the data, and my re-presentation of the values and beliefs guiding the recommendations of the three fields, the perspectives of marginalized peoples was valued, albeit not as fully as a direct inclusion of their voices into the data set.

These four principles—criticality, affirmative presentism, bricolage, and multilogicality—ground the conceptual work of critical historiography in the realm of educational practice. Privileging relationships, having an appreciation of simultaneity, drawing from diverse skill sets, and honoring individual perspectives are all part of my repertoire as a classroom teacher. Although in the next section I describe a primarily conceptual research project, this research is conceived within and intended for middle grades classrooms.

Techniques of Critical Historiography

The three main research techniques (methods) used in critical historiography are meta-analysis, critical interpretation, and asking unique questions. I describe each technique, and introduce some context of how I used each one in my research.

Meta-analysis. The first main technique—meta-analysis—has a meaning in critical historiography that is slightly different than the meaning used in the context of quantitative research. In the context of critical historiography, meta-analysis involves looking at the breadth of relevant data sources (e.g., written texts) for what has been included and what has been excluded. In addition, with foundational texts as sources of data, meta-analysis involves interpreting for ways in which the data sources reflect challenge and/or acceptance of dominant paradigms. "Meta-analysis instills a critical distance through which to create a bird's eye view of the entire slice of history while simultaneously producing an insider's perspective" (Villaverde, Kincheloe, & Helyar, 2006, p. 315). The purpose of this technique is to generate knowledge, in the form of a narrative or a conceptual model, based on the production of existing analyses of the related literature. My initial review of the literature is a meta-analysis (in the critical historiographical meaning) that generated a conceptual model of the significant interrelationships between applied developmental psychology, middle grades education, and spirituality/spiritual development. In my meta-analysis, I focused on what has been included. Then, in my data analysis, I focused on the other two parts of a critical historiographical meta-analysis: what has been excluded and how the foundational literature has challenged and/or sustained dominant paradigms. Meta-analysis was crucial to my research design in terms of how I was able to conceptualize and organize the convergence of the fields relevant to my inquiry.

Critical interpretation. Critical interpretation is a second technique of critical historiography (Villaverde, Kincheloe, & Helyar, 2006). In addition to the work of Villaverde, Kincheloe, and Helyar (2006), critical interpretation is also informed by the work of Henry (2006), who described contemporary educational historiography as the "revisioning [of] extant bodies of thought, analyzing existing data in new ways" (p. 339). Through Henry's (2006) work, I was introduced to Said's (1993) data analysis strategy of contrapuntal reading. Henry, like Kincheloe (2001, 2005), advocated bricolage as a research principle for rigorous inquiry, and it is from that perspective she cited Said (1993). Historiographical research is also informed by Rury (2006), who attested to the importance of hermeneutics in educational research: "Education is a complex, value-laden social phenomenon, of course; thus the role of interpretation has been especially important in the history of education" (p. 326). Maclean (1982) described how hermeneutics were applied by 19th century German historiographer Droysen in language that parallels my own application of hermeneutics: "It follows that historical understanding as a method is not an abstract academic exercise but rather the very basis of human praxis brought to the level of scholarly reflection" (p. 360).

What Henry (2006), Rury (2006), and Maclean (1982) drew attention to is the promise of conceptual work for practitioners. My critical interpretation of the data consisted of looking for evidence of prevalent paradigms for the middle grades concept, spirituality as a developmental domain, and holistic education. My sources of data for a critical interpretation were three to four foundational texts from each of the three fields. In a critical historiography, the conceptual work is grounded in artifacts from the field of practice (as is often true for purely qualitative research as well). In my critical historiographical research, I hope to have offered a practical language for thinking and talking about responding to the spiritual development of middle grades students.

Asking unique questions. I conclude this description of the techniques of critical historiography with the third technique, asking unique questions. This technique is deployed throughout the research process, including the drafting of results and how those results are situated within their socio-political context.

At the beginning of my research process, I engaged in this technique in the ways in which I framed this topic—as a scaffolding of overlapping fields constructed through my positioning apparently disparate ideas in proximity to each other. Given the uniqueness of how I view the topic of the educational relevance of the spiritual development of middle grades students, I considered this technique to be both strategic and complementary of my aims and intentions. Asking unique questions gave me direction and permission to challenge hegemonic beliefs about spirituality, academic writing and research, and human development theory and research.

I also employed the technique of asking unique questions when crafting narratives to describe the results of my data analysis and as a framing device for the discussion of my findings. Villeverde, Kincheloe, and Helyar (2006) described asking unique questions as "an inquiry based method [which] is at the core of a meaningful research endeavor; it fuels curiosity, and recognizes problematic practices and beliefs before considered 'natural' or part of the 'norm'" (p. 315). My composition of the narrative descriptions of the prevalent paradigms for the three (hi)stories of the middle grades concept, spirituality as a developmental domain, and holistic education was guided by this technique's direction to explicitly interrogate the bases upon which claims were made within those (hi)stories. Asking unique questions also encourages the use of my imagination (White, 1987, as cited by Villeverde, Kincheloe, and Helyar, 2006) in order to articulate a discourse of possibility (Giroux, 1981). My discussion of the results of my research is framed by the possibilities suggested by including spirituality as a developmental domain relevant for the practice of middle grades education.

Within my discussion of the findings in the context of the middle grades, I addressed how the research illustrates Popkewitz's (1991) social epistemology by making links between my summative findings of three shared paradigms (Ecological Epistemology, Holistic Ontology, and Positivist Ontology) and their discursive interrelationship, and the constitution of two subjects of schooling: developmental domains in the context of middle grades reform and the relevance of spirituality in education. In relating social epistemology to reforms in education, Popkewitz and Brennan (1998) argued, "exploration of these reform themes...provides detailed evidence of the ways in which the connection of knowledge to power operates to constitute the subject[s] of schooling" (p. 23). By making the link between knowledge and power explicit in my discussion of the research findings, I re-present spiritual development and middle grades education in unique ways.

Finally, asking unique questions can be a strategy for lifting the veil on paradigms that were so deeply embedded in the researcher's consciousness that he is blind to their influence over his powers of interpretation and analysis. Choosing constructivist grounded theory coding strategies supported my intention to interrogate not only the normative frameworks of the middle grades concept, spiritual developmental theory, and holistic education but my own paradigms as well: "[grounded theory] coding should inspire us to examine hidden assumptions in our own use of language as well as that of our participants" (Charmaz, 2006, p. 47). Through my use of Charmaz's (2006) instruction for researcher memo-writing before, during, and after the analysis process, I documented my own transformation as a scholar, teacher, and educational leader. While my larger purpose in this research is to influence the field of middle grades education, I address in the final chapter how my endeavors in this project changed me as I entered into "...a space of transformation where previously excluded perspectives operate to change consciousness of both self and the world" (Kincheloe, 2008, p. 132).

Before turning to my research design using critical historiography, I want to re-emphasize the purpose of my research project: to illuminate what I see as an area of missed opportunity in the field of middle grades education—the potential for cultivating belonging through the explicit inclusion of the spiritual domain as a part of human development. As I saw it when conceptualizing this research, this oversight was connected to (dominant) cultural understandings about spirituality that are reflected in public education in the United States. By employing a research methodology that allowed me to unearth both the content of the paradigms influencing the related fields and the discursive interrelationships amongst those paradigms, I was able to challenge the illusion of inevitability regarding the exclusion of spiritual development from the middle grades concept. This research is important at this time when cultural understandings about spirituality seem to be shifting to reflect more inclusivity than during previous eras in academia (a bigger tent, so to speak). While my research design is certainly not the only way to explore the educational relevance of spiritual development in middle grades education, based on my professional experiences as a middle and secondary classroom teacher and as an emergent scholar in higher education, a critical historiography felt both timely and responsive to the needs of the field of middle grades education.

Research Design for Critical Historiography of Relevance of Spiritual Development

Conceptual framing for research design. In the previous chapter, I identified three significant interrelationships amongst the fields most directly related to the absence of spiritual development in the middle grades concept of developmentally responsive education. The diagram that follows represents the conceptual framework I rendered, borrowing from Popkewitz's (1997) metaphoric language for historiographical research in education: "My traveling among different sets of ideas is to think of them as part of a scaffolding, to think of them as a grid or overlay of historically formed ideas, whose pattern gives intelligibility to today's debates" (p.18).

Figure 4.1

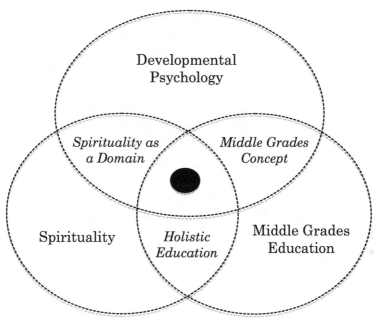

When I lay the three outer fields over one another in a Venn dia-gram, not only do the three significant interrelationships emerge, but a blank area in the center also becomes visible. It is this blankness I sought to fill with knowledge of what, if any, para-digms were shared amongst the different sets of ideas. Was a pattern there, which, as Popkewitz suggests, could cut through the inevitability that saturates contemporary agreements about the relevance of spiritual development in public education? Could the pattern, if there was one to be interpreted, suggest the educational relevance of the domain of spiritual development, and do so with sufficient specificity to be practical for middle grades teachers and advocates? The line of logic I followed in these questions paralleled the logic I deciphered in my original interpretation of how an over-lap of the fields of middle grades education and applied developmental psychology yielded the middle grades concept of de-velopmentally responsive education for young adolescent learners.

I used the Venn model as a starting point from which to mani-fest a research design for a critical historiography of my guiding inquiry question, What is the educational relevance of spiritual development in middle grades education? My research interprets for the conceptual contents of the convergence of the three inner fields. These conceptual contents were framed as paradigms that oriented the (hi)stories of the fields of the middle grades concept, spirituality as a developmental domain, and holistic education. The paradigms of the (hi)stories were the major units of historiographical analysis. Before describing the data collection and analysis strategies used for the critical historiography, I disclose the construct of paradigm that guided my research design.

Defining paradigm. When using the term *paradigm* as a unit of historiographical analysis, I refer to the work of Kuhn (1996; with Conant & Haugeland, 2000). Kuhn (1996), in his historiographical account of the history of science, brought paradigm as a unit of conceptual analysis to the forefront of Western intellectual discourse (Burke, 2001). Kuhn described scientific inquiry as a collective endeavor to understand the natural world, a field of practice characterized by relative consensus disrupted by periods of paradigm "revolution" (p. 92). Kuhn (1996) described the relationship of paradigmatic beliefs with systematic inquiry as directive. He used the metaphor of maps to articulate the ways in which paradigms influence practice:

> Paradigms provide [natural] scientists not only with a map but also with some of the directions essential for map-making. In learning a paradigm the scientist acquires theory, methods, and standards together, usually in an inextricable mixture. Therefore, when paradigms change, there are usually significant shifts in the criteria determining the legitimacy both of problems and of proposed solutions. (p. 109)

In the second edition of *The Structure of Scientific Revolutions*, published in 1970, Kuhn offered further clarification of his definition of paradigm, as a response to the criticism that his use of the term was inconsistent in the 1st edition (e.g., Masterman, 1970). He wrote that he saw two definitions of paradigms. The first was sociological: "it stands for the entire constellation of beliefs, values, techniques, and so on shared by the members of a given community" (p. 175). The second usage was more scientific: "on the other hand, it [paradigm] denotes one sort of element in that constellation, the concrete puzzle-solutions which, employed as models or examples, can replace explicit rules as a basis for the solution of the remaining puzzles" (p. 175). In the example I cited about paradigms as maps, both usages are illustrated—paradigms are, according to Kuhn, acquired and sustained within a shared intellectual community through education and application. For me, Kuhn's definition(s) of paradigm reflects Popkewitz's construct of a social epistemology: "A social epistemology enables us to consider the word *learning* not as standing alone, but as embodying a range of historically constructed values, priorities, and dispositions toward how one should see and act toward the world" (Popkewitz & Brennan, 1998, p. 9). Like Kuhn's (1996) construct, a social epistemology considers paradigms as discursive practices, i.e., tacit rules that are socio-historical constructions.

Kuhn's (1996) theory regarding the role of paradigms in the natural sciences is a compelling one for critical historiographical research in the social sciences. Shortly after he died in 1996, an edited collection (Kuhn, Conant, & Haugeland, 2000) of his work from the last decade of his life reflected refinement but not repudiation of his seminal 1962 theory. In an essay on the natural and social sciences, Kuhn addressed the ways in which his theory regarding paradigm wars could be applicable in both sets of disciplines: "No more in the natural than in the human sciences is there some neutral, culture-independent, set of categories within which the population—whether of objects or of actions—can be described" (p. 220). In my research, I applied Kuhn's theory on the role of paradigms within an academic field as a framing device that complements Popkewitz's (1991) social epistemology framework. An implication of that decision was that I interpreted the data for evidence of paradigms.

Interpreting paradigms as a unit of historiographical analysis is akin to a historian's use of artifacts as sources of data. Historians use artifacts to tell a story; historiographers use paradigms to interrogate how a history has been constructed. As artifacts, paradigms are examples of historically contingent practices. For example, Husen (1999) described paradigms as a social and cultural practice: "a paradigm could be regarded as a cultural artifact, reflecting the dominant notions about scientific behavior in a particular scientific community...at a particular point in time" (p. 31). Knowledge of a paradigm, as constructed by the researcher, becomes a unit of historiographical analysis.

Popekewitz's (1991, 1997) construct of a social epistemology also reflected the historiographer's treatment of paradigms as cultural artifacts, but with the added element of praxis, or action based on reflection (knowledge). Popkewitz (with Brennan, 1998) reframed knowledge "as social practice that generates action and participation" (p. 5). My position as a historiographical researcher in education is that knowledge of the paradigms guiding the (hi)stories of the middle grades concept, spirituality as a developmental domain, and holistic education will potentially generate action among middle grades advocates. At the very least, given the lack of consensus regarding what is meant by the signifier *spirituality/spiritual development*, clarified knowledge of the paradigms and their discursive interrelationship facilitates a conversation amongst middle grades advocates seeking a more holistic implementation of the middle grades concept.

Accordingly, I see great value in the historiographical enterprise of trying to identify dominant historical paradigms in the fields that guide and inform practice in the middle grades. First, the act of naming the basic beliefs privileged in education, and other social science fields that influence education, challenges the ways in which current practices and policies are seen as natural, predetermined, and inevitable (Kincheloe, 2008). Naming these basic beliefs allows for alternative and underrepresented perspectives, such as the relevance of spiritual development in public education, to be more seriously considered. Researchers Novoa and Yariv-Mashal (2003) bemoaned the ahistorical characteristic of research in education, characterizing it as "vaporous thinking" (p. 430).

> Not only is it impossible to analyse any educational problem without a clear understanding of its historical location, but this way of thinking—and here the metaphor of the *gas* is useful—occupies the totality of the space available, therefore eliminating the possibility of alternative methods and approaches. (p. 430)

A second reason for using paradigms as units of historiographical analysis relates to my research purpose. The topic of spirituality, and its educational relevance, lacks definitional clarity in the field of education in general as well as in the specific sub-field I am trying to influence, middle grades education. A systematic approach, such as the one I conducted—to interrogate rigorously the (hi)stories of spirituality as a developmental domain, the middle grades concept, and holistic education—offers the potential for illuminating areas of confusion and misunderstanding. From my review of the related literature, little knowledge has been produced on the inter-discursive nexus of the three aforementioned fields. I hope that the results of this research will address this gap in the field of middle grades education.

Challenges in the research design process. When crafting a research design for my study, I was hindered by was the relatively unchartered territory of critical historiography in educational research. I had few authors to rely upon for direction, especially once I began data analysis. In the following chapter, I describe my research methods in detail to offer the kind of guidance I lacked. I negotiated the challenge using academic, professional, and personal resources, some of which were recently acquired; some developed over a long career of practice.

One strategy I used to navigate the unchartered territory was to rely on the guidance provided by the established techniques I chose for my bricolage. As I have briefly referred to already, I drew from constructivist grounded theory (Charmaz, 2006), and a critical literary theory, contrapuntal reading (Said, 1993) to design data analysis strategies. Laying out the specific, well-established data analysis techniques of constructivist grounded theory before beginning data analysis proved helpful, and Charmaz (2006) was frequently consulted for direction. Also, I leaned heavily on the guiding principles of constructivist grounded theory, such as allowing the emergent themes to guide my analysis. My use of tables as analytic tools in focusing coding (as I describe in detail in the following chapter) is a strategy that emerged from the process organizing my analysis as it was produced and staying faithful to the emergent findings.

While I did not find an abundance of literature on critical historiography, Kincheloe's (2001, 2005, 2008) work on critical constructivism and the principles of critical historiography (i.e., bricolage) was invaluable to me during the research design and execution phases. Most of the scholars whose work I drew from (e.g., Kuhn, 1996; Popkewitz, 1997) were, like Kincheloe, prolific authors with a bounty of published works to serve as sherpas as I traversed new terrain.

I also compensated for the lack of specific guidance on critical historiography by drawing from my background as a historian and as a classroom teacher. Because of my academic training as a historian, I felt confident in my capacities for translating historiography in a piece of educational research. Because of my professional background as an educator, I felt comfortable with employing Kincheloe's (2008) principle of bricolage as a strategy for navigating divergent conceptual waters while still keeping my interpretive eye on the shore of classroom practice. In many ways, this research process reminded me of the theory/practice tension that comes with being a reflective practitioner. I frequently wrestled with the dynamics of praxis: the ideas behind my research processes and the actions I carried out as part of the process.

Finally, I offer a personal reflection on my own positionality in designing, executing, and discussing this research. I came to this study as an educator with almost 20 years of experience in schools. I have taught middle and high school social studies in both public and private schools in urban and suburban locales. All of the schools where I have worked embraced innovative pedagogy and organizational structures that fostered collegiality, creativity, and a strongly shared sense of purpose. Although my interest in and allegiance to critical pedagogy was strengthened as a result of my doctoral studies at my university, my lived identity as a radical, holistic educator was first nurtured at Oberlin College in the early 1990s where liberationist theologian bell hooks and sustainability pioneer David Orr taught. As a White, upper/middle class female, I possess insider status within the field of education; as a radical political activist with an impatience for closed systems, I am an outsider.

My background has both limited and strengthened this research project. As an educator with little experience in mainstream public schools, I have a limited ability to suggest implications for practice that might be effective in most public schools in the U.S. However, given my direct experience in schools that rewarded creative intellectuals and empowered participants, I have the capacity for divergent thinking when it comes to re-imagining middle grades education.

Data collection strategies. My interrogation of the (hi)stories of the middle grades concept, spirituality as a developmental domain, and holistic education began with a decision to treat foundational texts within those three fields as sources of data. The findings from my initial meta-analysis (see Chapters Two and Three) informed my selection of data for this research. I sampled three to four major, foundational works of authority using criteria described in Chapter Five. Each data set of three to four texts represented source material for a (hi)story of the field.

My decision to sample major foundational works from the wider scope of literature was a historiographical one. In seeking to interpret the paradigms of the (hi)stories of the middle grades concept, spirituality as a developmental domain, and holistic education, I treated foundational literature as historical accounts. Using specific foundational texts as representative of the (hi)stories of academic fields was a historiographical strategy used by Kuhn (1996). Historicizing foundational literature is also consistent with Popkewitz's (1991) social epistemology construct. Popkewitz's approach "entails placing particular events in schooling within a historical formation that presupposes relations of power/knowledge. Thus, the focus is on historical conditions, institutional practices, and epistemologies..." (p. 3). Some of my data explicitly incorporates historical background (e.g., Benson, 2006; Miller, 2007). An important implication of my decision to use foundational work as historical accounts is that my data selection process had to employ rigorous validation strategies. In Chapter Five, I provide an account of how I applied the principles and techniques of critical historiography to select texts for my study.

Data analysis strategies. To answer my main inquiry question, What is the educational relevance of spiritual development in middle grades education?, I created two subquestions to focus and define my analysis activities. I designed two rounds of data analysis for the first question, What prevalent paradigms underlie the academic discourse on spirituality as a developmental domain, the middle grades concept, and holistic education? For this level of analysis, I borrowed strategies from constructivist grounded theory (Charmaz, 2006). Initial coding was followed by focused coding; the final results of the first two rounds of data analysis were lengthy paradigms narratives for each of the three fields' (hi)stories. These narratives are reproduced as examples of critical historiographical findings in Chapter Six.

To explicate my rationale for drawing from constructivist grounded theory analysis strategies, I describe and explore the work of Charmaz (2006). My decision to borrow data analysis techniques from grounded theory, and constructivist grounded theory in particular, was influenced by the approach's safeguards against unproblematized researcher assumptions, perspectives, and preconceptions. These safeguards are (as I summarize them): *in vivo* codes, constant comparative analysis, coding each datum independently from the others, focused coding, and allowing for ambiguity during the data analysis phase. In short, by choosing to use critical historiographical research as a method for investigating my research question, my data analysis emphasized a critical constructivist interpretation of the data for socio-political beliefs, historically-contextualized values, and ontological and epistemological assumptions. The data analysis techniques and strategies of constructivist grounded theory gave me a vehicle for carrying out this focus in my critical constructivist interpretation.

Constructivist grounded theory, when compared with grounded theory methods advocated by Strauss and Corbin (1998) or other qualitative coding strategies, had many characteristics that were advantageous for this research. The approach allows for ambiguity during the research process, which was useful here given the plasticity of some of the major constructs relevant to my research (e.g., spirituality) as well as the unexplored conceptual territory into which I ventured. Charmaz (2006) was direct about the need for a high tolerance of ambiguity during constructivist grounded theory research:

Your observations and ideas do matter. Do not dismiss your own ideas if they do not mirror the data. Your ideas may rest on covert meanings and actions that have not entirely surfaced yet. Such intuitions form another set of ideas to check. Our task is to make analytic sense of the material, which may challenge taken-for-granted understandings. (p. 54)

In addition to being an advantageous strategy for my research, I also see Charmaz's call for researchers to be willing to hold loosely ideas in gestation as the qualitative validation strategy of researcher reflexivity (Creswell, 2007).

From Creswell (2007) I found another reason for this critical constructivist research study to borrow from constructivist grounded theory. He characterized constructivist grounded theory as being about "learning about the experience within embedded, hidden networks, situations, and relationships, and making visible hierarchies of power, communication, and opportunity" (p. 65). This point is not to say that other qualitative methods do not also employ strategies for illuminating subtle themes; Creswell's point here is that constructivist grounded theory techniques have an *emphasis* on bringing to the surface critical issues related to the ways in which power is replicated through unproblematized assumptions and worldviews. Charmaz (2006) argued this point when she wrote, "coding should inspire us to examine hidden assumptions in our own use of language as well as that of our participants" (p. 47) and initial coding "help[s] you refrain from imputing your motives, fears or unresolved personal issues to your respondents and to your collected data" (p 54). Grounded theory's emphasis on findings coming from the data, as opposed to seeking data to test a pre-conceived hypothesis, appealed to me as another means for addressing researcher reflexivity.

Grounded theory is used when the research purpose is to produce new knowledge, in the form of a theory. I did not produce a theory, nor was I researching a phenomenon described by human subjects, so my research is not exclusively grounded theory. However, in keeping with the critical principle of bricolage, it is appropriate and desirable for me to draw from "multiple methods of inquiry...with diverse theoretical and philosophical notions of the various elements encountered in the research act" (Kincheloe, 2001, p. 682).

I answered the second subquestion by utilizing an interpretive technique from postcolonial literary theory, contrapuntal reading (Said, 1993). The second subquestion—What are the inter-textual and inter-discursive relationships within the convergence of the paradigms of the three fields?—addressed the conceptual contents of the nexus of the three fields when their (hi)stories were laid out in a Venn diagram. To analyze the area of convergence of the three (hi)stories, I read across the data sets contrapuntally by analyzing paradigm narratives for evidence of inter-textual and inter-discursive patterns.

Contrapuntal reading is a technique used by literary theorists, borrowed by critical historiographers (e.g., Henry, 2006). Contrapuntal is the adjective form of counterpoint, a musical technique in which a central melody is harmonized with other independent melodies. Said (1993) described contrapuntal reading as a means of analyzing the "intertwined and overlapping histories" (p. 18) within (the reader's interpretation of) a text. The researcher reads with "a simultaneous awareness both of the metropolitan history that it narrates and of those other histories against which (and together with) the dominant discourse acts" (p. 51). Said's direction for adopting a "simultaneous awareness" strongly influenced how I framed one of my major findings in this research: my interpretation of a dynamic of paradox amongst dichotomous paradigms.

Said's (1993) postcolonial discourse analysis method is consistent with my critical constructivist researcher paradigm: "Informed by local knowledges from multiple social and cultural locations, critical constructivists avoid the grand narrative of Western discourses that are monological in their dismissal of histories and cultural concerns of non-Western peoples" (Kincheloe, 2008, p. 125). The technique of contrapuntal reading was not explicitly referenced by Popkewitz in his work on social epistemology (1991, 1997, with Brennan, 1998). However, the idea of contrapuntal reading is reflected in Popkewitz's (1991) analysis of "the multiple productive elements of power" (p. 14):

Fixed in the rhetoric of reform, the patterns of schooling and teacher education, and the sciences of pedagogy are multiple and regionally organized procedures, rules, and obligations that organize and discipline how the world is seen, acted on, felt, and talked about. Power, in this positive sense, rests in the complex sets of relations and practices by which individuals construct their subjective experiences and assume an identity in social affairs. (p. 14)

Popkewitz implicitly refers to Said's (1993) contrapuntal reading of texts by identifying the discursive function of educational reform rhetoric, paralleling Said's interpretation of the synergistic tension between discourses of imperialism and discourses of resistance.

The product of the final round of data analysis was a written interpretive narrative of the inter-textual and inter-discursive relationships between the paradigms of the three fields. Chapter Seven reproduces my narrative discussion of the discursive patterns both within and among the three (hi)stories. With these findings in hand, I composed a series of implications for classroom practice and further research; this work is offered in Chapter Eight.

For a quick reference overview of the data analysis design, I included a detailed delineation of the activities conducted during each of the three rounds in Appendix A.

Research Integrity

Discussions of limitations and my positionality as the researcher comprise this last section of Chapter Four. As critical constructivist research, it would be inconsistent for me to interrogate the limitations and positionalities of the authors of the (hi)stories I analyzed without venturing into my own. In reflecting upon the limitations at various points throughout this study, three areas of weaknesses came to light: (a) the texts used as data sources, (b) my framing of certain aspects of the topic, and (c) a flaw in the research design and execution of critical historiography.

Limitations of the data sources. The first area of limitation is associated with the texts used as data sources in three ways: (a) personal bias in text selection, (b) cultural homogeneity of data sources, and (c) inconsistency in depth across the three fields. The first two ways offer some foreshadowing about my values and priorities—that is, my positionality—as a critical constructivist researcher; the third is simply an acknowledgment of the current status of the field of spirituality as a developmental domain within the developmental sciences.

In selecting foundational texts as data, I had to account for my own assumptions and researcher bias toward selecting texts that reinforced my own ideas about the relevance of spiritual development in middle grades education. My familiarity with the related literature (in the fields of applied developmental theory, spirituality as a developmental domain, holistic education, middle grades education, and the middle grades concept) strengthened my ability to select some texts over others as data that were foundational, serving as proxies for the (hi)stories of the fields. Hence, conducting a thorough review of the literature is one strategy I used to reduce the influence of my biases. In addition, I consulted with persons known to be experts in the three fields: Dr. Jack Miller, holistic education; Dr. Micki M. Caskey, middle grades education; and Dr. Robert Roeser, spirituality as a developmental domain. While each of these persons has his or her own perspectives regarding the relative influence of the potential texts, my goal as a critical constructivist researcher was to strive for trustworthiness in my data collection, not definitive validity.

Even though I have accounted for my own researcher bias, a second way in which this study is limited by the texts used as sources of data is that the texts included overwhelmingly represent White, middle-class authorship. Some voices are still left out that could be relevant contributions to the (hi)stories of the three fields. An example of a text that met all of my criteria, and would have explicitly included non-Eurocentric ideas about holistic education, is *Education for Awakening: An Eastern Approach to Holistic Education* (Nakagawa, 2000). This limitation becomes even more troubling in light of the literature on a culturally responsive theory of spiritual development which suggests that the predominance of Western theoretical and research paradigms is harmful to the efforts of an educational approach that addresses student spirituality (Juang & Syed, 2008; Lippman & Keith, 2006;

Mattis, Ahluwalia, Cowie, & Kirkland-Harris, 2006; Nicholas & DeSilva, 2008; Owen Wilson, 2005).

My decision to use written texts that are recognized as authoritative in the field of middle grades education as data sources is strategic given the audience for this research. But in making that strategic decision, did I reinforce the deployment of power in favor of Euro-centric values? The absence of voices directly from historically marginalized groups is a deficit in this piece of research. My selection of a critical historiographical approach, which employs criticality as an underlying principle (Villaverde, Kincheloe, & Helyar, 2006), is an attempt to honor my positionality as a critical constructivist researcher. Criticality sees historical discourses as socially constructed interactions between individuals and societal structures that are influenced by power and privilege. The critical perspective allows the researcher to identify and interrogate the predominance of Western theoretical paradigms, creating a discourse of possibility (Giroux, 1981). I also tried to account for the critical historiographical principle of multilogicality by using contrapuntal reading as one of my data analysis strategies. However, given the limitations of my interpretive abilities to hear the voices of historically marginalized people in the data, I think a more successful way to honor multilogicality would be to use texts written by "other people's children" (Delpit, 2006).

A third limitation related to the texts used as data sources has to do with the inconsistency of the breadth and depth of scholarly literature across the three fields. Based on my review of the literature, I found a substantive body of work on the middle grades concept, a slightly less substantive body of work on holistic education, and a much sparser body of work on spirituality as a developmental domain. The range in depth, breadth, and rigor within the foundational texts limited my capacity for selecting texts across the three fields that represented the same levels of authority. For example, within the field of spiritual development, Benson and Fowler are considered authorities and advocates. But, in my review of the literature, I found a smaller number of authors who could have met that criteria than I found in the middle grades or holistic education fields. That compromise is reflected in the fact that of the three spiritual development texts, only one (Benson) refers explicitly and exclusively to a theory of spiritual development. Fowler used the term faith development, and Oser, Bucher, and Scarlett combine spiritual development with religious development in their synthesis of the field. The scarcity of work on spiritual development is a limitation of this research, as well as a limitation within the field of spiritual development at the current time.

Framing the issue. A second area of limitation is the two ways I have framed central constructs related to my research question. The first way has to do with how human development is constructed by middle grades advocates; the second is the pre- dominance of literature that views spiritual development as positive. I address both of these and how I accounted for this area of limitation in this research.

A conceptual limitation of this research is my decision to accept how middle grades advocates frame human development. The dominant message from middle grades advocates (e.g., NMSA, 2010) is that human development occurs in distinct domains; people at different life stages have distinct developmental needs. I made the decision to follow the developmental framework employed by the advocates of the middle grades concept because they are the primary audience for my research. However, in adopting the prem- ise that human development can be known and understood through a structural model, I also adopt the limitations of that stance.

The conceptual framing of human development into distinct domains with stage-dependent needs is not neutral. In my review of the literature, I found recent work that directly countered the middle grades' emphasis on developmentally appropriate educa- tion on the grounds that adolescence, and its associated claim for being a distinct period of human development, is a social construct (Vagle, 2012). Claiborne (2007) challenged the underlying assump- tions of pedagogy that is based on the construct of developmental readiness. Claiborne's work raised questions about the cultural implications of pedagogy that is based on a construct of human de- velopment as natural, progressive, and focused on the individual (pp. 431–432). Webster (2013) illustrated a third argument against the construct of developmentally appropriate education by contest- ing the notion of developmental needs. He challenged the viewpoint that education should be responsive to developmental needs be-cause it implies that young people are merely "becomings" not "beings" (p. 5) with current worth and integrity. I find these claims to be valid, persuasive, and sound, even as they fundamentally challenge the premise of this research.

My awareness of this framing limitation from an early stage of research design and problem-posing was a resource. In wrestling with the dialectical challenge presented by Vagle's (2012) work, I was careful to not reify my own constructs of human development through this research. It also helped me during the first round of data analysis—initial coding—by inserting a distance between my own assumptions and beliefs and the texts I interpreted for as-sumptions and beliefs. These challenges reminded me that any program, position, or policy in education is one of a "universe of alternatives" (Sarason, 1982, p. 102), not a natural given.

A second way in which my framing of central constructs limits this study is in my treatment of spiritual development as positive. In my review of the literature, I observed some, but very little, consideration of the dark side of spiritual development. In her emerging research on the dark side of human spirituality, de Souza (2012) framed her new work on aspects of youth spirituality that inhibit healthy human growth. Working with Hay and Nye's (2006) construct of spirituality as relational consciousness, de Souza explored aspects of spiritual expression that reflect a sense of separateness. Like de Souza's earlier work (2006), I also identi-fied the absence of the spiritual domain of human development from education contexts as a problem. But in doing so, I assumed that its inclusion could only promote healthy human development and thriving. From my reading of the literature, the dark side of human spirituality is one of the edges of the field of spiritual de-velopment to which future work will have to respond. While this study itself does not directly account for this framing limitation, hopefully future, field-based studies will draw from the knowledge generated in this work to inform constructs of spiritual develop-ment that include its negative implications.

Flaw in research design and execution. While critical his-toriography worked as a method for interpreting for prevalent paradigms of academic fields and inter-discursive patterns amongst the fields, my execution of the method fell short in terms of more fully situating these paradigms in their socio-historical context. When I rendered the final results for the conceptual nexus of the three fields, my analysis procedures had not given me sufficient findings on its social, political, and historical context. A consequence of this weakness is a lack of conclusions and implications about the potential for inclusion of spiritual development as a possible means of enhancing the capacity for middle grades educators to be more culturally responsive to young adolescents. The question of the potential inter-discursive relationship between culturally responsive teaching and student spiritual development is still highly potent. I hope to investigate it in future research.

In reflecting upon this failure to generate sufficient findings on the socio-political contexts of the (hi)stories, I suspect that the problem rests with my decision to select text passages for initial coding that focused on the main content and ideas of the three fields. I excluded text passages that addressed socio-historical context, thinking I would apply a direct contrapuntal reading— without subjecting those passages to initial and focused coding—as an analysis technique during the third round of data analysis. However, in the transition between constructivist grounded theory techniques and contrapuntal reading, I lacked a plan for incorporating text that had not been through initial and focused coding processes into the third round of analysis. This is where I lost ground in terms of positioning myself to render findings that allowed me to make claims regarding culturally responsive teaching and spiritual development.

What all of these areas of limitation have in common is the discursive relationship between constructs of spirituality and spiritual development and responsive teaching that honors the dignity and integrity of all students, but especially those who come from groups whose knowledge has not been valued in public schools in the United States. In my estimation, the issue of how teaching that is responsive to young adolescent spiritual development can be informed by cultural awareness is still paramount even though this study has not provided much new knowledge with which to generate action.

Chapter Five

Research Methods Illustrated

IN this chapter, I offer a detailed account of my research methods for a critical historiography. I begin with a description of the validity strategies used during data collection, and then outline the specific processes used during the three rounds of data analysis: initial coding, focused coding, and contrapuntal reading. This account of my specific processes was rendered using the memos I wrote before, during, and after data analysis. Because of the uniqueness of my research design, I decided to include an appendix with artifacts from my data analysis processes. I include these artifacts not only as documentation for this account of my research methods during data analysis but also as references for future critical historiographical research projects.

Throughout this research, consistent with the principles of critical historiography, I have generated results that were then used as source materials for further loops of the hermeneutic cycle. The results of each round of data analysis were:

1. Initial Coding: initial codes for content and interpretations of beliefs, values, and assumptions (BVAs)
2. Focused Coding: 15 paradigms categories and thick narratives for each paradigm
3. Contrapuntal Reading: 3 meta-paradigms

Except for the paradigm narratives, these results/source materials are included in this chapter. The paradigm narratives are both *results* of the first two rounds of my data analysis as well as *source materials* used during the third round of data analysis. The paradigm narratives are presented in Chapter Six because they represent the findings I used to answer my first research subquestion: What prevalent paradigms underlie the academic discourse on spirituality as a developmental domain, the middle grades concept, and holistic education? I suggest that the reader study one or two of these narratives (in Chapter Six) before reviewing my account of my contrapuntal reading process in the last section of this chapter. A narrative account of the results of contrapuntal reading is also presented in Chapter Six.

Meta-Analysis: Data Collection/Text Selection

One of the three techniques of critical historiography is meta-analysis. Meta-analysis, as I described in the previous chapter, involves interpreting for ways in which (hi)stories reflect acceptance and/or challenge of dominant paradigms. In a critical historiography, the sources of data are related literature; in the case of my research on the relevance of the domain of spiritual development in middle grades education, the related literatures were foundational texts from three fields: the middle grades concept, spirituality as a developmental domain, and holistic education. Each of those fields represented a significant interrelationship between larger fields related to my issue: applied developmental psychology, middle grades education, and spirituality.

In establishing a set of criteria for data collection, I recalled a lesson from quantitative research: if my inputs are garbage, my analysis will be garbage as well (M. Hara, personal communication, 2011). Although I recognize that my findings will not represent a generalizable "truth" about the world "out there" (a standard desirable by many practitioners in education), the standards of historiographical research require just as much rigor, integrity, and reliability as any other method in educational research. Indeed, as my primary audience is one that resides in a dominant cultural context that is skeptical of spirituality as an educational concern, I was doubly motivated to establish criteria for my inputs (i.e., foundational literature) that meet validity, or trustworthiness, tests.

Historiography is neither a qualitative nor a quantitative method, though a historiographer may liberally draw from both research paradigms. For addressing validity issues, I turn to Creswell (2007), an authority in the field of qualitative research. He strongly recommends that investigators explicitly specify their validation strategies as a goodness test for research. Even Wolcott (2001), who rejects validity on the grounds that it is not relevant for a qualitative paradigm, addresses the matter directly even if only to refute it. Therefore, I address validation strategies recommended by Creswell (2007) in my description of my research techniques.

I used the following criteria to select data sources from the fields of the middle grades concept, spirituality as a developmental domain, and holistic education. I employed the term *field* to describe a bounded theoretical and empirical area of academic study. This description is qualified by my acknowledgment that boundaries between academic disciplines are human constructs (Kincheloe, 2008) and therefore, are subject to debate. From a social epistemological perspective (Popkewitz, 1991), academic fields are a description and embodiment of the "relation of knowledge and power that structures our perceptions and organizes our social practices" (p. 1). Certainly for the data used in this research, Popkewitz's characterization of academic fields as embodiments of how knowledge is organized as a social practice held true—this phenomenon was seen most clearly in the field of holistic education, which was the most self-conscious about its construction (of the three fields included in this research). With these qualifications and clarifications in mind, I employ the term *field*.

The data sources were:

- Published as a written text;
- from one of the following three fields: spirituality as a developmental domain, the middle grades concept, and holistic education;
- descriptive of the main theories, constructs, and/or ideas of the field;
- written by a recognized authority in the field; and
- written by an advocate of the field.

I now elaborate on the finer points of these criteria for data selection. "Published as a written text" refers to works that have been published in either peer-reviewed journals or as a book. While I could have accessed the publication's content electronically, I did not select data that was only published electronically because I wanted to limit my data sources to texts that had been subjected to a more rigorous review process before being published.

From conducting my literature review, or, as I have described it previously in this section, my meta-analysis, I was confident in my informed ability to (a) categorize a data source as belonging to one of the three fields and (b) distinguish descriptive literature that speaks to the major ideas of the field from literature that is more narrowly focused.

In my literature review, I observed a range in the breadth and depth of specific pieces of literature. The programmatic and empirical literature was focused primarily on a specific study, such as Greene et al. (2008), "Caught in the Middle Again: Accountability and the Changing Practice of Middle School Teacher," or program implementation, such as Cohen (2005), "Journal Writing in Mathematics Education: Communicating the Affective Dimensions of Mathematics Learning." The theoretical literature ranged from an expansive treatment of the work's topic, such as Benson (2006), "The Science of Child and Adolescent Development: Definitional, Theoretical, and Field-Building Challenges," to a highly focused discussion, such as Ryoo et al. (2009): "Critical Spiritual Pedagogy: Reclaiming Humanity Through a Pedagogy of Integrity, Community, and Love." Drawing upon my knowledge of the literature, I selected literature that was theoretical (not empirical or programmatic), comprehensive (wide in scope), and descriptive (of the major ideas of the field) to use as data sources.

In the process of determining whether or not a text met the criteria "descriptive of the main theories, constructs, and/or ideas of the field," three texts were seriously considered, but rejected from this research because I did not think they met this criteria. Nel Noddings' (2005) seminal text, *The Challenge to Care in Schools: An Alternative Approach to Education*, was suggested by my consultant on the Holistic Education data set; I also recognized it as a hugely influential text for educators and scholars who describe themselves as holistic. However, the Noddings (2005) work is not, in my analysis, descriptive of the field of holistic education as much as it is a significant contributing text for holistic practitioners. I acknowledge that in any comprehensive bibliography of texts for holistic educators, Noddings' (2005) work should be included. However, for this research, I determined it did not meet the descriptive criteria.

A second text for the Holistic Education data set, Huebner (1985), was rejected for inclusion as well. In the case of Huebner (1985), my concern was that this work was more closely tied with exploring curriculum theory rather than describing the field of holistic education. Additionally, although Huebner may be influential in the circle of curriculum theorists in the United States, his work is not widely recognized by middle grades educators. In my review of the literature on the middle grades concept, I rarely saw Huebner cited.

The final text that was rejected on the grounds of not describing the main ideas of the field was a publication by King and Roeser (2009). Like the Noddings (2005) text, the King and Roeser (2009) piece is something that should be included as a key reading in a bibliography for adolescent development and/or contemplative pedagogy; but it does not fit the descriptive criteria established for this research. In selecting texts for the spirituality as a developmental domain data set, I made a distinction between texts that focus on spirituality as a developmental domain and those that have a more limited focus (i.e., adolescent spiritual development), rejecting those with a limited focus from this study.

The last two criteria address the ambitious task of claiming that a source carries authority and advocacy, included because my primary audience for my research is people working within the field of middle grades education. So, I considered sources of data that are considered authoritative as a communication strategy, i.e., texts to which my audience would be more receptive. The advocacy criteria were important because I was looking for literature (data) that is not merely descriptive but also foundational—that is, influential—in its respective field.

With this research, I assign no definitive claims regarding authority and advocacy. However, to make well-informed decisions, I applied specific strategies for ascertaining authority within and advocacy for the fields, seeking to meet Rury's (2006) standard of "sufficiency" (p. 330) in terms of historiographical research.

Here are the tests I applied to the authors of potential data:

- number of publications in peer-reviewed journals; and
- professional position/history in the academic community.

Here are the tests I applied to the publication itself:

- number of times cited by other authors in peer-reviewed journals; and
- number of times used in syllabi for courses in education (holistic education and middle grades concept texts) and psychology (spirituality as a developmental domain texts).

I also conducted:

- consultations in person or via email with academics I recognized as experts in each of the three fields.

The tests for the degree of a data source's authority and advocacy met two of Creswell's (2007) eight validation strategies. For qualitative research, Creswell recommended two as the minimum number to utilize in a qualitative study. The first—triangulation—I addressed by using multiple sources (i.e., publications and record of professional history) to discern the authority of the sources of the data.

A second strategy—peer review—I addressed by consulting with expert scholars in each of the three categories of data to verify the appropriateness of my data selection, based on the aforementioned criteria. I consulted: Dr. Micki M. Caskey (middle grades concept); Dr. Robert W. Roeser (spirituality as a developmental domain); and Dr. John (Jack) P. Miller (holistic education). The first two are tenured faculty at Portland State University in Oregon; the third is a tenured faculty member at the University of Toronto in Ontario, Canada. All three are nationally and internationally recognized as expert scholars in their respective fields. After determining strong candidates for inclusion in each data set, I sent an email to each consultant with an abstract of my dissertation research proposal, my list of potential texts, and these five questions:

1. In what ways does each text represent the major theories, constructs, and/or ideas of holistic education (middle grades concept/spirituality as a developmental domain)?
2. In your opinion, is the text authored by an authority in the field? Please explain.
3. In your opinion, is the text authored by an advocate of the field? Please explain.
4. Although I am not conducting a chronological historiography, do my selections adequately represent a sampling of major works between 1965 and 2012?
5. Given my goal of limiting the selections to four texts, would you make any additions or subtractions to the list?

Two of the three consultants (Dr. Caskey and Dr. Miller) responded in writing; the third, Dr. Roeser, was not able to respond in writing but was available to meet with me in person to discuss my data selections. For that consultation, I took notes during and immediately following the conversation.

Following these steps, I selected four texts from the field of the middle grades concept and three from the fields of spirituality as a developmental domain and holistic education.

Middle Grades Education Data Set:

- Alexander, W. M., Williams, E. L., Compton, M., Hines, V. A., & Prescott, D. (1968) *The emergent middle school.* New York, NY: Holt, Reinhart, & Winston.
- Lounsbury, J. H. & Vars, G. F. (1978) *A curriculum for the middle school years.* New York, NY: Harper & Row.
- Carnegie Council on Adolescent Development's Task Force on Education of Young Adolescents. (1989) *Turning points: preparing American youth for the 21st century.* Washington, DC: Carnegie Council on Adolescent Development.
- NMSA (2010) *This we believe: Keys to educating young adolescents.* Westerville, OH: Author.

Spirituality as a Developmental Domain Data Set:

- Fowler, J. (1981) *Stages of faith: The psychology of human development and the quest for meaning.* New York, NY: Harper.
- Benson, P. L. (2006) The science of child and adolescent spiritual development: Definitional, theoretical, and field-building challenges. In E. C. Roehlkepartain, P. E. King, L. Wagener, & P. L. Benson (Eds.), *Handbook of spiritual development in childhood and adolescence* (pp. 484-497). Thousand Oaks, CA: Sage.
- Oser, F. W., Scarlett, W. G., & Bucher, A. (2006) Religion and spiritual development throughout the lifespan. In W. Damon & R. M. Lerner (Series Eds.) & R. M. Lerner (Volume Ed.), *Handbook of child psychology,* vol 1: *Theoretical models of human development* (6th ed:, pp. 942-998). Hoboken, NJ: Wiley.

Holistic Education Data Set:

- Miller, R. (1997) *What are schools for: Holistic education in American culture.* Brandon, VT: Holistic Education Press.
- Kessler, R. (2000) *The soul of education: Helping students find connection, compassion, and character at school.* Alexandria, VA: Association for Supervision and Curriculum Development.
- Miller, J. (2007) *The holistic curriculum* (2nd ed.). Toronto, ON: University of Toronto Press.

After finalizing my text choices, I strategically sampled passages of the longer texts to analyze. The longer texts were: Alexander, Williams, Compton, and Hines (1968)[1]; Lounsbury and Vars (1978); Fowler (1981); Kessler (2000); Miller (1997); and Miller (2007). The four remaining texts were analyzed in their entirety. Decisions about which passages of the longer texts to

---

[1]   Cited as Alexander (1968) for the remainder of this text.

include were made in accordance with my research purpose: to articulate the educational relevance of the domain of spiritual development in middle grades education by means of interpreting for the conceptual contents of the nexus of the fields of the middle grades concept, spirituality as a developmental domain, and holistic education. Because I was beginning by interpreting for paradigms, I selected passages of the texts that focused on the main ideas, constructs, and/or theories of the related field of study. During this process, I also kept a log of text selections that might be used for a direct contrapuntal reading—portions of text that directly addressed socio-historical issues related to the field. However, as I explained in the previous chapter, the selections for a direct contrapuntal reading were never analyzed.

For each text, I documented (a) the initial selections of text passages for analysis, (b) my rationale for my selections, and (c) any changes I made to the initial selections. In that documentation process, I also revisited some of the choices I had made about which texts to include as data in this study. For example, after initial coding of NMSA (2010) and Carnegie (1989), but while making selections for Alexander (1968) and Lounsbury and Vars (1978), I wondered if I had already collected enough data on the middle grades concept to move forward in the next round of analysis. I made the decision to keep Alexander (1968) and Lounsbury and Vars (1978).

Typically, I used these passage selection memos to reaffirm the purpose of my overall research and the specific methods I was using to address my main research question. For example, when re-evaluating my selections for Fowler (1981), I wrote:

> I agree with all of my initial selections [from Fowler]. But I want to add the italicized stage summaries at the end of each chapter in Part IV. I still think I should be focusing on the paradigms that undergird the *theories* on spirituality as a developmental domain; but I think that some of that analysis can be done by interpreting for the beliefs, values, and assumptions reflected in the *descriptions* of the stages. I liken the descriptions of the stages to the content of the middle grades concept. (i.e., NMSA's 16 characteristics).

The stages I referred to in the above memo were Fowler's stages of faith development. His descriptions of the stages were lengthy and not focused as much as other sections of his text on spirituality as a domain of human development. As I noted in one of my text selection memos, keeping the initial coding manageable was a consideration when making passage selections. As it was, the timeline for initial coding (three weeks for all ten texts) was completely unrealistic. It took me 15 weeks of focused time to complete the initial coding for all three data sets.

Critical Interpretation: Initial and Focused Coding

As a technique of critical historiography, critical interpretation involves the hermeneutical process of interpreting texts for meaning. In the context of this research, I interpreted three sets of (hi)stories, or foundational texts, for paradigms. Interpreting for paradigms involved two rounds of data analysis. In crafting the bricolage for this critical historiography, I drew from the research tradition of constructivist grounded theory (Charmaz, 2006).

This section has two parts: in the first, I briefly review the procedures of constructivist grounded theory (Charmaz, 2006) as they were applied in this study. In the second section, which is further divided into three parts, I describe the processes of initial coding and focused content coding I used for each of the three data sets. My descriptions are organized by data set and presented in the same order I conducted these first two rounds of analysis: (a) middle grades concept; (b) spirituality as a developmental domain; and (c) holistic education.

Constructivist grounded theory procedures. I applied hermeneutics in my initial two rounds of analysis of the data by interpreting the data (Rury, 2006) from the fields of the middle grades concept, spirituality as a developmental domain, and holistic education. The data from each field (the three to four texts) comprised one data set; in total, I had three data sets. As a bricoleur (Kincheloe, 2001, 2005), I borrowed initial coding strategies from constructivist grounded theory (Charmaz, 2006) to generate codes for the content (main ideas, theories, and constructs of the field) and to interpret for beliefs, values, and assumptions (BVA interpretations).

Initial coding and BVA interpretation occurred during the first round of data analysis. I coded one text at a time by passage level. The length of each passage varied, depending on the content of the passage and the text itself. For example, in a shorter text (e.g., NMSA, 2010) the main ideas, theories, and constructs were expressed more densely than in a longer text (e.g., Fowler, 1981). Therefore, I made the decision to initial code smaller datum (passage) for the denser text. The initial codes and the BVA interpretations served as indirect evidence for categories of paradigms, and were the source materials used in the second round of data analysis.

In constructivist grounded theory (Charmaz, 2006), initial coding involves analyzing the data for implicit meaning, tacit knowledge, and assumptions using codes that capture actions and processes. Although Charmaz described initial and focused coding processes with data that are transcripts of interviews, her guidelines for coding worked for my data as well. In constructivist grounded theory coding, the researcher approaches the data without an extant theory in mind. Researchers are advised to use gerunds as codes instead of nouns to avoid making codes into topics too early in the analysis process. In my initial coding, I tried to use only gerunds; however with some data, I chose to use nouns as initial codes because they seemed to capture my interpretation. The emphasis on fidelity to the data by avoiding naming topics too early seems greater in grounded theory than found in other qualitative coding strategies. Therefore, it was more useful for my research purposes.

One specific initial coding technique is *in vivo* code names (Charmaz, 2006). *In vivo* codes "serve as symbolic markers" (p. 55) of the language and meaning of the authors of the texts. *In vivo* codes are as close to the actual language used within the data as possible. For example, an initial code from Miller (2007) was "merging reason and intuition" (p. 8). The datum that this *in vivo* code came from is: "A more holistic approach calls for a merging of reason and intuition. When these two elements are connected, student thinking is enriched" (Miller, 2007, p. 8). In this example, I used an *in vivo* code by quoting directly from the datum.

Charmaz (2006) offers three suggestions to keep in mind when applying *in vivo* coding as an initial coding technique: "Those general terms everyone 'knows' that flag condensed but significant meanings; a participant's innovative shorthand term that captures meanings or experience; [and] insider shorthand terms specific to a particular group that reflect their perspective" (p. 55). Charmaz's strategies kept my analysis grounded in the data and, at the crucial initial stage of data analysis, enabled me to produce analytical codes that were reliable for further analysis. Initial codes were refined, verified in terms of how well they capture the data, and expanded in the next round of data analysis, focused coding.

Focused coding, also an analytic technique of constructivist grounded theory (Charmaz, 2006), occurred during the second round of data analysis. The purpose of focused coding is:

> ...to synthesize and explain larger segments of data. Focused coding means using the most significant and/or frequent earlier codes to sift through large amounts of data. One goal is to determine the adequacy of those codes. Focused coding requires decisions about which initial codes make the most analytic sense to categorize your data incisively and completely. (pp. 57–58)

Focused coding, as implied by the preceding quotation, is not a linear process. Constant comparative analysis is used as part of focused coding—it is an iterative form of data analysis that involves looping back and forth between the data, the codes, and the "emergent" categories (e.g., Charmaz, 2006, p. 45). Refinement of the categories is part of the purpose of focused coding. Examples of specific constant comparative methods are: comparing data with other data for similarities and differences, analyzing within data comparisons, making sequential comparison between data coded early on and data coded last, and comparison within each data set (Charmaz, 2006)—in my case, different texts.

For this research, I went through two sub-rounds of focused coding: using just the initial codes, I constructed focused *content* codes (FCCs). Then in a second sub-round of focused coding, I analyzed the beliefs, values, and assumptions interpretations that accompanied each initial code by categorizing all the BVA interpretations by the FCCs. This process of data analysis was strongly guided by the technique of constant-comparative analysis. I rendered paradigm categories from the two sub-rounds of data analysis; I composed brief paradigm memos immediately following focused coding to document my analysis. After completing initial and focused coding for all three data sets, I wrote thick descriptions of the paradigms in each of the three fields, as interpreted through my critical constructivist lens. In these narratives, the paradigm categories were illustrated by quotations from the texts as evidence supporting my interpretation of the data.

I now turn to a description of the analytical procedures I went through for this research. Because this study uses a research approach—critical historiography—not common to educational scholarship especially as it relates to K–12 settings, I have chosen to report in detail the analytic procedures I employed and to make transparent the two levels of interim codes that led to the paradigms categories and their resulting descriptions. I also relate some of the tensions and issues I navigated in the process. A detailed account of processes and tensions creates credibility for the findings described in Chapter Six, and further contributes to the usability of this approach by other educational researchers who may not initially see it as an option in a world that privileges empirical studies.

Because I analyzed the data one data set, or field, at a time, I present each in the same order, addressing methods and issues that arose for each data set. For each data set, I provide frequency data for the initial codes (ICs) and beliefs, values, and assumptions interpretations (BVA interpretations); depict the analytical processes of focused coding in a critical historiography; and identify the paradigm categories.

Middle grades concept. For this data set, 220 initial codes were generated during the first round of interpretive analysis. For each initial code, which described the *content* of each datum, excerpts from the same selection of text that illustrated the initial code were identified and documented on the coding sheets. I selected 293 quotations to illustrate the initial codes. Each datum was also interpreted for the beliefs, values, and assumptions, using a critical constructivist interpretive lens. In the Middle Grades Concept data set, I documented 135 interpretations of beliefs, 189 interpretations of values, and 71 interpretations of assumptions. (See Appendix B for a slice of the initial coding data analysis table I employed to document and manage my analysis.)

My analysis of the body of initial codes yielded eight focused content codes (FCCs) that reflected themes in the content of the middle grades concept as rendered from the four texts. Developing the final eight FCCs involved looping back and forth amongst the ICs of all four texts, as well as referencing the quotations as needed to further refine and distill the FCCs, to ensure that I captured the main themes of the middle grades concept. The eight FCCs for this data set were:

1. The middle grades as a critical period, for individuals and for society
2. School mediates growth and development/Developmentally responsive education/Process over product
3. Integration and interrelationships among domains and types of knowledge
4. Relationships (people)/collaboration and community
5. Intrapersonal development/Courage and empowerment
6. Social constructivist learning theory
7. Middle grades as educational reform
8. Differentiation/Seeing the sum, seeing the parts

As this was the first set of data I analyzed, the names of these FCCs were less refined than the FCCs of the other two data sets. A tension I experienced in the focused coding process was between distillation of analytical expression and fidelity to the data. In my process of analyzing the body of initial codes, I sought to group together content themes that were related (i.e., 'Relationships (people) and Collaboration and Community') even if that made the FCCs cumbersome. I decided to use FCC names that retained the subtle distinctions of the themes. With the knowledge that my goal in the hermeneutic circle was to develop a manageable number of paradigm categories, I also wanted to keep the number of FCCs manageable without over-generalizing the content themes in the process. Another factor in my thinking about the FCC names for this data set was an awareness that the process of crafting FCCs was not the final product in the overall research project. Focused coding—in this research, as in a more traditional constructivist grounded theory research project—is an important, but still intermediary, step in a larger interpretive analytical process. Categories, at this stage of analysis, are emergent (Charmaz, 2006). In reviewing my focused coding several months afterwards, I chose to leave the labels as I had constructed them at the time.

Another tension I navigated during this part of the data analysis was focusing on *content* and capturing that aspect of the data. In my research notes, I documented moments when I worked through distinctions between describing content as processes, i.e., FCC 'school mediates growth and development' and labeling the data with terms and concepts not used in the texts. The latter suggested data analysis that emphasized naming *topics* over describing processes. Social constructivism was described in many places in the texts, and hence, I include it as one of the final eight FCCs, but the term 'social constructivism' was not used in most of that data. As a strategy for effectively communicating to my audience using terminology with which I assumed they would be familiar, I chose to depart from *in vivo* coding for two of the focused content codes: 'Social constructivist learning theory' and 'Differentiation.'

As I moved to the next round of data analysis—interpreting for paradigms—I was aware of the need to produce a set of FCCs that conveyed the substance of the middle grades concept without inserting too much of my interpretation of the beliefs, values, and assumptions that guided the advocates of the middle grades concept. The development of focused *content* codes functioned as a validity strategy, as well as an analysis technique, to keep the paradigm categories firmly grounded in the content of the middle grades concept. As units of historiographical analysis, the paradigm categories needed to reflect the particular ideas and positions of the middle grades advocates.

I used the eight FCCs to categorize the 395 BVA interpretations (see Appendix C for a slice of the focused coding data analysis table I employed to document and manage my inquiry).

At the end of the categorization process, a small number of BVA interpretations were left uncategorized (i.e., did not "fit," according to my analysis, with one of the eight FCCs). Accounting for the un-categorized BVA interpretations in this data set proved to be a valuable check on my fidelity to the data. However, in keeping with Charmaz's (2006) counsel to be comfortable with ambiguity during this stage, I decided to allow those uncategorized BVA in-terpretations to remain unaccounted for as I moved on to the next phase of interpretive data analysis.

Once most of the BVA interpretations were categorized by FCC, I began to analyze those tables to articulate paradigms for the middle grades concept. During this last round of analysis, the FCCs were re-evaluated once again as part of the process of devel-oping paradigm categories. For example, the FCC 'Middle Grades as critical period' corresponded to very few supporting BVA inter-pretations from three of the four texts; only the analysis of Carnegie (1989) yielded frequent BVA interpretations. However, there were sufficient initial codes to support 'Middle grades as a critical period' as an FCC. In my analytical notes on this FCC I wrote, "I don't think this data reflects a complete [focused content code] category. Right now it is a partial category...the uncatego-rized BVA statements are related to this data...Turbulence of ya [young adolescents], turbulence of society, threats, fears, per-ils...[As a paradigm] this category could include 'mgc as ed reform' It is also related to, but separate from, 'Nurturing the Nature'" (Analytic Notes, May 24, 2012). By screening the eight FCCs with the BVA interpretations, I was in a position to suggest paradigm categories that were supported by the data. My analysis of the BVA interpretations categorized under the FCCs 'Middle grades as critical period' and 'Middle grades as educational reform' sug-gested the paradigm category "Perceiving Perils." I used my handwritten notes, taken mostly on the hard copies of the catego-rized BVA interpretations, during this phase of interpretive analysis as a resource for developing paradigm categories (e.g., applying the term 'perils' as part of one of the final middle grades concept paradigm categories).

In the course of analyzing the FCC-categorized BVA interpreta-tions for paradigms, I began to account for the BVA interpretations from this data set that I had not categorized by FCC. After developing some initial ideas about potential paradigms, I went back through the uncategorized BVAs with the nascent paradigm categories in mind. Thirty of the 64 uncategorized BVAs (e.g., "Belief—race, SES, family structure, geographic location, and ELL impact educational opportunities/experiences"; BVA interpretation from Carnegie, 1989, pp. 20–21) seemed to correspond with the emergent paradigm category "Perceiving Perils." This analysis lent support to the robustness of the emergent paradigm category and is a good example of how I applied the constant-comparative method to establish the trustworthiness of my data analysis. Some BVA interpretations (e.g., "Value—aligning [teacher] preparation with purpose/function of mg schools"; BVA interpretation from Alexander, 1968, pp. 97–99) were left uncategorized in one of the eight FCCs and did not seem to support the emergent paradigm categories, according to my analysis.

After analyzing the BVA interpretations as categorized by the eight FCCs, accounting for uncategorized BVAs, and re-examining the FCC categories, I rendered five paradigm categories: *Separating and Re-Integrating, Nurturing the Nature, Perceiving Perils, Be-Coming Together,* and *Empowering Education.*

Spirituality as a domain of human development. For this data set, 117 initial codes were generated during the first round of interpretive analysis. For each initial code, which described the content of each datum, excerpts from the same selection of text that illustrated the initial code were identified and documented on the coding sheets. I selected 147 quotations to illustrate the initial codes. Each datum was also interpreted for the beliefs, values, and assumptions, using a critical constructivist interpretive lens. In the Spirituality as a Developmental Domain data set, I documented 123 interpretations of beliefs, 69 interpretations of values, and 43 interpretations of assumptions.

During my process of interpreting beliefs, values, and interpretations for the Oser, Scarlett, and Bucher (2006) text, I faced a research decision. This text is unique from the other texts in my research in that, as a chapter in a handbook on child and adolescent development, it includes a review of the literature on the prevailing scholarly explanations of child and adolescent spiritual development. According to the memo I wrote on October 10, 2012, I needed to decide which author's perspective I was interpreting for beliefs, values, and assumptions. Therefore, the decision I had to make was: Am I interpreting for the BVA of Oser, Scarlett, and Bucher? Or, am I interpreting for the BVA of the authors Oser, Scarlett, and Bucher have identified as prominent contributors to the field of spiritual development? My decision and my rationale are reflected in this quotation from my research journal: "I think (from a researcher perspective) it's OK to switch the focus of my BVA interpretation b/c [because] THE AIM of the data collection and data analysis is to create a picture/story of the field of spiritual development" (October 10, 2012). In my analysis, I shifted the focus of my BVA interpretation between the authors of the chapter and the authors referenced in the chapter. Although the various theories on spiritual development were critiqued by Oser, Scarlett, and Bucher (2006), the inclusion of the specific theories and their authors in an authoritative handbook in the field of developmental sciences was interpreted by me as primary evidence of how the "story" of the field of spirituality as a domain of human development is told. Critical questions such as Whose voice is heard? Which knowledge is legitimized? were still relevant in my interpretation of this text for beliefs, values, and assumptions.

My analysis of the body of initial codes yielded five focused content codes, which reflected themes in the content of the field of spirituality as a domain of human development, as rendered from the three texts. As with the previous data set, developing the final FCCs involved looping back and forth amongst the ICs of all three texts, as well as referencing the quotations as needed to further refine and distill the FCCs to ensure that I captured the main themes of the field. The five FCCs for this data set were:

1. Constructing spirituality (in the academy)
2. Theorizing about human development
3. Paradox as a heuristic
4. Crucibles of spiritual development
5. Contents of domain of spiritual development

In an effort to craft focused codes that distilled my analysis without sacrificing my fidelity to the data, I used a new strategy during this phase of coding. After generating lists of potential focused codes and applying constant comparative analysis in conjunction with memo-writing, I constructed a table that categorized the longer list of focused codes with my potential FCCs. The longer list of focused codes represented the sub-categories for each FCC; trying to sort the subcategories by the focused code categories enabled me to account for the data and to test the strength of the FCCs. The table became a tool of my data analysis process.

Table 5.1

Subcategories by Potential Focused Content Codes

Constructing spirituality	Theorizing about human development	Paradox as a heuristic	Crucibles of spiritual development	Contents of domain of spiritual development
Function/role of [spdev]/ spirituality	Relying on empiricism	Paradoxes abound	Social constructivist epistemologies	Lenses/ Frameworks/ Orientations
Needing scholarship	Universal process of human development	Heuristic	Interplays: between domains; person and cultural context	Myth-making/ Narratives
Spirituality and Religion as constructs	Stage-structural and developmental systems	Domain independent/Interdependent	Crucibles	Transcendence
Historical/ Contemporary perceptions about spirituality	Structures vs. content of spdev	Creating/ Inheriting	Interplays	Pathways
	Strengths emphasized over deficits	Universality/ Diversity		Trust/Mutuality/Attachment

The table illustrates one way I sorted through the emerging codes using inductive reasoning. As a snapshot of my data analysis, it also illustrates how I developed an emergent interpretation of the paradigms for this data set. For example, as a content code, FCC 'Crucibles of Spiritual Development' foreshadowed the paradigm category "Seeing Crucibles." In this phase of my analysis, I captured the specific 'crucibles' that were identified as part of spiritual development (e.g., interplays between person and context). In the next phase of analyzing the BVA interpretations for evidence of paradigms, I incorporated my content analysis to yield an interpretation that made explicit how the authors saw crucibles as part of their explanations of the process of spiritual development.

In the process of categorizing the 235 BVA interpretations by the five focused content codes, I found that several BVA interpretations fit under more than one FCC. In my research journal I characterized this overlapping categorization as *fuzziness*, especially between the FCCs 'Constructing spirituality' and 'Contents of the domain of spiritual development.' When I went back to review the initial codes and corresponding quotations from the data, however, my rendering of these two focused content codes as distinct from each other was affirmed by the data. I added a parenthetical clarification of "in the academy" to the FCC 'Constructing spirituality' as a result of re-analyzing the ICs and quotations. I accounted for the fuzziness in BVA categorization by labeling the multi-categorized BVA interpretations using italics and colors.

In hindsight, I was not too surprised to experience BVA interpretation overlap between the focused content codes that captured the data on definitional aspects of spirituality. From my review of the literature on spirituality in education and theories of spiritual development, I was aware that definitional ambiguity in Western cultures was a major theme in the empirical, theoretical, and programmatic literature. Therefore, beliefs, values, and assumptions related to constructs of spirituality in an academic context were bound to show up in focused content codes that addressed data reflecting the construction of spirituality. For the purposes of this research, parsing the distinctions in terms of aligning content with beliefs, values, and assumptions was less strategic than allowing for areas of overlap in this stage of data analysis. As with the data set on the middle grades concept—where I encountered BVA interpretations that did not "fit" into one of the FCCs—my decision to allow for ambiguity at this stage was guided by the principles of constructivist grounded theory.

In the course of analyzing the FCC-categorized BVA interpretations for paradigms related to spirituality as a domain of development, I was able to clarify the boundaries of my analytical codes that captured data on defining spirituality by re-framing these data in the language of paradigms. My research memos on emergent paradigms for the categorized BVA interpretations from the FCC 'Contents of the domain of spiritual development' illustrate my analytical process in this transition from focused content codes to paradigm categories. When documenting my analysis of the patterns in the BVA interpretations, I interpreted two subcategories: (a) ways of characterizing *what* happens during spiritual development; and (b) ways of characterizing *how* spiritual development happens. In my memo from October 22, 2012, I observed:

> It's interesting that what emerged is those 2 subcategories...because I don't think I would have 'captured' the data in such a way before sitting down to review the BVA [interpretations]. I still see a major distinction between [a] describing the paradigms behind *theorizing* about spdev [spiritual development] and [b] describing the paradigms behind the *theories* of spdev [spiritual development]. Because this [arrow pointing to the former subcategory] seems to be a major Focused Content Code. And I've observed that in my review of the literature on spdev theory, spdev research, spirituality & education...basically, wherever 'spirituality' is addressed in the social sciences.

In rendering the paradigm categories, the two categories that resulted from the part of my analysis described above are: *Legitimizing Spiritual Development* and *Aligning Heart and Will*. The other three paradigm categories—*Mapping the Human Journey*, *Allowing Paradox*, and *Seeing Crucibles*—encompassed some of the definitional themes as well.

Holistic education. For this data set, 100 initial codes were generated during the first round of interpretive analysis. For each initial code, which described the content of each datum, excerpts from the same selection of text that illustrated the initial code were identified and documented on the coding sheets. I selected 108 quotations to illustrate the initial codes. Each datum was also interpreted for the beliefs, values, and assumptions, using a critical constructivist interpretive lens. In the Holistic Education data set, I documented 93 interpretations of beliefs, 98 interpretations of values, and 39 interpretations of assumptions.

When I began the first round of initial coding, I only analyzed the J. Miller (2007) and R. Miller (1997) texts because I had second thoughts about including the Kessler (2000) text in my data set. I hesitated because the focus of Kessler's text is less on the *field* of holistic education and more on classroom-based practices to implement holistic education. I made the decision to proceed with the first three rounds of interpretive analysis (initial coding, focused content coding, and categorizing BVA interpretations by FCC) without the Kessler text. After doing so, I did not feel like I had analyzed sufficient data to render paradigm categories. I based this decision on my review of the focused content codes and categorized BVA interpretations. My initial analysis of just the two Miller texts seemed incomplete in two emergent focused content codes: a cultural critique of education and ontological/epistemological beliefs. I made strategic selections from the Kessler (2000) text that focused more on the theory of holistic education than on specific classroom-based practices.

I interpreted the Kessler data for initial codes and beliefs, values, and assumptions. I then re-analyzed the entire set of initial codes that now included the Kessler data for focused content codes. I also re-categorized the BVA interpretations by FCC with the Kessler data in the set. In other words, I did not simply integrate the Kessler initial codes and BVA interpretations into the focused content coding analysis from just the J. Miller (2007) and R. Miller (1997) data analysis. I essentially started the focused content coding and BVA categorization all over from the beginning with the expanded data set. With the inclusion of the Kessler data, the

FCCs were more robust, and I was satisfied that I had analyzed sufficient data to interpret for paradigms.

I briefly compared the focused content coding and BVA categorization that resulted from the two data sets (one without Kessler, one with Kessler) to see if I could interpret any differences. The main difference I noticed was that with the inclusion of the Kessler data, the FCCs 'Educating in community' and 'Conceptualizing spirituality' were more substantially supported by the data in terms of both initial codes and BVA interpretations. I also noticed the ways in which Kessler's K–12 practitioner voice fleshed out the story of holistic education that was told by the higher education academics, John Miller and Ron Miller. My comparative analysis was brief, however, and only conducted as validation strategy for my analysis of the data.

In rendering the focused content codes, I employed the same procedures I used for the data set on Spiritual Development. After reading through the entire list of initial codes, I composed a list of potential FCCs based on my impressions (without referring back to the initial codes). Then, I went through the initial codes a second time, to create a new list of potential FCCs while concurrently referring to the initial codes. After revising both lists a third time while in constant contact with the initial codes and the quotations, I began to articulate potential main FCCs and subcategories of FCCs. As with the Spiritual Development data set, I categorized the subcategories by the emergent main FCCs in order to organize my analysis and evaluate the fidelity of my analysis to the data. For example:

Potential focused content code: **Spiritual Epistemology**

Subcategories: imagination as learning, honoring reason and intuition, seeing the whole from the parts, awareness of interconnection, re-connecting, meaning over information, knowing as spiritual task, inviting soul, establishing trust, learning as a process, not a product

At the conclusion of this phase of data analysis, I rendered five focused content codes for the Holistic Education data set:

1. Seeking Balance/Transforming Culture
2. Spiritual Epistemology
3. Educating in Community
4. Conceptualizing Spirituality
5. Re-Framing Accountability

I then categorized the beliefs, values, and assumptions interpretations by the five FCCs. I did not find as many BVA interpretations that overlapped with more than one FCC (as I had found in the Spiritual Development data set). The most frequent area of overlap was the BVA interpretations for the FCCs 'Re-framing accountability' and 'Seeking balance/transforming culture.' For the BVAs that did overlap, I used the same process of color-coding in the BVA by FCC table to keep track of that analysis. I used the BVA by FCC table to interpret for patterns that might reflect paradigms. As with the other two data sets, I documented initial impressions and emergent analysis with analytic memos in my research journal.

After analyzing the BVA interpretations as categorized by the five FCCs, accounting for the few uncategorized BVAs in this data set, and re-examining the FCC categories, I rendered five paradigm categories: *Claiming Ontological Truths, Knowing With Wholeness, Schooling for Cultural Consensus, Re-Framing Accountability*, and *Beliefs About What it Means to be Human*.

Critical Interpretation: Contrapuntal Reading

The third round of data analysis involved a contrapuntal reading (Said, 1993) of the paradigm narratives. Contrapuntal reading is a data analysis strategy that corresponds with the critical historiographical technique of critical interpretation and reflects the principles of critical historiography. In this section of my accounting of the research methods, I first describe the contrapuntal reading as a data analysis technique, then I describe the contrapuntal reading processes I devised for this research.

For readers unfamiliar with Said's (1993) work on contrapuntal reading, I offer an example from his application of this analytical technique in the context of his work in the field of literary theory. Applying a contrapuntal reading to Joseph Conrad's *Heart of Darkness*, first published in 1899, Said notes:

> Conrad is so self-conscious about situating Marlow's tale in a narrative moment that he allows us simultaneously to realize after all that imperialism, far from swallowing up its own history, was taking place in and was circumscribed by a larger history, one just outside the tightly inclusive circle of Europeans on the deck of the *Nellie*. As yet, however, no one seemed to inhabit that region, and so Conrad left it empty. (p. 24)

This passage reflects a critical historiographical approach akin to the one I used for this research. In his analysis of the text, Said addressed the positionality of the author by accounting for how Conrad's cultural status in England in the late 1800s affected his work: "your self-consciousness as an outsider can allow you actively to comprehend how the machine works, given that you and it are fundamentally not in perfect synchrony or correspondence" (p. 25). Said also named how the White narrator, Marlow, wields power over the text's (European) audience in their reliance upon Marlow as a source of authority on indigenous peoples of Africa. In later passages, Said addressed the ways in which he sees the interdiscursive relationship between the imperial discourse and the discourse of resistance when he interpreted the narrator's unwillingness to view "non-European 'darkness' [as] in fact a non-European world *resisting* imperialism so as to one day regain sovereignty" (p. 30).

Said was insistent on not polarizing the two forms of discourse into the binaries of oppressor and oppressed (a "rhetoric of blame," p. 18); instead he urged for a contrapuntal reading that sees the connections saying: "We must be able to think through and interpret together experiences which are discrepant, each with its particular agenda and pace of development, its own internal formations, its internal coherence and system of external relationships, all of them co-existing and interacting with others" (p. 32). Doing so, he argued, "enables us to appreciate [ideology's] power and understand [ideology's] continuing influence" (p. 33). Said's emphasis on connection over polarization directed my analysis of the data toward an interpretation of inter-textual and inter-discursive patterns within the categories of paradigms.

Said's direction aligned with my research purpose of better understanding educational relevance of spiritual development, as opposed to an investigation of the extent to which issues of spirituality have been silenced in education in the United States.

I had three reasons for my decision to draw from Said (1993) as a data analysis strategy in critical historiographical research. First, the technique of contrapuntal reading is consistent with the principles of critical historiography—for instance, criticality and multilogicality. In contrast to multilogicality, criticality emphasizes the constructed and regulatory nature of social and historical discourse (Henry, 2006; Popkewitz, 1991; Villaverde, Kincheloe, & Helyar, 2006) whereas the latter emphasizes the perspectives that have not been valued in the dominant discourse construction. Said (1993) acknowledged the former, criticality, and provides a discourse analysis strategy for hearing the voices of the latter, multilogicality.

Second, the contrapuntal strategy of reading for the tension between a discourse of imperialism and a discourse of resistance (Said, 1993) offered me direction as I interpreted for discursive practices within a convergence among the paradigms of the middle grades concept, spirituality as a developmental domain, and holistic education while being aware of the cultural/historical context in which these texts were produced and are read. Said described contrapuntal reading as "a procedure [that] entails reading the canon as a polyphonic accompaniment to the expansion of Europe" (p. 60). In my discussion of my findings, I address how the canons of the three fields I investigated could be read as an accompaniment to educational reform priorities in the United States.

Third, the metaphor of counterpoint fits well with my Venn diagram conceptual model of the inter-relationships between and among the related fields. My researcher's hunch during the design of this project, guided by Popkewitz's (1997) scaffolding metaphor, was that a better understanding of the educational relevance of spiritual development lies within a nexus of the three (hi)stories. But to illuminate its contents, a data analysis strategy that resembled counterpoint in music was useful as I sought to create melody out of disparate yet interrelated strands of harmony. Contrapuntal reading starts from the perspective that texts have many layers of meaning that can be deconstructed and then reassembled into a coherent narrative. Said's (1993) instruction to read contrapuntally—instead of univocally—reflects how, as a critical constructivist, I have conceptualized how a better understanding of the educational relevance of spirituality can be known through productive deconstruction of texts.

Although Said (1993) offered guidance on how to contrapuntally read a narrative, my use of the specific analysis strategy of interpreting for inter-textual and inter-discursive patterns is a reflection of how I operationalized contrapuntal reading for the purposes of this critical historiographical research. Said does not use the specific terms "inter-textual" and "inter-discursive," but I find similar meanings in his written descriptions of contrapuntal reading. Both Said and Kincheloe (2008) write about data analysis that is deeply critical in its emphasis on making explicit power dynamics and tacit rules as well as deeply constructivist in its subjectivist ontology.

When I first conceived of this research design, I wrote of inter-textual and inter-discursive as two *categories* by which to organize my analysis. However, when I actually began this analysis, I reconceived inter-textual and inter-discursive as two interpretive *lenses* by which to analyze the paradigm narratives. The inter-textual lens allowed me to interpret for textual expressions such as specific terms or phrases, metaphors or analogies, ideas, or positions that were commonly shared by the three data sets. Kincheloe's (2005) definition of inter-textual referred to "the complicated interrelationship connecting a text to other texts in the act of textual creation or interpretation" (p. 329). In my analysis of the paradigm narratives, I focused on the second part of the interrelationship (interpretation), while in my discussion of the implications of the conceptual contents of the nexus of the three fields, I incorporated the interrelationship that connected the texts in the acts of their creation (i.e., their historical contexts).

The inter-discursive lens allowed me to interpret for paradigms that were commonly shared by all three data sets. In this research, I defined paradigms as discursive practices in accordance with Kincheloe's (2008) definition of inter-discursive: "Discursive practices are defined as a set of tacit rules that regulate what can and cannot be said, who can speak with the blessing of authority and who must listen, whose socio-educational constructions are scientific and valid and whose are unlearned and unimportant" (p. 36). This definition was also in accordance with Kuhn's (1996) analogy of paradigms as maps as well as the rules for map-making. By combining Kincheloe's (2008) definition of discursive practices with Kuhn's (1996) definition of paradigms, I crafted a critical historiographical data analysis strategy that interrogated and made explicit the ways in which the ideas and positions of the fields have been constructed. By interpreting the results of my constructivist grounded theory analysis for commonly held paradigms, or inter-discursive patterns, I was able to generate knowledge about the conceptual nexus of the three fields as a strategy for exploring the educational relevance of the spiritual domain of development in middle grades education.

Here are the procedures I used for the contrapuntal reading of the paradigm narratives. During the third round of data analysis, I mainly worked with one of the products from the second round of the analysis: the thick narrative description of the paradigm categories. Because I was working with source material that was two steps removed from the data, it was very important that the first two rounds of data analysis had integrity. As mentioned before, this is why I chose to use constructivist grounded theory techniques for initially coding the data and for refining those initial codes and generating categories.

During the contrapuntal reading of the paradigm narratives, I employed the constant-comparative method to return to the focused content codes, the BVA interpretations, the quotations I had selected from the texts, the initial codes, and even back to the texts themselves as a series of checks on my interpretation of the narratives. Even though I had used quotations to illustrate the initial codes and BVA interpretations, I often returned to the full passage from which I had extracted an excerpt of text, to confirm (or reassess) how I interpreted the context and meaning of the data. This is in accordance with both Charmaz (2006) and Creswell (2007), who recommended keeping descriptions of the results of qualitative analysis grounded in the data by quoting and citing generously from the data. Citations linked with specific claims served as documentation of my past analysis and facilitation for the final round of analysis. This process was facilitated by my decision to use extensive in-text and parenthetical citations in the paradigm narratives.[2]

During initial and focused coding, I kept a record of potential inter-textual patterns. For example, while analyzing the Holistic Education data set, I interpreted two potential inter-textual patterns between the Holistic Education initial codes and the Middle Grades Concept initial codes: intra-personal teacher growth and education as developmentally responsive. I kept memos to document my leads; upon completion of all initial and focused coding, I had a list of six potential inter-textual patterns.

I used these six potential inter-textual patterns as starting places for the contrapuntal reading of the paradigm narratives. My first steps were to expand upon these patterns and identify other potential shared *themes*, using text from the paradigm narratives. Because I had re-conceived of the inter-textual and inter-discursive as interpretive lenses, I shifted the level of analysis upward/outward to capture over-arching themes that might be interpreted for inter-textual and inter-discursive patterns. I re-read through the paradigm narratives and identified themes that were common to all three fields (e.g., Human Development) and then explored in writing that theme from an inter-textual perspective and from an inter-discursive perspective. Using the example of the Human Development theme, one of the potential inter-textual patterns was 'conceptions of the developing human.' I then interpreted six potential inter-discursive patterns within that theme: 'growth influenced by internal and external processes,' 'developmental theory as normative,' 'integrated domains of development,' 'each domain has a function,' 'universal aspects, diverse expressions,' and 'responding to development.' (I provide these results as examples to illustrate my process; a much fuller explication of them can be found in Chapter Seven.)

---

[2]   For the sake of readability, in Chapter 6 I chose to remove most of the in-text and parenthetical citations. Appendix D includes excerpts from two paradigm narratives with the citations left in place, as an illustration of my strategy for future researchers.

My next step was to create a tool for organizing and making sense of my data analysis as it expanded. I used a table to organize and keep track of my analysis process; Table 5.2 is a modified excerpt from that table.

Table 5.2

Analytical Tool for Contrapuntal Reading Across Paradigm Narratives

	Theme	*Inter-textual*	*Inter-discursive*
	Epistemology	What is knowledge?	Ecological metaphor/ framework, Ecological epistemology
Data from MGC paradigm narratives	p. 21 *Be-Coming Together*, as a paradigm code, encompasses the meeting place between learning and interpersonal relationships, where collaboration is both a means and a goal.		
	p. 23–24 In my analysis, locating a source of authority within classroom teachers reflects an epistemological belief (and therefore paradigmatic) about whose knowledge "counts" when crafting curriculum theory.		
Data from SpDev paradigm narratives	p. 35 Benson goes on to claim that spiritual development occurs because of and is influenced by, "...the ecologies one chooses to be the primary crucibles for development" (p. 490).		
	p. 37 *Seeing Crucibles*, as a paradigm code, captures the fundamental valuing of interaction, the assumption that something of substance happens in the 'in-between' space, and the belief that human development occurs because of and within these crucibles.		
Data from HolEd paradigm narratives	p. 46 Knowing is described as subjective, multidimensional, and interconnected (e.g., Miller, 1997, pp. 199–201; Miller, 2007, pp. 190–192).		
	p. 50–51 Miller (2007) calls this "organic accountability" (p. 193), reflecting the ways in which advocates of holistic education reject the factory/machine metaphors of teaching and learning in favor of metaphors that emphasize biology, nature, and ecology.		

To test the robustness of my analysis, I used cells in the table (represented here as the last three rows) to document and keep track of text from the paradigm narratives; the page numbers cited for each datum are from a draft hard copy. As I did with the quotations from the data during initial coding, the quotations from the paradigm narratives were meant to illustrate data that I was connecting to the inter-textual and inter-discursive patterns, not to represent all of the text that supported my analysis. In other words, while in some cells I included more than one quotation from the paradigm narratives, I did so to more illustrate how I interpreted each specific excerpt as part of the whole pattern, not to make a claim regarding the quantitative amount of text that supported my analysis.

As a researcher new to critical historiography, this process was an interesting part of the hermeneutic cycle: working with the results of data analysis that had multiple layers of data compression, as well as constant-comparative looping between raw data (the texts), initial codes, focused content codes, and paradigm narratives. I was aware more than ever of the dual challenge of returning to the data (texts) to maintain fidelity while simultaneously synthesizing vast amounts of data analysis to enable clarity of expression. The principles of constructivist grounded theory (Charmaz, 2006), such as using constant comparative analysis and allowing for ambiguity during the process, were helpful guides as I navigated the complex terrain. The use of tables to document, organize, and evaluate my data analysis was a useful validity strategy as well as an analysis tool.

After working with the potential inter-textual patterns (documented during initial and focused coding) I applied contrapuntal reading to the paradigm narratives, adding potential themes, inter-textual and inter-discursive patterns as I interpreted the narratives. The documentation of the inter-textual and inter-discursive patterns on the table marked a return to my initial conceptualization of the inter-textual and inter-discursive patterns as *categories* by which to organize the results of my analysis. At the conclusion of this round of data analysis, I identified 19 potential themes. Distributed amongst the themes were 18 potential inter-textual patterns and 24 potential inter-discursive patterns. At this stage, I still considered these themes and patterns as potential results. For example, eight of the potential inter-discursive patterns

were not fully supported by evidence from all three sets of paradigm narratives (e.g., the inter-discursive pattern 'developmental
theory as normative' was not supported by analysis of the Holistic
Education data set).

The next step of my analysis was to review the table and construct claims about the contents of the conceptual nexus between
the fields of the middle grades concept, spirituality as a developmental domain, and holistic education. In this phase of data
analysis, I used visual organizers to document and work with my
evolving analysis. I read over all entries in the table, took notes in
my research journal as I was analyzing, then drew initial visual
outlines for the inter-textual and inter-discursive patterns that
were supported by my analysis of the paradigm narratives. Using
these outline-memos, I drew more complex representations of the
conceptual relationships between the patterns. From the outline-
memos, I rendered eight inter-textual patterns and eight inter-
discursive patterns that were supported by data from all three
data sets and created a visual model that was more formalized
than the outline-memos as another way to work with the results. I
used labels to capture the patterns and give myself a concise way
to write about my findings (e.g., integration as an inter-discursive
pattern; empiricism as an inter-textual pattern). I created a digital
version of the visual model to work with my emergent findings; I
moved various text boxes around as I tried to conceptualize the
interrelationships between the inter-textual and inter-discursive
patterns, which I consider a primary level of analysis. That analysis yielded an interpretation of three primary paradigms:
Ecological Epistemology, Holistic Ontology, and Positivist Ontology.

A secondary level of concurrent analysis involved accounting
for the discursive interrelationship between two of the meta-
paradigms, Ecological Epistemology and Holistic Ontology, and
with a third meta-paradigm, Positivist Ontology. I say discursive
interrelationship, not inter-discursive relationship, to distinguish
between the patterns that are inter-discursive between the three
fields/data sets (inter-discursive relationship) and the discursive
interrelationship between Ecological Epistemology/Holistic Ontology and Positivist Ontology that occurs *within each field*. In the

latter, a contrapuntal reading yielded an interpretation of a complex discursive dynamic between Ecological Epistemology/Holistic Ontology and Positivist Ontology that I characterize as paradoxical. Into my digital visual model, I inserted as a theoretical bridge between Ecological Epistemology/Holistic Ontology and Positivist Ontology a quotation from Said (1993) about reading for the disparate harmonies with a melody—what he characterizes as a "simultaneous awareness" (p. 51) of not only the content of the dominant discourses and the discourses of resistance but also the ways in which both discourses act "against which and together with" (p. 51) each other. In my critical historiographical analysis, I accounted for the both positivist and holistic ontologies within the conceptual nexus of the three fields. Each has its own harmony, but together they form a (conceptual) counterpoint melody.

In addition to three primary paradigms, I also interpreted five secondary paradigms, four of which were closely related (textually and discursively) to the primary Ecological Epistemology and Holistic Ontology paradigms: (a) social constructivism/situated cognition; (b) knowing as alignment; (c) integration; and (d) interconnection. I interpreted seven inter-textual patterns total; four were also related to the Ecological Epistemology and Holistic Ontology paradigms and the associated four secondary paradigms. The fifth secondary paradigm—empiricism—was related to the Positivist Ontology primary paradigm and three additional inter-textual patterns.

In a subsequent round of constant-comparative analysis that involved composing memos for each inter-discursive and inter-textual pattern, I revised my re-presentation of my analysis by a further reduction of the data. As I wrote about the secondary inter-discursive patterns (e.g., knowing as alignment), I decided that it was neither helpful nor clarifying to make a distinction between primary and secondary paradigms: my interpretation of the content and influence of the secondary paradigms was expressed in my description of content and influence of the three primary paradigms. Also, conceptually, I had trouble making a sharp distinction between what constituted a primary from a secondary paradigm. I came to understand that what I called the secondary paradigms were elements of the primary paradigms. So, in effect, my memos were repetitive. I revised the visual analytic model/tool for exploring the interrelationships between inter-discursive and intertextual patterns (see Appendix E for the final version of the visual analytical model).

To conclude this description of the specific procedures used to analyze the data and begin to transition to a report of the results, it seemed fitting to return to Kincheloe's (e.g., 2005, 2008) call for a thick description of the results of critical constructivist research. The following passage from his 2005 publication illustrates his (and my) rationale for doing so as part of research findings:

> Complexity in the context of cultural inquiry demands that the researcher develop a thick description that avoids the reductionism of describing the 'functional role' of an individual. Such a 'literacy of complexity' understands the intersecting roles and social locations of all human beings and the multiple layers of interpretations of self, contexts, and social actors involved in rigorous research. (p. 327)

My analysis process in this research at times felt like the "literacy of complexity" that Kincheloe described. Sorting through the many layers of interpretations, accounting for my researcher reflexivity, and navigating a unique methodology in educational research while also seeking to avoid reductionist analysis that reified emergent findings was a complex task indeed. But, as a research methodology, critical historiography proved to be strategic and useful in serving the purposes of this research, precisely in its allowance for a literacy of complexity.

Chapter Six

Paradigms of the (Hi)stories

CARDINAL questions for historiographical research in education that is guided by critical constructivism are: Who speaks with authority, and who is expected to listen? What worldviews and perspectives can be interpreted from the ways in which a (hi)story is told? What epistemological assumptions ground theories about learning? How does the construction of knowledge in schools—which is shaped by powerful historical, cultural, and political forces—in turn shape teachers and students? From an interrogation of a (hi)story, what can be understood about the hybridity of teaching and learning, of knowledge production and youth development?

When it comes to communicating results of critical constructivist research, Kincheloe (2008) wrote, "When critical constructivists produce knowledge, they are not attempting to reduce variables but to maximize (Knobel, 1999) them. Such maximization produces a thicker, more detailed, more complex understanding of the social, political, economic, cultural, psychological, and pedagogical world" (p. 3). In this chapter, I describe the results of my first two rounds of analysis of the data through a series of in-depth narratives on the paradigms for the three (hi)stories. The results of the third and final round of analysis, the conceptual contents of the area of paradigmatic convergence, are presented in Chapter Seven. As with the accounting of the research methods in Chapter Five, I organized the narratives by data set, in the same order I analyzed the data. These narratives were constructed after the first two rounds of data analysis were completed for all three data sets.

Prevalent Paradigms

The end result of the initial and focused coding is a claim regarding the paradigms that are prevalent for each of the fields included in this research. These findings addressed my first research sub-

question: What prevalent paradigms underlie the academic discourse on spirituality as a developmental domain, the middle
grades concept, and holistic education? These results represent yet
another level of the hermeneutic cycle, as I move deeper within the
boundaries of each paradigm category, exploring edges, dimensions, and intersectionality. Table 6.1 shows the paradigm
categories for all three data sets. This set of results became a unit
of historiographical analysis for the final round of data analysis, to
be described in the second section of this chapter.

Table 6.1
Paradigm Categories

Middle Grades Concept	Domain of Spiritual Development	Holistic Education
Separating and Re-Integrating	Mapping the Human Journey	Beliefs About What it Means to be Human
Nurturing the Nature	Aligning Heart and Will	Knowing With Wholeness
Be-Coming Together	Allowing Paradox	Schooling for Cultural Consensus
Perceiving Perils	Seeing Crucibles	Re-Framing Accountability
Empowering Education	Legitimizing Spiritual Development	Claiming Ontological Truths

Epistemological and ontological issues dominate these paradigm categories, with the field of holistic education most deeply
steeped in discussions on knowledge, learning, and reality. Holism,
as a perennial philosophy, stresses a particular perspective on reality and knowing that lies in contrast to the dominance of
technocratic educational discourse. So, in defining holistic education, it is not surprising that epistemology and ontology are
frequent topics. The (hi)story of spiritual development primarily
invokes ontological issues, especially in regards to being able to
define and describe the developmental processes that are spiritual.

The authors' perspectives on epistemology are invoked in the descriptions of spiritual developmental processes. One of the main themes of that (hi)story is that ways of knowing are deeply connected with spiritual development. In the foundational texts on the middle grades concept, epistemological issues are referenced when describing the content of recommended practices with young adolescents. Ontological issues are referenced when middle grades advocates make claims about the nature of the stage of young adolescence.

As an artifact of critical constructivist research, the narratives address cultural, historical, and political themes as well. My critical interpretation is woven throughout the paradigm narratives; when cultural, historical, and/or political issues are particularly important to my rendering of the paradigm narratives, my interpretation is more explicit. Examples of paradigms categories that reflect explicit critical interpretation are *Perceiving Perils* and *Empowering Education* (middle grades), *Legitimizing Spiritual Development* (domain of spiritual development), *Schooling for Cultural Consensus, and Re-Framing Accountability* (holistic education).

Because my research strategy was to interpret for paradigms, I emphasize in the narratives the deepest layers of beliefs, values, and assumptions that influence the (hi)stories of the three fields. However, at times I also describe in detail the content that resulted from the paradigms, as a means of further explication of the ways in which the paradigms were operating. This approach is consistent with Kuhn's (1996) definition of paradigms as both maps and rules for map-making. In that analogy, a better understanding of the rules for map-making results if one can also see the maps. This analogy is particularly apt for this research, the purpose of which is to study the "maps" of the three related fields into order to find theoretical common ground that suggested a rationale for the relevance of spiritual development in middle grades education.

Note: Any use of italics within direct quotations is a representation of the original authors' use of italics. I did not add emphasis to any of the direct quotations.

Middle Grades Concept

In this section on the findings from the Middle Grades Concept data set, I describe the content, boundaries, and interconnections of my interpretation of the paradigms that guide the advocates of the middle grades concept. I rendered five paradigm categories: *Separating and Re-Integrating, Nurturing the Nature, Perceiving Perils, Be-Coming Together,* and *Empowering Education.* In this section on the middle grades paradigms, I chose to present the findings by starting with paradigms that primarily address onto-logical issues, before moving into paradigms that encompass epistemological perspectives. This organization mirrors a main theme of the (hi)story of this field: Because of certain ontological claims about the reality of human development, certain epistemo-logical perspectives are considered preferable for middle grades education. I end with the paradigm categories that draw in cul-tural, socio-historical, and political issues. I make these distinctions within the order of the paradigm narratives with very broad strokes: None are as cut and dried as I have described in this introduction to this section.

Separating and re-integrating. *Separating and Re-Integrating* as a paradigm category reflects a sequence of beliefs: (1) a holistic ontology that is *a priori,* (2) man's separation of con-structs is negative, and (3) a call for educators to re-integrate constructs. NMSA (2010) used the term holistic to characterize knowledge, human development, and implementation of the ele-ments of the middle grades concept (e.g., "When teachers help them see the many connections...student recognize the holistic na-ture of all knowledge" p. 22). Constructs that have been wrongly separated are: life from school, personal from academic, and knowledge into disciplines. Re-integration of these constructs is believed to be best for young adolescent learning. Teachers control and determine the re-integration through curriculum and instruc-tion: "Effective middle grades schools provide experiences, studies, and units...that are specifically designed to be integrative; for that is how learning is maximized" (NMSA, 2010, p. 21).

Middle grades advocates assume characteristics of human development are domain-specific. However, middle grades advocates also believe successful middle grades education treats the developmental domains as interrelated: "...the goal of intellectual development is not pursued at the expense of the social, emotional, and physical development of the individual" (Alexander, 1968, p. 85). A connection between this category and *Empowering Education* is the critique of distinguishing extracurricular learning activities from other curricula in a way that privileges the core academics. In the data, learning activities categorized as extracurricular are seen as tending to developmental domains not typically targeted in academic learning activities. Erasing the privileged status of traditional academic courses over extracurricular activities by no longer treating the latter as extra, or outside of, the curriculum, is in keeping with the paradigmatic view that human development involves distinct yet unequivocally interrelated domains.

Nurturing the nature. The *Nurturing the Nature* paradigm category encompasses positivist beliefs about human development, as reflected by my use of the term nature, and feminist values about adult interactions with young adolescent learners in a school context, as reflected by my use of the term nurture. The title of this paradigm category is also a play off of the debate in the later part of the 20th century over competing influences on human development: nature vs. nurture. Based on my analysis of the four texts, middle grades advocates have resolved this debate by upholding stage-based, positivist theories about the primacy of nature (inherent, biologically-determined mechanisms), while simultaneously triumphing the potential of developmentally-responsive schooling (environmental, contextual factors). For middle grades advocates, early adolescence is a stage of human development with outcomes that depend upon, among other environmental factors, what happens in middle schools. An irony of this paradigm is that the student-centered construct of developmentally responsive education is informed by adult-generated knowledge about young adolescent development. Students, the young adolescents themselves, were not cited as sources of authority about their experience of human development. Based on my more comprehensive review of the literature on middle grades education, it is fair to claim that the *prevalent* paradigm reflects a reliance on adults for knowledge about young adolescent development. However, some literature does acknowledge, and in some cases even draws from, young adolescents as sources of authority about their development as it pertains to their education (e.g., Doda & Knowles, 2008).

Human development is essentialized in the data: Development can be known, described, empirically studied, and intentionally responded to in ways that facilitate positive growth. Growth and development are used synonymously in the data, implying a tacit understanding of human development as an upward trajectory (e.g., a "path," with "turning points," Carnegie, 1978, p. 14). Developmental characteristics are either explicitly or implicitly referred to as a 'fact' (e.g., "...precocity is a distinguishing characteristic of many transescents [young adolescents] today, a fact that must be considered in designing a curriculum for this age group," Lounsbury & Vars, 1978, p. 35).

According to middle grades advocates, given the distinct attributes of young adolescents, successful middle grades education can be and must be responsive to those attributes. Attributes are also described in the data as needs. For example, "a volatile mismatch exists between the organization and curriculum of middle grade schools, and the intellectual, emotional, and interpersonal needs of young adolescents" (Carnegie, 1989, p. 32). Caring relationships that provide support and foster hope and belonging are valued as being developmentally responsive.

Nurturing, as the paradigm category suggests, is a process not an event. In the data, the politics of caring are sometimes implied by terminology, as the use of the term advocacy in this datum: "advocacy is not a singular event or a period in the schedule, it is an attitude of caring that translates into actions, big and small, when adults respond to the needs of each young adolescent in their charge" (NMSA, 2010, p. 35).

Be-coming together. *Be-Coming Together*, as a paradigm category, encompasses the meeting place between learning and interpersonal relationships, where collaboration is both a means and a goal. A metaphor from the data to describe this category is the middle school as a "finding place" (NMSA, 2010, p. 20). Closely related to the feminist values introduced in *Nurturing the Nature*, this paradigm category also emphasizes processes of learning and human development over outcomes of learning and development.

In the data, being known and cared for is asserted to be the best educational approach for young adolescents: "Teaching and classroom learning, for the most part, occur in relationships. The extent of learning which results is directly related to the quality of those relationships" Lounsbury & Vars, 1978, p. 6). Middle grades advocates analogize successful schools as being like home in that the students perceive that they belong: "the middle grade school proposed here...creates [a] community of adults and young people embedded in networks of support and responsibility..." (Carnegie, 1989, p. 36).

The teacher attitude that students are human be-ings rather than human do-ings is seen as desirable and even essential for the purpose of maximizing learning potential: "since young adolescents learn best through engagement and interaction, learning strategies should involve students in dialogue with teachers and one another..." (NMSA, 2010, p. 23). This paradigm orients middle grades practitioners to prioritize process over product, a stance that is operationalized in several specific recommendations, such as the emphasis of formative over summative assessment.

The title of this category is a play on words—becoming is *in vivo*: "the basic educational objective of the middle school is neither skills nor knowledge, but simply 'becoming'" (Lounsbury & Vars, 1978, p. 4). In separating *be-* from *-coming* I seek to emphasize my finding that middle grades advocates emphasize the dual processes of coming together in community and seeing each person as a separate learner. An irony I interpreted in the data is the stance that because of the diverse expressions and rates of young adolescent development, learning needs are unique to each student, and that the uniqueness of their needs is best met through collaborative learning activities.

Perceiving perils. The *Perceiving Perils* paradigm category captures the various ways in which the middle grades concept is justified by the authors' emphasis on threats to young adolescents and to United States society. My use of the word "perils" is deliberate: peril as a term invokes moral turpitude and situations that are life threatening and beyond personal control. NMSA (2010) uses an analogous term: "hazards" (p. 6). People subject to perils are vulnerable; vulnerability is one of the *defining* characteristics of young adolescents in the data. People subject to perils need protection; in the data, the protectors are the adults, not the young adolescent peers. The proactive strategy for protection is the middle grades concept.

A consistent theme across the four texts is the theme of young adolescence as a critical period given the perils or complexities of contemporary society. A variance in this theme is the source of this danger in contemporary society. For example, in Lounsbury and Vars (1978), the source of the peril is "a pluralistic society undergoing a value crisis so severe that it threatens the very foundations of our government" (p. 37). In Carnegie (1989), the "pluralism" that Lounsbury and Vars obliquely referred to is more specifically identified as "...a source of social unrest in this nation as the relative size of minority groups increases in coming years" (p. 48). I characterize this perspective as a paradigm as opposed to simply descriptive of content because the perception of perils—be they societal or developmental—is foundational to the construction and rationale for the middle grades concept. In both of the above examples, each threat was connected to an aspect of the middle grades content. For Lounsbury and Vars (1978), the antidote was curricular content that was responsive to young adolescent development and societal context; for Carnegie (1989), an exploration of interdisciplinary themes "...offer[ed] one way of dealing positively..." (p. 48) with the social unrest.

The volume on that alarm gets turned up as the expression of the middle grades concept moves from 1968 to 2010. In the later data (i.e., Carnegie, 1989), the perils of contemporary society are linked with the concept of equity. Diversity/equity is absent from Alexander (1968), introduced in Lounsbury and Vars (1978), hammered on in Carnegie (1989), and softened (but very much present) in NMSA (2010). "Equity" as a term is not indexed in Alexander (1968) or Lounsbury and Vars (1978). The term appears six times in my initial codes for Carnegie (1989) and twice in NMSA (2010). The paradigmatic relationship between equity and the middle grade concept is further explored in the paradigm category *Empowering Education*.

Finally, throughout the data are claims to the critical nature of early adolescence in terms of personal growth and the health, stability, and prosperity of society in the United States in the later 21st century. These claims overlap with the positivist perspective on human development, as described in *Nurturing the Nature*.

A strong relationship exists between *Perceiving Perils* and the previous category, *Be-Coming Together*. The latter is described as the response to the alarm bells sounded in *Perceiving Perils*. There is an interesting irony in this inter-categorical relationship: the use of fear tactics to motivate trusting relationships.

Empowering education. The *Empowering Education* paradigm category encompasses teacher self-efficacy, learning theory, and the middle grades concept as educational reform. In this category, empowerment is both personal and collective and occurs at classroom, school, and societal levels. This category and *Be-Coming Together* overlap: The strongest area of overlap is the function and value of teacher intrapersonal development. Seeing one's own humanity in order to see the humanity of others is emphasized in the 1968 and 1978 data as a necessary disposition or attitude. In the 1989 and 2010 data, teacher intrapersonal development is characterized in terms of external, observable actions of caring and well-being. The middle grades teacher is valued as a core element of the middle grades concept; internal, personal transformation is believed to have external benefits for teaching and learning in schools.

Teachers are empowered by middle grades advocates by being seen as the primary authorities on curriculum and instruction. In the data, testimonials from teachers were legitimized as evidence for the validity of the middle grades concept. Teacher authority was also reflected in specific recommendations of the middle grades concept. For example, in the Carnegie (1989) report, one of the recommendations is: "Decisions concerning the experiences of middle grades students should be made by adults who know them best" (p. 54). In my analysis, locating a source of authority within classroom teachers reflects an epistemological, and therefore paradigmatic, belief about whose knowledge counts when crafting curriculum practice and theory.

Another area of this paradigm category is learning theory. Subjectivist epistemologies dominate the data. Social constructivist and situated learning theories prevail. Learning happens when (a) the learner is an active participant in authentic learning contexts; (b) when the learner is perceived by the teacher and by him/herself to have worthwhile assets; and (c) learning occurs in and through community. Beliefs and values about learning are also reflected by the learning activities that are considered legitimate. In the middle grades concept, academic curricula are not privileged over extracurricular activities: "considering, as we do, the total program of learning opportunities to be the curriculum, the term 'extracurricular' is not really an appropriate category for any learning opportunities" (Alexander, 1968, p. 65).

The middle grades are believed to be a potent site for reform of education in the United States, beyond just the middle grades. I interpreted a difference over time regarding the purpose of the reform. In the earlier two texts (i.e., Alexander, 1968; Lounsbury & Vars, 1978), the purpose of the middle grades concept as reform was to innovate education in the United States. In the latter two texts (i.e., Carnegie, 1989; NMSA, 2010), the purpose of the reform was to increase equity in education. For either purpose, I interpreted an explicit critique of the factory models of education in 21st century schools: "[Middle school] ought not to be an 'institution,' a teaching factory, but rather a center for learning and growing, a place especially designed for young adolescents where they are 'at home...'" (Lounsbury & Vars, 1978, p. xii).

Understanding metaphors to be signposts for paradigms, the distinction between school as factory and school as home is significant to the task of articulating the prevalent paradigms of the middle grades concept. The significance lies in how the epistemological and ontological perspectives guiding the middle grades concept, which value caring relations and constructivist learning theories, are related with the paradigms guiding the next (hi)story, spirituality as a developmental domain.

Spirituality as a Domain of Human Development

In this section on the findings from the Spirituality as a Domain of Human Development data set, I will describe the content, boundaries, and interconnections of my interpretation of the paradigms that guide the advocates of this field. The five paradigm categories for this data set are: *Mapping the Human Journey, Aligning Heart and Will, Allowing Paradox, Seeing Crucibles,* and *Legitimizing Spiritual Development.* I begin the narratives with the paradigm that influences how the authors conceive of human developmental theory in general (*Mapping the Human Journey*) before then turning to the paradigm that influences the contents of spiritual development theory in particular (*Aligning Heart and Will*). As a continued exploration of the contents of spiritual development, I describe two paradigms, *Allowing Paradox* and *Seeing Crucibles,* which depict the authors' lenses through which the (hi)story of spiritual development is constructed and explained. Finally, I situate the (hi)story within its cultural, social, and political context of the developmental sciences by describing the paradigm guiding the authors' argument for the addition of a domain of spiritual development: *Legitimizing Spiritual Development.*

Mapping the human journey. The paradigm category *Mapping the Human Journey* reflects a major theme in the data: theorizing about human development. An important part of the (hi)story of the domain of spiritual development is how the storytellers explain human developmental processes and outcomes, i.e., "Central, then, to a theory of spiritual development are conceptions of the developing person" (Benson, 2006, p. 487). Human development is allegorized in the data as a road that all persons travel, reflecting the perspective that human development is a universal phenomenon. Empiricism is highly valued as a tool for knowing more about human developmental processes and outcomes, reflecting positivist ontology. In some data the value placed on empiricism is reflected in specific datum, for example, Oser,

Scarlett, and Bucher's (2006) reference to "the results of careful and thoughtful studies" (p. 976); in some data the value is inferred, such as Fowler's (1981) use of a large body of mixed-methods research upon which his theory of faith development is based.

Two approaches to explaining human development are cited: stage-structural theory and developmental systems theory. In the data, stage-structural theory and developmental systems theory are valued when used in conjunction with each other. For example, Oser, Scarlett, and Bucher (2006) refer to these two frameworks as "paradigms" which are "theoretically compatible" (p. 943). In the data, each approach is believed to be necessary, but not sufficient without the use of the other (e.g., Fowler, 1981, p. 90: "the stages tell only part of the story"). Benson (2006) encapsulated the two frameworks as "three dynamics of human development" (p. 485): core processes (stage-structural theory), context (developmental systems theory), and goals (addressed in both approaches). Throughout the data, the role of context in human development, as an influence on outcomes and an impetus for developmental processes, is perceived as significant. My analysis of the role of context and environment on spiritual development will be further explicated in the narrative on the paradigm category *Seeing Crucibles.*

Mapping the Human Journey includes the authors' humanistic perspective that human development occurs from a strength-based orientation, rather than a deficit-based orientation. In other words, human development is not viewed as incomplete people getting better through more development. An example of this perspective is found in a datum from Fowler (1981): "Each stage has the potential for wholeness, grace and integrity and for strengths sufficient for either life's blows or blessings" (p. 274).

The data reflect a willingness to accommodate cultural variations in how people develop. However, the dominant paradigm is human development theory as normative, with distinct patterns or stages that can be identified using empirical methods:

> Our empirical studies have aimed at testing whether there is a predictable sequence of formally describable stages in the life of faith. The hypothesized stages with which we began, however, and the versions of

them that have withstood empirical scrutiny exhibit an indisputably normative tendency. (Fowler, 1981, p. 199)

Within the normative framework, the function of each domain of human development is privileged as a criterion for determining the legitimacy of a phenomenon as developmental. How the function of spiritual development is described by the data will be addressed in the narrative on the paradigm category *Legitimizing Spiritual Development*.

Aligning heart and will. The name for the second paradigm category, *Aligning Heart and Will*, is *in vivo*. The phrase originates from Fowler (1981), who characterized faith development as "an alignment of heart and will" (p. 11). This paradigm category illustrates the contents of spiritual development—as distinguished from the *Legitimizing Spiritual Development* category—which captures how the data reflect a focus on constructing a theory of spiritual development more than the contents of such a theory. The category name refers to my analytical categorization of how spiritual development is conceptualized in the data: what develops (goals, functions) and how it develops (processes). In this narrative, I first explore the paradigm category's title. Then, I divide my description of the related results into those two categories in which spiritual development is conceptualized, what develops and how it develops.

The term *aligning* captures the joint influence of the two prevailing developmental frameworks: (a) human development as adaptation (from developmental systems theory) and (b) human development as restoring equilibrium (from state-structural theory). *Heart and will* capture the aspects of being human that I interpret as central to the story of spiritual development theory—in terms of the what and the how. Finally, the category *Aligning Heart and Will* also captures the data that reflect a holistic paradigm. In a holistic paradigm, alignment is a dynamic, ongoing process in which healthy human developmental systems are distinguished from each other but seen as deeply interconnected to each other, to ecologies, to transcendence. A datum that illustrates the emphasis on alignment of heart and will is Oser, Scarlett, and

Bucher's (2006) assessment of Fowler's (1981) theory of spiritual development:

> [Fowler's] stages take into consideration an individual's development with respect to major developmental tasks including identity achievement, cognitive development, moral judgment, symbol formation, social perspective taking, and locus of control. For Fowler, the development of faith and the development of persons are so intertwined as to be, to a large extent, one in the same. (p. 959)

In this datum, the authors' use of the phrase "one in the same" speaks most clearly to me of the holistic perspective. Seeing the parts and the whole simultaneously is a holistic lens by which to understand, explain, and explore phenomena. As a lens, holism echoes the use of paradox as a heuristic that also requires holding apparent binaries as mutually co-influencing.

I continue my explication of this paradigm by first exploring how the texts convey what is developing as part of the domain of spiritual development. Then, I turn to the authors' conceptualization of how spiritual development happens.

The act of clarifying the contents of spiritual development is reflected in the data as a task that is complex but possible, using empirical methods of inquiry and scholarship (see *Legitimizing Spiritual Development*). In the data, the contents (the 'what' that is developing) of spiritual development are characterized as qualitative growth in the capacities for making meaning, creating order, constructing myths or narratives, and creating or applying an interpretive framework/orientation. Two data that illustrate these characteristics of spiritual development include:

- "Prior to our being religious or nonreligious...we are concerned with how to put our lives together and with what will make life worth living." (Fowler, 1981, p. 5)
- "Spiritual development as a process of actively constructing a view of the self in the context of self-transcending myths and frames." (Benson, 2006, p. 489)

In Fowler's (1981) description of the stages of faith development, a central theme is the process of using stories (received and self-told) as a means of organizing a personal sense of meaning and purpose. The different ways in which stories are used is a main element in Fowler's theory of what happens in the domain of spiritual development. In Fowler's Mythic-Literal Stage (approximately ages 8–11), "...the meaning is both carried and 'trapped' in the narrative" (p. 149). In a later stage, the Conjunctive Stage, which not all adults reach according to Fowler's theory, the capacity for using narratives as a source of personal meaning and purpose looks qualitatively different: "...the rise of the ironic imagination—a capacity to see and be in one's or one's group's most powerful meanings, while simultaneously recognizing that they are relative, partial and inevitably distorting apprehensions of transcendent reality" (p. 198). Here, the capacity for tolerating and appreciating paradox is defined as a key outcome of spiritual development.

One datum makes an explicit cultural distinction when referring to the types of interpretive frameworks created as a part of a person's spiritual development. Benson (2006) distinguished between the personal interpretive frameworks, associated with European or United States' cultural paradigm, and the collective interpretive frameworks, associated with "...other social and cultural locations..." (p. 487).

Spiritual development is also described as the ways in which people of different ages (a) cope with challenges and successes, (b) value and commit to beliefs about what is sacred, and (c) experience connection within themselves, with others, with the environment, and with a sense of transcendence. A lengthy and complex datum from Fowler (1981) illustrated the complex expressions with which advocates of a theory for the domain of spiritual development try to sum up these three aspects of spiritual development:

> ...*faith* is: people's evolved and evolving ways of experiencing self, others and world (as they construct them) as related to and affected by the ultimate conditions of existence (as they construct them) and of shaping their lives' purposes and meanings, trusts and loyalties, in light of the character of being, value and power determining the ultimate condition of existence (as grasped in their operative images—conscious and unconscious—of them). (pp. 92–93)

In this datum, aspects of the prevalent paradigms of this (hi)story are addressed: human development as an ongoing journey, the use of secular linguistic constructs as a strategy for legitimizing spiritual development theory, the use of paradox heuristics as a device for understanding developmental processes, and spiritual development as occurring within crucibles.

Fowler (1981) characterized spiritual development as a process of re-integrating the capacities and strengths of previous stages of development: "Try to imagine the whole process as dynamically connected, each successive spiral stage linked to and adding to the previous ones. Each stage...marks the rise of a new set of capacities or strengths in faith. These add to or recontextualize previous patterns of strength without negating or supplanting them" (p. 274). Spiritual development as a process of deeper levels of integration echoes the strength-based humanistic perspective on human development referred to in the narrative on *Mapping the Human Journey*. The (hi)story of this field characterizes the domain of spiritual development as a critical component of the process of intrapersonal integration, again reflecting a holistic paradigm.

In addition to these aspects of what develops, spiritual development was characterized as a "perfecting" (Oser, Scarlett, & Bucher, 2006, p. 947) process over the course of a lifetime, although I interpreted variations in the criteria for perfection. These variations range from Fowler's (1981) criteria for the final stage of faith development: "...inclusiveness of community, of radical commitment to justice and love and of selfless passion for a transformed world, a world made over not in *their* images, but in accordance with an intentionality both divine and transcendent," (p. 201), to Benson's (2006) notion of developing persons being able to know and explain "...what is good, important, and real..." (p. 487), to Oser, Scarlett, and Bucher's (2006) argument that perfecting is a process of moving from "narrow-minded...behavior and thinking into open, fully integrated...spirituality" (p. 943). While the data on perfecting reinforce my claim that a normative paradigm outweighs the call for embracing diversity of developmental expression and patterns (see *Mapping the Human Journey*), the variations I interpreted in the data belie a more subjectivist epistemology than a normative paradigm might otherwise suggest.

In addition to conceptualizing what is developing in the domain of spiritual development, the authors address a second component of the contents of a theory of spiritual development: how development is activated, sustained, and expressed. Like the data referred to in the narrative on *Mapping the Human Journey*, advocates of the field of spiritual development wrestle with fundamental notions of how human development occurs. The results of my analysis show significant conceptual overlap between this paradigm category and the category *Seeing Crucibles* in this area.

One example of this overlap is the relationship between the processes of spiritual development and a developing subject's cultural context. For example, Benson (2006) identified the joint processes of creating and inheriting as of paramount significance in determining the outcome and process of spiritual development:

> Culture informs the texts that are inherited; the language that shapes one's thinking; the symbols that are accessible; the rituals that command attention and focus the person on culturally sanctioned definitions of person, cosmos, and transcendence; and the degree of normative permission there is for one to consciously and actively engage one's spiritual development. (p. 492)

From this datum, and others, I interpret that advocates of a field of spiritual development believe the domain of spiritual development can be stimulated by specific elements of a person's environment. The discursive effect of cultural context on spiritual development is vividly illustrated in the Benson datum in his reference, for instance, of how language shapes thinking.

The category label *Aligning Heart and Will* suggests a previous period of misalignment. In my analysis, the data address multiple causes of the misalignment and multiple explanations for the ways in which a developing subject responds to that experience. Periods of misalignment are described in the data as disequilibrium between person and context, as well as between different domains of development such as cognitive and moral. Fowler suggested that without disequilibrium, a developing subject might not transition to another stage of faith development. One of his research findings was that it is not uncommon for persons to reach equilibrium (alignment) at his third stage of faith development, the Synthetic-Conventional Stage. This finding supports his claim that not all persons move beyond what he theorizes as a third stage of faith development.

Finally, the authors cite, in one form or another, the existence of an innate drive as a motivating force for human development. This drive is connected to what is developing in the spiritual domain: an evolving sense of personal meaning and purpose. One datum from Benson (2006) described the processes of development in relation to its contents: "...meaning, purpose, obligation...and contribution (knowing and affirming why one matters) *pull* persons into spiritual development...and the animating forces within the person...*push* the person forward. Hence, spiritual development is energized by both push and pull..." (p. 492). What exactly these animating forces are is addressed indirectly in the data; in another datum, Benson (2006) used the metaphor of an "engine" (p. 485) to describe "developmental press" (p. 488). Fowler (1981) attributes the innate drive to critical self-reflection and creative imagination: "Disillusionment with one's compromises and recognition that life is more complex than Stage 4's logic of clear distinctions and abstract concepts can comprehend, press one toward a more dialectical and multileveled approach to life truth" (p. 183). In this datum, I interpreted a developmental perspective that places importance on disequilibrium and values integration.

Allowing paradox. The third paradigm category, *Allowing Paradox*, captures my analysis of how paradox is used and valued as a heuristic by advocates for the field of spiritual development. As a paradigm, paradox heuristics challenge binary thinking by suggesting that clarity comes from allowing two things to be true, not from adherence of one or the other. For this paradigm and others in the Spiritual Development data set, I interpreted evidence that suggests a paradigm shift, with some aspects of the traditional scientific paradigm upheld (e.g., thinking in binaries) while aspects of a different paradigm arise (e.g., embracing paradox). In the data, paradox is offered as a heuristic, or conceptual model, for clarifying a theory of spiritual development. This paradigm category differs from *Seeing Crucibles* (discussed later) in that the emphasis is less on the interaction between two constructs and more on the conceptual act of holding as true two seemingly opposite or contradictory constructs.

I interpreted many examples of paradoxes used in the data as a device either for explaining the *contents* of spiritual development theory or for directing how to *theorize* about spiritual development. Scholarly and personal writing is offered by Fowler (1981) as a means of adhering to the criteria of academic research and writing while simultaneously honoring the intimacy of spiritual development: "I am committed to rigorous examination and clarification of the meanings we share. This intends to be a book of responsible scholarship and research. But to communicate and to bring its truths to expression we will have to write and read in personal ways" (p. xii). In this datum, Fowler reinforced the binary of scholarly and personal by drawing attention to them as disparate types of formal communication. But at the same time, Fowler critiqued the privileged status of what is considered scholarly by insisting that a complete understanding of spiritual development theory is incomplete without a personal voice.

Two paradoxes are invoked frequently in the data: (a) the explanatory power of a formal theory that maintains fidelity to the peculiarities of personal experiences, and (b) universal patterns with diverse manifestations. A datum from Oser, Scarlett, and Bucher (2006) illustrated these similar paradoxes: "...there are meaningful ways to attend to individual and cultural differences while still attending to what is universal and normative. We need to find ways to attend integratively (*sic*) to both diversity and general principles" (p. 990). The two prevailing frameworks of human development—stage-structural theory and developmental systems theory—are also presented as a paradox heuristic. In my analysis, the advocates treat both frameworks as necessary, but insufficient without the other. This claim about a theory's completeness echoes Fowler's (1981) claim that spiritual development theory is incomplete without both scholarly and personal writing.

Other paradoxes presented as heuristics are: serious play, intuitive and counterintuitive ontologies, rationality and passion, and knowing self through transcendence of self. In a datum from

Oser, Scarlett, and Bucher (2006), there is a direct reference to the use of heuristics in understanding spiritual development theory: "Whatever the ways, the effort is the same, explaining not only the development of acts, thoughts, and feelings, but also explaining the development of persons. In general, critics forget that stages and structures are heuristic instruments for understanding this development" (p. 957). This datum reflects a tone of defensiveness in the authors' rationale for the use of heuristic devices in this field, connecting this paradigm category to *Legitimizing Spiritual Development.*

Allowing Paradox, like the category *Seeing Crucibles*, reflects a deeply constructivist perspective of learning in two ways. First, the learner (i.e., the developing subject) is viewed as an active agent, not a passive recipient of transferable information. Secondly, the student of spiritual development theory is asked to actively hold two binaries as a means of understanding the processes and contents of the domain of spiritual development. This latter point reflects the constructivist perspective (Dewey, 1902, 1916) on using inquiry to formulate adaptable dispositions with which to solve current and future problems.

Seeing crucibles. *Seeing Crucibles* is closely related to, but distinct from, the use of paradox as a heuristic. The name of this paradigm category is *in vivo*, reflecting the authors' claims that spiritual development occurs within and as a result of interactions between separate entities. Captured in this category are ontological and epistemological perspectives that are subjectivist. The term crucible appeared in Benson (2006): "...it [spiritual development] also includes the myths learned on Grampa's or Grandma's lap and in the crucible of peer relationships, family, and community" (p. 490). Benson went on to claim that spiritual development occurs because of and is influenced by, "...the ecologies one chooses to be the primary crucibles for development" (p. 490). In the field of chemistry, substances in a crucible are subjected to strong forces (e.g., high heat) resulting in the melting and re-forming process of alchemy. As a metaphorical term in the data and in this analysis, a crucible conceptually symbolizes the space of interaction between two or more forces in which the participating entities are irrevocably altered or transformed.

Crucibles are places of alchemy, a combination of the contents of the interaction and the resulting outcome(s) of the interaction. Throughout the data, the significance of a developing person's interaction with cultural and social context is explored in multiple ways. Crucibles are viewed as bidirectional influences, adaptations, and "interplays" (Benson, 2006, p. 490). One datum refers to the bidirectional interplay between person and environment as a process of creating and inheriting: "the myths and narratives that organize and give direction to our lives involve a lifelong creative process in which persons actively create (whether the activity is conscious or not) a story, using source material that can come from many institutions and relationships" (Benson, 2006, p. 490). Oser, Scarlett, and Bucher (2006) referred to the crucible between parent and child as a process of "...co-constructing their spiritual identities" (p. 978). In these ways, spiritual development is framed as a type of social constructivist learning theory.

Another way in which spiritual development is seen as both a process and product of interactive transformation is in its relationship with other domains of human development. Human development is viewed as having separate domains whose growth and maturation are interrelated not only in terms of overlapping focus areas, but also in terms of stimulating further development. For example, all three data sources cite how shifts in cognitive capacities influence and are caused or accompanied by shifts in spiritual capacities.

Other important, though less frequent, interactions that reflect the paradigm *Seeing Crucibles* are: (a) academics and practitioners in the field of spiritual development, (b) structures and contents of spiritual development, and (c) spiritual development theory and theories for other domains of human development. For example, intentionally created interactions between academics/researchers and practitioners/clinicians generate a more useful theory for and applications of spiritual development (Benson, 2006).

In sum, this analytic category is intended to capture the conceptual tools employed by advocates of the field of spiritual development as a means of articulating the paradigm. *Seeing Cru-*

cibles portrays the fundamental valuing of interaction, the assumption that something of substance happens in the 'in-between' space, and the belief that human development occurs because of and within these crucibles.

Legitimizing spiritual development. The influence of positivist ontologies interpreted in the first paradigm category, *Mapping the Human Journey*, was also interpreted in the data supporting the final category, *Legitimizing Spiritual Development*. The authors of the (hi)story defended theorizing about spiritual development within and in response to the parameters of empirical criteria rooted in the social sciences. In my rendering of this paradigm, I analogized the authors' arguments for a scientific theory on the domain of spiritual development as five defensive walls. These walls, each of which I explicate in this narrative, are the conceptual scaffolding for this paradigm category. I used the metaphor of defensive walls (from medieval castles) to illustrate my interpretation of the defensive tone of the texts, and the complex layers of the building blocks of logic, discourse analysis, and empiricism used to erect a formidable argument for spiritual development as a field in psychology.

Within these walls, a theory of the development of spirituality is described. I have already described the (hi)story of what happens in the domain of spiritual development and how it happens in *Aligning Heart and Will*; here I review a few aspects of spiritual development that are protected by the defensive walls. Spiritual development is described as involving the whole person, experienced in multilayered interactions, and occurring across the lifespan.

On the first defensive wall, a distinction is made between spirituality and religiosity:

> Spiritual development is a universal domain of development that can be dramatically informed by ideas and practices that are theological and/or religious. But, explicit in the definition is the possibility that spiritual development also occurs independent of religion and/or conceptions of sacred, ultimate, or alternative forms of reality." (Benson, 2006, p. 486)

Fowler (1981) also made this distinction in his theory by referring to the structure of faith development versus the contents of faith development, the latter being more potentially related to specific religious beliefs. The distinction between spiritualty and religion implies, in my interpretation of the data, positivist ontology. Spiritual development is privileged as an essentialized human developmental process, whereas religion is viewed as a social construct that is, therefore, excluded as a developmental process. By holding spiritual development apart from religiosity, even while acknowledging that the latter may overlap with the former, advocates of a theory of the domain of spiritual development are playing by the same map-making rules (i.e., empiricism) as those who have historically discounted spirituality as ineligible for inclusion in the social sciences. Therefore, in my analysis, the paradigm shift illustrated by this defensive wall is paradoxical—the traditional paradigms of the developmental sciences are being both challenged and reaffirmed by (hi)story of the field of spiritual development.

A significant exception in the data to this distinction between religiosity and spirituality is Oser, Scarlett, and Bucher (2006), whose review of the prevailing theories on spiritual development includes theories on religious development as well. In my more comprehensive review of the literature on the field of spiritual development, however, I found this synonymous treatment of spiritual and religious development to be an exception. Oser, the lead author, has written a large body of work on the development of religious judgment; it is possible that he was more inclined to collapse spiritual and religious judgment because of his pre-existing record of scholarship. In their justification of this categorization, Oser, Scarlett, and Bucher (2006) offered the following perspective:

>...if separated from religious development, the contents of spiritual development seem less fixed, and the steps toward higher, more complex levels seem less evident. There is today no theory of pure spiritual development. That is why in this chapter...we use *religious* and *spiritual* as highly overlapping entities, which can be taken mostly together. (p. 943)

The authors identify experiences of/relationship with transcendence as the main area of overlap (p. 953). Based on my review of the literature on spirituality as a developmental domain, as well as the literature on spirituality and education, Oser, Scarlett, and Bucher's (2006) strategy of collapsing religious and spiritual development is not representative of the strategy employed for the purpose of legitimizing the field of spiritual development in the developmental or social sciences. I noted—in my interpretation for beliefs, values, and assumptions—that the authors' criteria of a pure theory of development also reaffirms a positivist ontology by implying that theories can be pure, i.e., uncontaminated by subjective epistemologies.

The second defensive wall constructed to legitimize a theory of spiritual development is a call for additional empirical scholarship. The perspective that there is a dearth of empirical literature was confirmed during my review of the literature. What is significant, as part of an analysis for prevalent paradigms, is not the actual lack of empirical scholarship in this field, but the perception that there is a lack as well of the argument that more empirical literature would legitimize a theory of spiritual development: "Another potential criterion for effective field building is...growing the rigor of theory, measurement, and research" (Benson, 2006, p. 493). This defensive wall affirms empiricism as an influence on the (hi)story of this field.

The third defensive wall is a clarification of the differences between faith and belief, interpreted most strongly in the Fowler (1981) data. Fowler introduces his theory with an explanation of the historical evolution of the linguistic conceptions of the two terms. In this evolution, faith becomes linguistically synonymous with belief. Fowler claimed that the significance of this evolution lies in noting the discursive ways in which faith has come to be understood as a cognitive, voluntary action: "...so pervasive is the impact of secularizing consciousness that even religionists and persons of faith have tended to accept the culture's truncation of belief into assent to a set of propositions or commitment to a 'belief system' " (p. 13). Oser, Scarlett, and Bucher (2006) made a similar argument regarding the relationship between power and knowledge: "The consequences of conflating faith and belief have been to marginalize religion and to dismiss spirituality as something less than rational" (p. 956). Fowler (1981) argued that the linguistic meaning of faith has a historical precedent to its post-Enlightenment meaning, whereas faith is understood not as a concept but as an affective orientation: "faith involves an alignment of the heart and will, a commitment of loyalty and trust" (p. 11). Other data affirmed the strategy of distinguishing between faith and belief by seeing them as culturally bound discursive constructs in order to legitimize the field of spirituality as a developmental domain.

The fourth defensive wall is a claim that spiritual development is a universal phenomenon: "Spiritual capacity is inherited capacity, a product of brain development" (Oser, Scarlett, & Bucher, 2006, p. 969). Universality is reflected in the data as an accepted criterion for determining whether or not spirituality, like cognition, is something that develops. Benson (2006), while distinguishing between spirituality and spiritual development, made the analogy with cognition explicit: "[Spiritual development] is not isomorphic with the term *spirituality*. There are linkages, of course, but they are also as different as cognition is from cognitive development" (p. 485). Fowler (1981) describes the capacity for spirituality (faith) a quality with which "...we are endowed at birth" (p. xiii). This claim of universality in the data as a source of legitimacy is presented alongside concerns about constructing a theory of spiritual development that addresses issues related to cultural diversity (e.g., Oser, Scarlett, & Bucher, 2006, p. 990). I accounted for this data in my narratives on the paradigms *Allowing Paradox* and *Seeing Crucibles*.

Finally, the role of spiritual development for the individual subject is addressed, as the fifth defensive wall, reflecting the use of function as a criterion for developmental theories in the social sciences (as introduced in the narrative on *Mapping the Human Journey*). The emphasis in the data on the function(s) of spiritual development illustrates the authors' strategy for legitimizing theories on the domain of spiritual development in a Western context that wants to account for the functionality of phenomena. In the data, the function of spiritual development is viewed in different ways: as a process of holistic intrapersonal integration, as a foundational orienting framework for one's life, and as a basis for thriving. My analysis of these data was more fully described in the narrative on the paradigm category *Aligning Heart and Will.*

The paradigms guiding the Spiritual Development data set are suggestive of a potential paradigm shift away from Enlightenment criteria for what is counted, or legitimized, as scientific knowledge. A subjectivist epistemology is reflected in the data: Spirituality and religion are identified as social constructs that have discursively affected how spiritual development has historically been treated in the social sciences. The discursive nature of the language of spirituality is reflected by the authors' attention to the fluidity of spirituality as a linguistic term. The context of an action (e.g., ringing a bell) can determine whether or not the action is labeled by the participant(s) or the observer(s) as spiritual. However, as described in the narrative *Mapping the Human Journey,* I found evidence of reaffirmation for the same positivist paradigms that have historically been used to discount academic study on human spirituality, i.e., a reliance on empiricism. The potential importance of the paradoxical discourse represented by these narratives are further explored in my analysis of the contents of the convergence of the paradigms of the three data sets.

Holistic Education

In this section on the findings from the Holistic Education data set, I describe the content, boundaries, and interconnections of my interpretation of the paradigms that guide the advocates of holistic education. I rendered five paradigm categories: *Beliefs About What it Means to be Human, Knowing With Wholeness, Schooling for Cultural Consensus, Re-Framing Accountability,* and *Claiming Ontological Truths.* For this data set, I begin with what I perceived to be the grounding paradigm, *Beliefs About What it Means to be Human,* and the only paradigm category label for which I did not use a gerund. Epistemological issues are the focus of the next paradigm, *Knowing With Wholeness.* Although for the previous two data sets I concluded with the paradigm categories that were explicitly situated within a cultural, social, and political context, cultural-political issues were paramount for this data set. There-fore, *Schooling for Cultural Consensus* and *Re-Framing Accountability* are presented in the middle. I conclude with one of the surprise findings, the strong influence of positivist ontology in the (hi)story of holistic education, as represented in *Claiming Ontological Truths*.

Beliefs about what it means to be human. The first paradigm category, *Beliefs About What it Means to be Human*, has multiple areas of overlap with the four other paradigms in the Holistic Education data set. This paradigm strikes me as both a beginning point and an ending point, suggesting the same spiral model of human development that was reflected in the data. The Spiritual Development data set included a paradigm on theorizing about human development; the texts from the Holistic Education data set show theorizing about *being* human. These data reflect the perspective that one can be fully human, with the opposite also being true—that one can be incomplete. For the holistic educators represented in this data, any belief about what it means to be human that does not include spirituality and spiritual development is incomplete.

In my analysis, the main metaphor/imagery regarding what it means to be human is wholeness, which is viewed as the human ideal. Wholeness is seen as both a means for human happiness and fulfillment and as the natural state of being human. Human development is presented as a process of integration and "unfolding" (Miller, 1997, p. 197), with developmental domains described as highly interactive with each other. These data reflect humanistic psychology in its emphasis on the appearance of human assets and strengths during growth instead of the Freudian emphasis on moving beyond human deficiencies:

> American education is built on the premise that children's development must be controlled to ensure an orderly society. Rodgers, and humanistic psychology in general, dissented on just this point: Their central claim was that the natural unfolding of the human being can and should be trusted. (Miller, 1997, p. 197)

Data that overlap with this paradigm category and the category *Schooling for Cultural Consensus* include an argument that the purpose of schooling should be to promote healthy human development, including spiritual development.

One significant consequence of believing humans to be complete as they are at any given point in time is a valuing of stakeholder voices as part of schooling. Kessler (2000) expressed this perspective most frequently (e.g., pp. xv–xvi). Accordingly, the holistic beliefs about what it means to be human overlap strongly with the paradigm category for *Re-Framing Accountability*. In that paradigm category, students are described as active agents in their learning, capable of knowing what they need, and deserving of care and trust. An implication of this paradigm category overlap is that holistic beliefs about being human are much different from the beliefs about being human suggested by the dominant notions of accountability in education.

I also found overlap in the data around beliefs about what it means to be human with knowing and knowledge (*Knowing With Wholeness*). The strongest topic of overlap concerned learning in genuine community. Miller (2007) advocated deep listening among members of the school community to facilitate learning. Kessler (2000) offers specific strategies for sharing sacred questions in peer groups to foster knowledge of self and others.

In the (hi)story, an implication of the holistic beliefs about what it means to be human is that education should look different than it does now. Miller (2007) explicitly distinguished *holistic* education from present day schooling as an approach that addresses spiritual issues in the classroom (p. 6). Miller (1997) expressed this point in the following datum: "Acknowledging the spiritual dimension of human existence places education in an entirely different light" (p. 87). Kessler (2000) took this point to its ultimate conclusion: "...even in our secular, high-tech world, our spirits hunger for answers. To me, the most important challenge has always been not *whether* we can address spiritual development in secular schools but *how*" (p. ix).

Knowing with wholeness. In the data, schools were described as places where learning happens, among other things, but learning was clearly expressed as one of the main activities in schools. In taking the position that one major purpose of school is to promote holistic human development (i.e., inclusive of spirituality), a spiritual epistemology is reflected in the data as the second of the five paradigm categories, *Knowing With Wholeness.* Epistemological beliefs are paradigmatic—beliefs about knowing and knowledge form the "map" as well as the "directions essential for map making" (Kuhn, 1996, p. 109). So, in describing my analysis of these data, I argue that spiritual epistemology guides not only the specific vision of holistic education but also provides the criteria by which education is evaluated and critiqued. This is significant in this research project because a major content theme of holistic education is a strong critique of hegemonic practices in education in the United States and elsewhere.

The spiritual epistemology of holistic educators is captured by the name for this paradigm category: *Knowing With Wholeness.* In the (hi)story of holistic education, the construct of human wholeness is defined by its contrast with current educational practices. The authors claim that current practices treat knowledge and knowing as fragmented, with rationality privileged over intuition. A datum from Miller (1997) illustrates the way in which wholeness is contrasted with fragmentation:

> As the well-known saying goes, a whole (a phenomenon-in-context) is always greater (more complex, more integrated, more meaningful) than the sum of its parts. This...flies directly in the face of the dominant epistemology of the modern age. Reductionism is atomistic and fragmenting; it argues that we know what is fundamentally real by dissecting things into component parts. (p. 81)

How advocates of holistic education view the consequences of the influence of reductionist epistemology on schooling will be further explored in the narrative on *Schooling for Cultural Consensus.*

From the holistic perspective, knowing involves integration—of self and of domains of knowledge, and with nature and within relationships. Knowing is described as subjective, multidimensional, and interconnected. Processes of learning are privileged over products of learning, as vividly illustrated by a datum from Kessler (2000, pp. 1–5) describing how a group of adolescent students dealt with a critically ill peer while on retreat. Knowledge is described in the data as fluid, dynamic, and highly context-dependent. Situated cognition and constructivist, (specifically, social constructivist) learning theories are represented in the data: "...knowledge is co-created as students construct their own meaning and ways of knowing" (Miller, 2007, p. 6).

While knowing is primarily construed in the data as an inner process, many data describe the influence of external forces such as institutions, teachers, and peers. These data suggested a spiritual epistemology that includes the belief that processes of knowing and knowledge can be taught as a result of routines that occur outside of a person. Holistic educators view inner and outer processes of knowing as two sides of the same coin, not as opposing binaries. The data from Kessler (2000) is particularly strong in this regards: The entire premise of her work is that teachers can promote healthy human development as part of learning in schools through seven gateways or entry points to students' inner lives. In addition to the interactions between teacher and students, this paradigm category is closely related to the paradigm *Re-Framing Accountability*, which captures the perspective that knowing occurs through the crucible of relationships in genuine communities.

The significance of including an epistemological perspective in the (hi)story of holistic education is raised by Kessler (2000), Miller (1997), and Miller (2007): *how* one knows and *what* one knows guides one's responses to the world. For example, in one datum Miller (1997) explicitly characterizes knowing as "a spiritual endeavor" (p. 220) because it involves meaning-making in relationship to self and others. For advocates for the field of holistic education, epistemological issues are central to their vision and critique of education in the United States: "Holistic education appears anti-intellectual—indeed, thoroughly nonsensical—from within the 'transmission' position, but from the viewpoint of 'transformation,' modern society's way of understanding and measuring intellect is a shriveled and inadequate caricature of the human mind's capacities" (Miller, 1997, p. 200).

Schooling for cultural consensus. The third paradigm category, *Schooling for Cultural Consensus*, captured how advocates of holistic education view the relationship between power and knowledge in schools. The first term of this paradigm category (schooling instead of education) is intentional: In the data, the authors wrote more on what happens in schools than on the universal practice of education. The distinction is subtle, but I hope to convey the (hi)story's focus on the particular (schools) over the universal (education).

Part of the strategy used by holistic advocates is to make explicit the ways in which constructs of knowledge are influenced by people and institutions that hold power. The latter part of the category label, cultural consensus, is a partial *in vivo* code from Miller (1997). Miller used a construct of "cultural consciousness" (Tart, 1986) to frame his exploration of the dominant cultural values that are highly influential in schooling, yet remain largely tacit (Miller, 1997, p. 2). What Miller (1997), Miller (2007), and Kessler (2000) argued is that schooling builds, reinforces, and reproduces certain values and beliefs. In this narrative, I describe the various ways in which the authors of the (hi)story of holistic education make their case.

This critical argument is paradigmatic because it is a starting point for the remainder of the holistic treatise. Consistent with both critical theory and postmodernism, a cultural consensus is an agreement by most or all participants in a society about what is good, true, and real; the power of this agreement, or consensus, is purposively sustained though various actors, including institutions such as schools. The authors in this data set echoed the critical perspective that education is not neutral: "...school reflect[s] the prevailing *worldview* of American society—the basic, and largely implicit, epistemological and moral assumptions that guide the formation of social practices and institutions" (Miller, 1997, p. 2). This perspective is a significant piece of how the story of holistic education is told. For advocates of holistic education, dominant cultural assumptions in the U.S. about epistemology and ontology threaten the dignity and integrity of society as well as the dignity and integrity of individuals.

In bringing the first and second parts of the category together, *Schooling for Cultural Consensus* captured the data on the possibility of being able to define and articulate dominant cultural values, especially as they relate to the purpose(s) of schooling. I interpreted a strong critique of the ways schooling in the United States (and Canada) is negatively affected by dominant cultural values. In the (hi)story, schooling was criticized for overemphasizing economic outcomes and privileging individual achievement over collaborative processes. Fragmentation of knowledge and coercive social control were critiqued on the grounds that those practices alienated teachers and students. Finally, holistic advocates accused schools of intentionally ignoring human spirituality: "Many communities decided years ago that the inner life of our children was simply not the business of public schools. Many classrooms are 'spiritually empty' not by accident, but *by design*" (Kessler, 2000, p. xi).

The critique of the ways in which dominant cultural values harm schooling is supplemented by alternative cultural values that could be sustained through schooling. The (hi)story reflects a vision of schooling that draws on humanistic psychology, balances rationality with intuition, and nourishes all domains of human development. In response to the ways in which the dominant epistemology fragments knowledge and alienates teachers and students, the storytellers of holistic education emphasize schooling that cultivates an awareness of interconnection: "We hope to foster in our students a deep sense of connectedness within themselves and to other beings on the planet" (Miller, 2007, p. 199).

Within the data is a bridge between this paradigm category and the following one, *Re-Framing Accountability*. This theoretical bridge is that if schooling has the power to indoctrinate certain cultural values and beliefs that shape perceptions of reality, it is in schools that hope for a better future lies. One datum captures this point well, in articulating education as a means of transforming individual perception and social integrity: "A 'revolution of the sensibilities'—that is, a transformation of consciousness, a fundamental shift in the cultural epistemology that defines reality—is considered primary. And this is an 'inward' revolution, requiring the active effort of individual persons throughout society" (Miller, 1997, p. 199).

Re-framing accountability. A telling aspect of the fourth paradigm category, *Re-Framing Accountability*, is the tacit acceptance of accountability as legitimate criteria for evaluating educational endeavors. Like the reliance on positivistic ontology for critiquing current hegemonic practices in schools (see *Claiming Ontological Truths*), using accountability, even in its reframing, suggests a continuity with the paradigms held by those who support what the authors refer to as traditional education in the United States.

That said, I interpreted a conception of accountability quite distinct from the more common understanding and application of accountability in the United States (i.e., the standards movement of the 1990s, NLCB of the 2000s, the Common Core of the 2010s). In my analysis of the data, accountability has been co-opted from empiricized products taken from single-point evaluations of recipients of information to an engaged sensibility, an orientation of interconnectedness, and a deep sense of presence in the classroom communities. In one datum, Miller (2007) called this collection of attributes "organic accountability" (p. 193), reflecting the ways in which advocates of holistic education reject the factory/machine metaphors of teaching and learning in favor of metaphors that emphasize biology, nature, and ecology. The complete datum from Miller (2007) illustrated how holistic advocates use ecological metaphors: "Genuine community creates what we might call an *organic accountability*. Because people are communicating with one another in an open and transparent manner, problems regarding student behavior and performance can be dealt with directly..." (pp. 193–194).

From a critical constructivist lens, the holistic re-framing of accountability shifts the source of power and empowerment away from policy-makers who may or may not be intimately connected to classroom realities and toward the students, teachers, and building-level administrators who cultivate and are nurtured by quality relationships. Therefore, student and teacher efficacy and autonomy is addressed as an accountability issue in several ways. For example, students are characterized as active agents in their learning. A critical need for teacher intrapersonal growth is identified as a means of increasing efficacy. Teachers and students are characterized as authorities in schooling. Schools are also described as needing to be held accountable through a shared sense of purpose and large vision: "The deeper the integration between thought and action, the more powerful effect on the teachers. The vision should provide a sense of direction for the school and be open enough so that the teachers can share in its vision and development" (Miller, 2007, p. 198). In sum, in the (hi)story of holistic education, accountability is co-constructed in multiple layers of relationships and roles grounded in mutual trust.

It follows, then, that a main theme in this data was accountability through the authors' vision of a genuine community. In the (hi)story of holistic education, teachers and administrators should be responsive to students' needs for experiencing belonging; in several datum, responsiveness was defined as deep listening to student interests, questions, and hopes: "To listen completely and fully is a difficult challenge in a culture that values multitasking and speed; yet it is the beginning of being accountable to our students" (Miller, 2007, p. 193). Kessler (2007) included students listening to each other in intentionally sacred spaces as part of accountability through community. Relationships should be seen as relevant to learning, and student privacy should be acknowledged and honored in the holistic re-framing of accountability in schooling.

In my analysis of the data, schools are not analogized as factories with products but as living, dynamic organisms in need of flexible care and co-existing within a larger context. Change, in the re-framed notion of accountability, is natural and should be embraced as an opportunity. The content of curriculum should be integrated with student experiences and interests: "Transformational learning acknowledges the wholeness of the child. The curriculum and the child are no longer seen as separate but connected" (Miller, 2007, p. 11). Instruction should build from democratic collaboration in authentic contexts as a means of providing ongoing support for an organic accountability.

Finally, in articulating criteria for success, outcomes to which school should be held accountable, currently realized as scores on standardized achievement tests, are replaced by a commitment to fullest human potential. A holistic understanding of what it means to be human that includes intuition, artistic sensibilities, and transcendence prevails throughout the data. Notions of fullest human potential are also captured in the paradigm category *Beliefs About What it Means to be Human.*

Claiming ontological truths. The final paradigm category, *Claiming Ontological Truths*, was a surprise finding in my analysis. I held the impression that the adherents to holistic education claimed a subjectivist ontological orientation; there are multiple truths that various individuals hold, depending on social contexts—such as culture and history—as well as individual traits. However, throughout the data, there were claims to the existence of a single Truth, reflecting a more positivist viewpoint than I had anticipated. For example, Miller (2007, pp. 193–194) and Kessler (2000, pp. 6–8) distinguish between community and communication that is genuine and that which is not. My finding is less focused on the criteria they suggest about determining whether or not something is genuine and more the claim that it is possible to evaluate—and therefore critique—communities and communication on the basis of genuineness. In this example, I am framing *genuine* as a synonym for *real*. Miller (1997) also used dichotomous rhetoric in his characterization of some types of human interactions as more "natural" and "normal" than others (p. 220). Again, what types of interactions he classifies as more natural and normal (e.g., cooperation) is less my focus in this paradigm category than his claim there is a natural type of human interaction. Other examples from the data include explicit references to "complete" and "incomplete" ways of knowing (Miller, 1997, pp. 197–201) and a "fundamental reality" to nature that can be known (Miller, 2007, pp. 3–6). It is worth noting that I also interpreted expressions of subjectivist ontology in the data (see *Schooling for Cultural Consensus*), but in my overall analysis, positivist ontology was the more prevalent paradigm.

The positivist ontological stance is significant to this critical constructivist research. Positivist ontology seems to contradict the plea of holistic educators for a broader ontological perspective when considering the relevance of spirituality in the social sciences. The potential contradiction lies in my observation that scholars (in education and the developmental sciences) have historically ignored spirituality/spiritual development on the grounds that spirituality cannot be studied/known using empirical tools. Accordingly, it is worth noting—as a piece of analysis for prevalent paradigms—that these attempts to challenge dominant cultural agreements fall back on the very same grounds for claims of reality that those who sustain hegemonic beliefs and values draw from: positivist ontology.

The significance of the thread of positivism alongside ontological and epistemological perspectives that appear dichotomous to positivist ontology is explored in more detail in the following chapter. These paradigm narratives represent findings that have significance on their own, but they also were used as a unit of further historiographical analysis. The paradigms were rendered in order to provide material with which to identify ideas and/or perspectives commonly held by advocates of the middle grades concept, spirituality as a developmental domain, and holistic education.

Chapter Seven

Dynamic of Paradox

THE conceptual framing for this critical historiography emerged after my review of the literature of the academic fields I saw as related to my research topic, the relevance of the domain of spiritual development in a developmentally responsive model of middle grades education. I drew three overlapping circles, with each circle representing the three large academic fields related to my topic, developmental psychology, middle grades education, and spiritualty. When these circles are arranged in a Venn diagram, the areas of overlap illustrate the ideas, positions, beliefs, values, and assumptions of each of the significant interrelationships among two fields at a time: the middle grades concept, spiritual development, and holistic education.

Figure 7.1

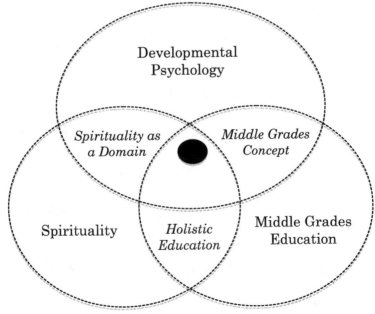

The goal of this critical historiographical study was to use data collection and analysis strategies that enabled me to make a claim regarding the conceptual contents of the nexus of the intersectionality of the paradigms of the significant interrelationships, the space in the middle of the Venn diagram created by the overlapping circles. This chapter describes what I rendered in the nexus. The knowledge produced from this critical historiography represent the final findings of this study.

In my description of the nexus, I distinguish between two types of discursive patterns: (a) the types of paradigms and (b) the dynamic amongst the paradigms shared by all three fields. What I found, in other words, is that not only were specific types of paradigms common to all three fields (Ecological Epistemology, Holistic Ontology, and Positivist Ontology), but also a pattern of paradigmatic interactions that was common to all three fields—a dynamic of paradox. These paradigms interacted with (and against) each other *within* their respective academic fields as part of how practitioners and advocates in the three fields decided what was important, valued, and sustained. My interpretation of a *pattern of interaction* that was also part of the conceptual nexus was an unanticipated finding is this research. I had expected and hoped to make claims about shared paradigm types; I had not anticipated being able to make claims about patterns of interaction amongst the paradigm types.

The results of this critical historiography are reported in two sections: I first identify and describe, using supporting evidence from all levels of data analysis, the three paradigms I interpreted as being common to all three fields. To distinguish these findings from those of the previous section and to capture their foundational qualities, I refer to them as meta-paradigms. Second, I identify and describe the dynamic of paradigm interaction that was common to all three fields.

Common Meta-Paradigms Across the Three Fields

In this section, I describe the meta-paradigms common to the three fields. Two paradigms—Ecological Epistemology and Holistic Ontology—expressed influence over the main ideas, positions, and beliefs of the three academic fields. These two meta-paradigms determined the "story" of the fields: the problems that were identified, the knowledge that was privileged, the claims for reality that were legitimized, and the sources of authority that were acknowledged.

Alongside Ecological Epistemology and Holistic Ontology was a third meta-paradigm, Positivist Ontology. Although the characteristics of Positivist Ontology are dichotomous to the characteristics of Ecological Epistemology and Holistic Ontology, I interpreted an equally strong influence of Positivist Ontology over how the "stories" of the middle grades concept, spirituality as a developmental domain, and holistic education were conceived, framed, expressed, and argued.

The influence of these apparent contradictions in paradigms was expressed through a dynamic of paradox. That is, both were "true" and "valid" for the advocates of the three fields, and presented not as an argument to be resolved but as a complex scaffolding by which to challenge old rules and offer new visions within a discourse that would be acceptable within the socio-historical context of the United States in the late 20th/early 21st century.

For each meta-paradigm, I begin by summarizing its main elements and tacit rules before providing more detailed evidence in support of my analysis. The evidence is organized around my interpretation of the paradigm narratives for inter-textual and inter-discursive patterns. In my description, I characterize the inter-discursive patterns as the main components of the meta-paradigms; the inter-textual patterns are referred to as inter-textual patterns.

Ecological epistemology and holistic ontology. Ecological Epistemology as a meta-paradigm category encompasses a perspective on knowledge, knowing, and learning that emphasizes interconnection and integration, draws from the natural world when using metaphoric language, and privileges transformational and transactional models of learning over transmission models. While the label I am using for this meta-paradigm is *in vivo* (e.g.,

Benson, 2006, p. 490), the term was employed by Bateson (1972, 1979) and others (e.g., Cajete, 1994; Orr, 1990, 1992) as well. I am familiar with some of this work and the authors' construct of an ecological epistemology. However, my description of the paradigm category I interpreted as Ecological Epistemology is grounded in the data and data analysis from this research. Had I knowingly borrowed constructs and language from Bateson or others I would have given proper attribution to their work.

Acting in tandem with Ecological Epistemology is the meta-paradigm Holistic Ontology. As a meta-paradigm category, Holistic Ontology embodies an interconnected view of reality, a view that sees truths about the world as essentially interdependent with each other. A holistic ontology embraces a reality of wholeness that is *a priori* to the Enlightenment illusion of fragmented knowledge and separate selves. Accordingly, the present is imbued with integrity; ongoing processes are privileged over single-point products; and wholes are foregrounded from parts.

Applying Kincheloe's (2008) definition of discursive practices, here are the ways Ecological Epistemology and Holistic Ontology share "tacit rules that regulate..." (p. 36):

- What can and cannot be said: What can be said is that human beings are interconnected with each other, the natural world, and the cosmos; this interconnection implies a leveling of authority; and something of import and value occurs within and as a result of interactions. What cannot be said is that people are essentially separate entities whose individual actions are isolated; that the natural world is distinct from and subjugated to human existence; and knowledge can be reduced into fragments that can be transmitted from one entity to another.
- Who can speak with authority and who must listen: Authority emanates from participants, intuition, experience, and collaboration. Those who must listen are proponents of hegemonic scientific and educational practices that alienate, demoralize, and oppress human dignity and integrity.
- Whose socio-educational constructions are scientific and valid: Humanist psychologists/educators, teachers/practitioners

(and sometimes students), people who are critically self-reflective, and voices that integrate personal and professional/academic experiences have scientific and valid socio-educational constructions.

- Whose socio-educational constructions are unlearned and unimportant: People who insist on treating human development and teaching as endeavors that happen in silos, reduce human learning to cognition, and compartmentalize human experiences have unlearned and unimportant socio-educational constructions.

Ecological Epistemology and Holistic Ontology were comprised of four components, which I had initially interpreted as interdiscursive patterns. The four components are: (a) social constructivism/ situated cognition, (b) knowing as alignment, (c) integration, and (d) interconnection. In my analysis of the paradigm narratives, as well as the focused content codes and BVA interpretations, the four components are themselves deeply interrelated with each other. For example, social constructivism/situated cognition and knowing as alignment are closely related. The former addresses learning theory while the later emphasizes processes of knowing. I made this distinction in my analysis because I interpreted the texts as making that semantic and conceptual distinction.

In my analysis, learning is characterized as resulting from and occurring within formal and informal collaboration and interactions (e.g., stories heard on Grandma's lap), constructed by active participants (e.g., democratic collaboration in authentic contexts) and dependent upon a dynamic of mutuality (e.g., integrative curriculum). A "learner" in the context of this data included students, teachers, and developing subjects.

Knowing as alignment was closely related to social constructivism/situated cognition as well as a third component, integration. Across the paradigm narratives, knowing was positively characterized as an ongoing process of alignment, also referred to as integration in ways that I interpreted as synonymous with alignment. The aligned and/or integrated entities identified in the data were: domains of self (identity, affect, spirituality), curricular content with disciplinary subjects as well as with the knowers, humans and nature, relationships with others (e.g., Miller, 2007, p. 8). As a component of Ecological Epistemology and Holistic Ontology, alignment reflects fluidity and movement rather than a state of stasis. The processes of human growth, learning, and knowing are emphasized over the outcomes or products.

The fourth component I interpreted from the paradigm narratives was interconnection. The influence of interconnection as a discursive practice was seen in how the stories of the middle grades concept, spiritual development, and holistic education privileged unified wholes (e.g., "the holistic nature of all knowledge," NMSA, 2010, p. 22) over "the dominant epistemology of the modern age[:] Reductionism [that] is atomistic and fragmenting..." (Miller, 1997, p. 81). Learning and human growth occur because of and within multiple points and types of interconnections, also referred to as *crucibles*. In all three of the data sets, fostering a strong awareness of interconnection was portrayed as desirable because, as claimed by the authors, it allowed for a genuine awareness of how things really are.

The tacit rules imposed by Ecological Epistemology and Holistic Ontology and their four specific components as described previously are reflected in the four inter-textual patterns I interpreted as associated with these two meta-paradigms. The first inter-textual pattern is 'conceptions of human development.' Each of the (hi)stories of the academic fields include a theory of human development that: (a) sees domains as interactive (e.g., cognitive growth stimulating spiritual growth in adolescence); (b) sees healthy development as a process of deeper integration of these domains (e.g., applying an interpretive framework for making meaning that draws from cognition, spirituality, emotion, and morality); and (c) favors a development theory that integrates stage-structural theory with developmental-systems theory (e.g., the promise of developmentally responsive middle grades education).

A second inter-textual pattern, 'affective parts of a person are important,' reflects the Holistic Ontology meta-paradigm that affirms a vision of humanity including emotional, moral, psychological, and spiritual aspects. I interpreted this inter-textual pattern as an explicitly stated challenge to the ways in which the authors perceived hegemonic privileging of the cognitive and physical aspects of being human. In addition to positioning affective aspects as equal to cognitive/physical aspects, the advocates of the three fields described healthy development and effective learning as dependent on caring relationships.

A third inter-textual pattern I interpreted across the three sets of paradigm narratives was the 'valuing of a person's inner life,' in terms of how a person makes meaning of their life and the degree of connection to one's deepest self. I interpreted this inter-textual pattern in two ways. First, the advocates of a theory of spiritual development—by connecting the domain of spirituality with the domains of cognition and emotion—call for increased recognition of spiritual development on the grounds that ignoring it jeopardizes the healthy development of other domains. This textual pattern is reflected in the other two data sets with claims that the intentional neglect of student/teacher inner life is harmful to academic (i.e., cognitive) growth. The second way this inter-textual pattern is manifest is in a characterization of the life-long process of making meaning of one's life as critical to healthy development and learning. One holistic education datum (Miller, 1997, p. 220) textually links meaning-making as a spiritual practice, as a means of situating spiritual development as relevant to schooling practices. I decided to join the two ways in which I categorized this inter-textual pattern because conceptually they are closely related; but the precise textual references to intra-personal integrity and making meaning in a personal and collective narrative were distinct enough to warrant differentiation in my description of this pattern.

The fourth and final inter-textual pattern is 'being inclusive while living in diverse communities' as a desirable outcome and guiding principle for on-going processes. As reflective of Ecological Epistemology, this inter-textual pattern describes individuals as living (and thriving or ailing) in larger, complex interrelated systems. In analyzing the ways in which the (hi)stories of the three fields were told, I interpreted a comfort with shifting back and forth between focusing on individual and diverse expressions of learning and development. In the Middle Grades Concept texts, this ease manifested in repeated recommendations for academic benefits for individual achievement through learning in diverse communities. In the Holistic Education texts, individual integrity was made possible through shared communal vulnerability and openness. In the Spiritual Development texts, the "best" theories of spiritual development drew from two distinct frameworks: those that emphasized internal structural growth and those that emphasized growth that happens because of and within external factors. I also interpreted a valuing of cultural diversity when it came to expressions of spiritual development (e.g., a Euro-centric personal narrative vs. a non-Eurocentric collective narrative) as well as in the establishment of a rationale for the middle grades concept and holistic education (as pedagogical approaches).

Positivist ontology. In my contrapuntal reading of the paradigm narratives, I interpreted the influence of a third meta-paradigm, Positivist Ontology. This meta-paradigm category captures a perspective that is firmly steeped in the principles of empiricism: Quantifiable truths about reality can be studied and verified through scientific methods of objective inquiry and systematic experimentation. In Positivist Ontology, claims can be made for truths that are 'right' and 'wrong' because it is possible to come to unambiguous answers using empirical methods of inquiry.

The discursive practices of Positivist Ontology are quite different from the discursive practices of Ecological Epistemology and Holistic Ontology. I again use Kincheloe's (2008) definition of discursive practices to frame my description of the "tacit rules" (p. 36) of the Positivist Ontology meta-paradigm for this data:

- What can and cannot be said: What can be said is that it is possible to know, define, study, and make claims about reality in the natural world and in human processes such as development and learning. Because of this, there are things that are true, genuine, and natural. It is possible to study phenomena in nature and human beings because it is possible for the investigator to be rational, objective, and neutral about the subject and methods used for investigation. What cannot be said is that truths about reality are subjective, or dependent upon the person making the claim;

phenomena from the human or natural world are contextually dependent; and there are truths about reality that cannot be known through empirical study.

- Who can speak with authority and who must listen: Authority emanates from a credentialed few, whose credentials are determined by their successful completion of a quantifiable program of legitimized study. Those who must listen are the majority of people, who live in the lower rungs of a highly stratified society and who, lacking intellectual resources, will benefit from the specialized expertise of the credentialed few.

- Whose socio-educational constructions are scientific and valid: Scholars who write and speak in neutral, objective language; adults (because of their superior cognitive abilities); and members of highly selective academic and political societies have socio-educational constructions that are scientific and valid.

- Whose socio-educational constructions are unlearned and unimportant: People who claim experience and/or intuition as valid sources of authority, and who believe truths to be partial, culturally determined, and/or subjective, and people who lack the valid academic credentials have socio-educational constructions that are unlearned and unimportant.

The primary component of Positivist Ontology, in my analysis of this data, is empiricism. In some data empiricism is explicitly called for, for example Benson (2006), who used it as a rationale for legitimizing a field of spiritual development theory. In other data, empiricism is strongly implied through claims of unambiguous truths, e.g., Miller (2007), who stated that there are "fundamental realities of nature" to which "education [must be brought] into alignment" (p. 3).

In addition to the categorical differences between Ecological Epistemology/Holistic Ontology and Positivist Ontology, I also interpreted a difference in the way the two sets of meta-paradigms were expressed in the (hi)stories of the three fields. In the former set, I interpreted that Ecological Epistemology and Holistic Ontology influenced the content of the (hi)stories. For example, one of the specific recommendations of middle grades advocates, the use of advisory groups, is explicitly related to the interconnection component of both meta-paradigms. However, in my interpretation of the way Positivist Ontology was expressed, I found that the connection was not in the *content* but in the *rationale* used to defend the content. The influence of Positivist Ontology was much more subtle. Yet, its influence ran just as deeply as the influence of Ecological Epistemology and Holistic Ontology.

I interpreted three inter-textual patterns that were associated with Positivist Ontology: 'threats,' 'Middle Grades Concept/Holistic Education and Spiritual Development as reform for the fields of Education/Developmental Sciences,' and 'defensiveness.' The common denominator in all three inter-textual patterns is an assertion that there is a "right" and a "wrong" way to educate students and conceptualize human development. While obviously any advocacy position may lay claim to a higher ground of authority, in all of the levels of my analysis of the data, from initial coding up through contrapuntal reading of the paradigm narratives, I was struck by the tone of vehemence in the authors' claim not just for authority but also by their claim that their position was closer to a real truth than the practices they argued against.

In the (hi)stories, two of the inter-textual patterns function as warnings about (a) potential and actual dangers facing society because of (b) the incompleteness of the culturally-dominant education/human developmental theory that only addresses certain domains/aspects of being human and compartmentalizes knowledge, learning, and growth. Both of these patterns, 'threats' and 'Middle Grades Concept/Holistic Education and Spiritual Development as reform for the fields of Education/Developmental Sciences,' are written in a tone that I interpreted as the third inter-textual pattern associated with Positivist Ontology, 'defensiveness.'

The authors of the three fields positioned their respective field of study as a potential reform for the greater fields under which they operate. For example, especially in the earlier Middle Grades Concept texts (e.g., Lounsbury & Vars, 1978), the recommended principles that would guide practices for the education of young adolescents are offered not only as good for that population but also for other grade levels. While the exact practice of integrated curriculum should look different for 14-year-olds vs. 8-year-olds, the principles guiding that practice—that is, connecting students with teachers, each other, their communities, and their inner lives through curriculum—are viewed by middle grades advocates as a potent reform for alienating curricular practices throughout K–12 education. In the Spiritual Development data set, a similar rationale is offered: "[it is]...a field...that is both rigorous and generates knowledge that becomes central to how the academic establishment thinks about human development," (Benson, 2006, pp. 492–493). The advocates of a theory on the domain of spiritual development reflect what both middle grades advocates and holistic education advocates argue: Further refinement and implementation of the principles and practices suggested in their field will rectify fundamental errors in the larger fields of education and the developmental sciences.

A datum from Miller (1997) illustrates the previous point and serves as an example of the defensiveness that I interpreted as one of the three inter-textual patterns associated with Positivist Ontology. In this datum, Miller linked individual and cultural transformation that could occur, and needs to occur, with the implementation of the principles (paradigms) of holistic education: "A 'revolution of the sensibilities'—that is, a transformation of consciousness, a fundamental shift in the cultural epistemology that defines reality—is considered primary" (p. 199). Another example of the data in which I interpreted a defensive tone is from the spiritual development data set. This statement from Oser, Scarlett, and Bucher (2006) was made in the context of explaining why spiritual development theorists draw from the stage-structural framework in their work, despite late 20th century critique of that framework as inadequate: "In general, critics forget that stages and structures are heuristic instruments for understanding this development" (p. 957). This datum in particular is also germane, as an example of the influence of Positivist Ontology, because the stage-structural framework carries an implication of universal, verifiable truths about human development. From my review of the literature on spiritual development theory, I concluded that one of the main criticisms of any theory of spiritual development was that trying to study spirituality using empirical principles was not possible. In other words, claims for a stage-based theory of spiritual development were desirable in order to be compliant with acceptable standards of scientific practice, but challenged by (a) the diverse manifestations of spiritual expression and (b) the lack of a universal definition of spirituality as a human phenomenon.

The third and final inter-textual pattern I interpreted during my contrapuntal reading across the paradigm narratives is the use of threats and invocation of current and/or future dangers as rationale for the positions advocated by the authors. The (hi)stories, in other words, were cloaked under an ominous cloud of peril, with looming disaster for the dignity and integrity of individuals and Western society. For example, Lounsbury and Vars (1978) indicated that they see the U.S. in the late 1970s as "...a pluralistic society undergoing a value crisis so severe that it threatens the very foundations of our government" (p. 37). When I first encountered this textual pattern during initial coding of the Middle Grades Concept data set, I was struck by the contrast invoked by the use of fear tactics to promote a vision of education explicitly grounded in trust, caring, and mutuality. In my analysis, this inter-textual pattern reflects the discursive practices of Positivistic Ontology because across all three data sets, the threats are grounded in claims about what is essential about what it means to be human, in terms of development, learning, and knowing, as well as claims about what is best for human societies. In my analysis, these are positivist ontological claims.

Dynamic of Paradox

As a result of a contrapuntal reading across the paradigm narratives, I interpreted a similar pattern of interaction between the three meta-paradigms. Within each respective field, Positivist Ontology acted discursively alongside and against Ecological Epistemology and Holistic Ontology. I characterized this pattern of interaction as a dynamic of paradox. In this dynamic, dichotomous paradigms are equally privileged by seminal authors of the (hi)stories of the middle grades concept, spirituality as a development domain, and holistic education. As a historiographical finding, this pattern of paradigmatic interaction might illustrate what Kuhn (1996, 2000) characterized as an initial stage of a paradigm shift: a time when questions and problems require new tools and rules for investigation, but the problem-solvers are still trying to use the old tools and rules because they are neither ready to let go nor able to envision what the new tools and rules might look like. In this last round of data analysis, I found evidence of some of Kuhn's hallmarks of a paradigm revolution, such as a qualitative change in how concepts/phenomena are labeled (e.g., personal meaning making as a spiritual act; caring as advocacy) and the criteria by which the concepts/phenomena are categorized (adding a spiritual domain of human development). Taking Kuhn's logic a step further, during a paradigm shift advocates of new paradigms (in this data, Ecological Epistemology and Holistic Ontology) would logically apply old paradigms (Positivist Ontology) in a society that might be more likely to pay attention if the dominant (old) discursive practices, or tacit rules, were being followed. Hence, during the multi-stage process of a paradigm shift, the discourse would be rife with paradox.

In my analysis of this data, I distinguished between a dynamic of paradox as a discursive interrelationship amongst the prevalent paradigms and a paradox in the content (ideas, positions, recommendations) of the fields. For example, in the Middle Grades Concept data set, a paradox in the content was the position that diverse individual student needs, due to the variance in rate of development, were best met through collaborative learning activities. This example of content paradox is different from a dynamic of paradox as a discursive interrelationship.

The dynamic of paradox involves the dichotomous tacit rules espoused by the meta-paradigms in ways that influence the content of the (hi)stories, *simultaneously* and without *cancelling out the other meta-paradigm(s)*. This finding is illustrated by a datum from the Holistic Education data set, in which positivist notions of accountability, as expressed in the context of U.S. education in the late 20th and early 21st century, are simultaneously affirmed and challenged by the authors' reframing of an "organic accountability"

(Miller, 2007, p. 193). The concept of organic accountability, as presented by the authors of the (hi)story of holistic education (especially Miller, 1997, and Miller, 2007), adhered to the tacit rules of Ecological Epistemology (e.g., learning through relationships) and Holistic Ontology (e.g., people are deeply interconnected with each other and with nature). Yet, their vision of new paradigms is explicitly framed within a Positivist-influenced construct (e.g., that it is possible and desirable to articulate and evaluate the products/outcomes of schooling).

Another example of my interpretation of a dynamic of paradox is how the advocates for a theory of spiritual development critique limitations imposed on the inclusion of spiritualty. The grounds on which advocates offered their critique are rooted in a subjectivist epistemology positing that scientific claims are reflections of culturally bound representations of truth, not essential or ahistorical Truths. The domain of spiritual development—so the (hi)story goes—has been excluded not because it has some essential qualities that violate rules of scientific scholarship, but because of "...a prevailing but outdated philosophy of science grounded in positivism" (Benson, 2006, p. 484). Yet, even as positivism is proclaimed outdated by Benson, in the same text he calls for more empirical work on spiritual development theory as a "criterion for effective field building..." (p. 493).

Invoking the 'myth' of neutrality, as illustrated previously in the developmental sciences, also occurs in the Holistic Education data set as a strategy for creating space for the inclusion of spirituality in an educational context. However, the grounds for claiming the importance of spiritualty are as ontologically positivist as they are ontologically holistic. In my analysis of the data, seeing the world as interconnected is not presented as one possible perspective; it is presented as the way things are. Development happens as a result of "natural unfolding" (Miller, 1997, p. 197) and because this is the way things are, a better education is one that prioritizes trust and mutuality (i.e., a holistic education) over social control and domination.

My analysis of the Middle Grades Concept data set revealed a similar line of logic: Problems are legitimized using positivist rules (this is they way things are), yet solutions are influenced by different paradigms. For example, because of the "fact" of the characteristics of young adolescents (Lounsbury & Vars, 1978, p. 35), middle grades education must be developmentally responsive to their unique and knowable needs, an assertion of a Positivist Ontological Truth. In identifying instructional strategies that are properly responsive, however, I interpreted the dual influence of Ecological Epistemology and Holistic Ontology: "When teachers help them see the many connections...students recognize the holistic nature of all knowledge" (NMSA, 2010, p. 22). This is an excellent example of the dynamic of paradox: Positivist Ontology directs descriptions of reality that can only be adequately addressed by solutions that embody Ecological Epistemology and Holistic Ontology.

Before concluding this section, I address one potential critique of my analytical logic. Perhaps, one might argue, a component of Holistic Ontology is positivism. Perhaps the data represented here is not simply trying to have it both ways, perhaps I have simply mischaracterized the elements of Holistic Ontology by not including positivist principles. To this criticism I respond: The positivist paradigm emphasizes a reality that can be known, studied, and described. The holistic paradigm emphasizes a reality that is interrelated at multiple points of connection between people, nature, and the cosmos. The presence of one paradigm does not necessarily negate or cancel out the other, but they are still dichotomous. They are still qualitatively different ways of seeing reality.

As I further discuss in the next chapter, my finding of paradoxical ontological paradigms and their accompanying epistemology is no small matter when it comes to articulating the educational relevance of the spiritual domain of human development in middle grades education. It is perhaps the lack of collective imagination around addressing spiritual needs in public schools in the United States that has limited its explicit inclusion in the middle grades literature on developmentally responsive education for young adolescents. I would argue that embracing paradoxes, especially ontological ones, requires significant individual and collective imagination. So far, the track record in U.S. education has leaned more toward reductionist dualism (Miller, 1997).

Chapter Eight

Establishing the Relevance of Spiritual Development in Education

IN this chapter, I offer conclusions and suggest implications for middle grades education and educational research. Drawing from the findings for both research subquestions, I address the focus of my inquiry: What is the educational relevance of spiritual development in middle grades education? Because this was a study conducted with a critical constructivist lens, attempts to answer the research question are framed within a certain set of assumptions: Knowledge production is influenced by the values of the producers and the context within which knowledge is produced; there is a symbiotic relationship between knowledge production and the deployment of power within a society; and education, as an institutional agent of knowledge transmission, is not neutral.

This chapter is organized into three sections. I introduce the discussion with a brief summary of the main findings. Then, I offer the conclusions based on the findings, focusing on situating spiritual development within the context of public education in the United States. Finally, I identify implications for establishing the relevance of spiritual development in the field of middle grades education. Because of the unconventional nature of critical historiography in educational research, I will also identify methodological implications for future researchers. In this chapter I also position this study within the larger context of the fields of middle grades education and educational research, explain how this work fills gaps in the knowledge base, and identify what gaps remain after this study.

Summary of Results

In this study, I used critical historiography to interpret for the prevalent paradigms guiding the (hi)stories of the fields of the middle grades concept, spirituality as a developmental domain, and holistic education. For each field, I rendered five prevalent paradigms from my analysis of three to four foundational texts from the three fields. Table 6.1, repeated here, summarized the paradigms for each field.

Table 8.1
Paradigm Categories

Middle Grades Concept	Domain of Spiritual Development	Holistic Education
Separating and Re-Integrating	Mapping the Human Journey	Beliefs About What it Means to be Human
Nurturing the Nature	Aligning Heart and Will	Knowing With Wholeness
Be-Coming Together	Allowing Paradox	Schooling for Cultural Consensus
Perceiving Perils	Seeing Crucibles	Re-Framing Accountability
Empowering Education	Legitimizing Spiritual Development	Claiming Ontological Truths

After articulating the prevalent paradigms for the three fields, I read across the narratives contrapuntally to interpret for inter-textual and inter-discursive patterns. In initially conceptualizing this research, I sought to describe the area of paradigmatic convergence amongst the three fields to be able to express what, if anything, was shared. The new knowledge—shared paradigms—would be used as a strategy for making a case for the relevance of spiritual development in the middle grades concept of developmentally-responsive education. As a result of my analysis of the paradigm narratives, I found three shared meta-paradigms as well as a shared pattern of discursive interaction. The three meta-paradigms within the nexus of the three fields are Ecological Epistemology, Holistic Ontology, and Positivist Ontology. Within each field, these three meta-paradigms had a pattern of interaction, a dynamic of paradox, which was similar. In other words, I found a discursive interrelationship within each field that was the same for all three (hi)stories.

Conclusions

Middle grades educators (and educators at the elementary and secondary levels) balk at the suggestion that the spiritual domain of development is relevant for several reasons. These reasons are connected to a cultural context that embraces scientific reductionism, a capitalist worldview, and aggressive nationalism, as well as the historical themes guiding the establishment of a system of public education in the U.S.—Puritan theology and restrained democratic ideology (Miller, 1997). However, in designing this research, I saw it as a problem that the middle grades concept of developmentally responsive education was not explicitly incorporating the spiritual domain. In framing the problem, I linked the phenomenon of alienation to the relevance of spiritual development. I saw inclusion of spiritual development as a potential strategy for increasing belonging. The conclusions I drew from my findings provide a theoretical bridge between the muddied comprehension of spirituality in an educational context and a more holistic implementation of developmentally responsive middle grades pedagogy.

In my discussion of the conclusions I drew from these findings, I focus on addressing my main inquiry question: What is the educational relevance of the spiritual development in the middle grades concept? Before offering my conclusions, I revisit what I mean by relevance. Relevance implies that a construct or idea is germane to the context. Relevance is subjective, although groups can have strong consensus on relevance that appears on the surface to be objective, neutral, and/or empirically based. This consensus is based on the group's values, shared history, and purpose. Relevance, as a subjective construct, can shift over time and when individuals from a group find themselves in new contexts. While the concept of relevance, like paradigms, can appear so tacit as to be essentialized, at its core relevance is a social construction and therefore subject to debate. However, to claim that an idea or a construct has relevance is to grant it legitimacy. Therefore, while relevance is a subjective designation, because of its potential for authority, it is desirable to possess.

Seen in this light, my research question about the educational relevance of spiritual development is actually a critical interrogation of the tacit understandings that guide education in general and the middle grades concept in particular. As such, it is also a critical interrogation of which knowledge and cultural values are privileged. So, when I characterize teachers' comprehension of spirituality in an educational context as *muddied*, my word choice is deliberate: Teachers' understanding of human spiritual development has been subjected to larger historical and cultural forces that have framed knowledge in and for schools within tightly proscribed reductionist boundaries. The act itself is alienating, as human beings are forced to reconcile the dissonance between the steely rules about which facts and skills merit inclusion in classrooms, and an aspect of their humanity which involves seeking personal meaning within a larger narrative, as well as experiencing transcendence and interconnectedness.

I have organized the discussion of my conclusions around three areas of relevance: educational, cultural-historical, and methodological. The first two conclusions address my main research question directly. In reviewing the findings, I identified the way in which spiritual development is relevant in middle grades education: as a source of enrichment for two components of the middle grades concept—caring relationships and constructivist learning theory. The educational relevance conclusion is nested within a second conclusion on the cultural-historical relevance of spiritual development in an educational context: evidence that suggests a paradigm shift in U.S. academia.

Finally, my conclusions about educational and cultural-historical relevance are made possible by the strength of these historiographical findings, and so I close my discussion on conclusions with a review of methodological relevance of this study to the topic of spiritual development in education. By using a critical historiographical approach with my research question, I was able to generate reliable findings that supported a clear articulation of how spiritual development is theoretically relevant to the middle grades concept.

Educational Relevance: Caring Relations and Constructivist Learning

At its roots, the field of middle grades education was a different image of the same landscape: the distinctness of the education of young adolescents within a K–12 system. While Hall (1904) introduced the concept of a pedagogical relationship between stage of development and education in the early 20th century, it was not until the 1960s that educators of young adolescents called for a systemic reorganization of K—12 education that acknowledged the distinctness of the middle grades. As I found in my interpretation of the prevalent paradigms of the middle grades concept, one of the main criteria for establishing relevance for a middle grades education was knowledge of young adolescent development. The paradigm category *Nurturing the Nature* captures how human development is viewed as an essentialized construct, a view consistent with development theory throughout most of the 20th century. The cited middle grades advocates use this perceived objective reality of human development as a source for their claim that middle grades education needs to do a better job being responsive to the students' developmental needs. In my analysis of the data from the middle grades concept, the passion for an educational model that tends to the needs, interests, and abilities of young adolescents is fueled by this allegiance to the *Truth* of the stage-based developmental distinction. I found this passion whether the authors were curriculum theorists, members of organizations dedicated to middle grades education, or representatives from the highest levels of government and education.

For middle grades advocates, the certainty with respect to conceptions about human development meant that the distinct needs of middle grades students could be known and translated into the middle grades concept of developmentally responsive education. Two main components of the middle grades concept, caring relationships and constructivist learning theory, show the strongest potential for being enriched by teacher knowledge of adolescent spiritual development processes.

Need for caring relationships. The results of this research suggested that the primary developmental needs of young adolescents are identified as relation-based, reflecting the cumulative influence of the paradigms *Nurturing the Nature, Be-Coming Together*, and *Empowering Education*. For example, a common recommendation for practice is collaborative learning activities, which are described as best for middle grades students because their developmental need for social interaction with peers is addressed.

My interpretation of the primacy of the relation-based needs of young adolescents is also reflected through metaphor. The metaphor of school as home dominates the discourse on the middle grades concept. In a home, parents hold the responsibility of making their children feel wanted, loved, and understood. The home metaphor contrasts sharply with the factory metaphor, which has dominated U.S. education for over a century. In a factory, managers hold the responsibility of making their workers be productive, compliant, and skilled. When considering all five of the prevalent paradigms of the (hi)story of the middle grades concept, and the distinction between homes and factories, I note the value placed on care, as conceived of and described by Noddings (2005). In her seminal work on care as an educational approach in public schools in the United States, Noddings made the case that "...the basic caring relation is an encounter" (p. 16). As such, caring relations between teachers and students have mutuality; in each encounter, one participant gives care, but there is an equally important participant who receives the care. Middle grades advocates, in my analysis, see the world through a similar lens of mutuality, grounded in a deep and abiding love for the participants in education, the process of learning, and promise of youth. A datum from Lounsbury and Vars (1978), whose own compassion, generosity, and grace as leaders in the middle grades movement has been well-documented, illustrates my summative claim: "Core[1] requires that the teacher treat each pupil with humaneness and respect. In turn, the student becomes aware of his own humanity and of his relationships and responsibilities to other human beings" (p. 59).

If caring relationships are a central developmental need for middle grades students, then a relevant educational experience for young adolescents is awareness of that dynamic of mutual caring and responsibility for each other. If a teacher's role is to create conditions in which learning happens, and learning for young adolescents is dependent upon their perception that they are caring people who are also cared for, it is relevant for teachers to create conditions in which students can cultivate awareness of that perception. In drawing these conclusions, I am not discounting other adult-generated conditions related to the need for caring relationships, such as class schedules and team grouping that facilitate each student being well-known by at least one adult.

Cultivating awareness of one's interconnection to others is one of the primary activities privileged in the foundational literature on the domain of spiritual development and holistic education. In both of these fields, this awareness is characterized as a spiritual experience. The literature on spiritual development and holistic education offers strong rationale for the importance of awareness of interconnection: healthy development, thriving, and integrity are examples of desirable outcomes. Middle grades advocates do not use the term *spiritual* when addressing the students' relational need for experiencing belonging and care within their school communities. However, drawing from the shared Ecological Epistemology paradigm that values learning as dependent upon interconnection could be an entry point for middle grades educators seeking to integrate a more holistic knowledge of young adolescent development.

In my analysis of the results, holistic educators, middle grades advocates, and proponents of a theory of spiritual development share a strong commitment to supporting human growth and

---

[1]   The authors' 1978 reference to core curriculum is specific to the middle grades concept and entirely different from the current usage of core curriculum as part of a national standards movement.

learning that is grounded in caring relationships. When establishing the educational relevance of spiritual development, the challenge is not finding agreement on the importance of student intra- and interpersonal relationships and the students' sense of place within something greater than themselves. What I conclude, based on my historiographical findings, is that the challenge lies in finding a culturally shared conception of students' inner lives that is honored in systemic ways in public schools in the United States.

This conclusion leads to the next topic in my discussion: learning. The shared Ecological Epistemology paradigm that privileges awareness of interconnection also provides the three fields of the middle grades concept, spirituality as a developmental domain, and holistic education a sense of convergence around learning theories. A second conclusion I reached from the results of this research is that there are both opportunities and limitations for seeing spiritual development as relevant for the middle grades concept, when learning theory is the shared focal point.

Constructivist learning theory. A shared Ecological Epistemology suggests educational relevance through a common perspective on learning theory. From my analysis of the findings, I characterize this shared perspective in even stronger terms: as a commitment. This conclusion is construed as both an opportunity for integration of the spiritual domain with the middle grades concept, as well as a challenge for its inclusion in public education in the United States.

The common commitment is to constructivist learning theory, and its subcategory, social constructivist learning theory. The paradigms from the data sets that demonstrate this commitment are: (a) *Be-Coming Together* and *Empowering Education*, from the middle grades concept; (b) *Seeing Crucibles* and *Aligning Heart and Will*, from spirituality as a developmental domain; and (c) *Knowing With Wholeness* and *Beliefs About What it Means to be Human*, from holistic education. Two aspects of constructivist learning theory are important to articulating the educational relevance of spiritual development: the role of the learning environment and the primacy of inquiry as a learning activity and as an acquired disposition.

The significance of the role of the learning environment, especially with pedagogy influenced by constructivism/social constructivism, is part of the parallel that suggests how spiritual development is relevant for middle grades education. Spiritual development theory emphasizes that factors external to the developing person, such as the stories told by caregivers, are a significant influence on the process and outcome of human growth. For example, Fowler (1981) stipulated "How these capacities [for faith] are activated and grow depends to a large extent on how we are welcomed into the world and what kinds of environments we grow in" (p. xiii). Likewise, theorists from the middle grades and holistic education are adamant about the importance of the role of the environment for students (e.g., middle grades advocates citing non-developmentally responsive classrooms as hazardous). The conclusion I draw from these findings is that an opportunity for integration of knowledge about adolescent spiritual development may come from the fields' shared understanding (as influenced by both Ecological Epistemology and Holistic Ontology) around the interrelationship amongst student learning, human growth, and the design of the environment within which learning and development occur.

The second element of constructivist learning theory that is valued by all three fields is the primacy of inquiry. As a learning activity, inquiry is recommended as a main element of a successful middle grades curriculum. For example, Alexander (1968) emphasized "...the importance of the student's own investigation" (p. 78) in his summary of four essential components of a developmentally responsive middle grades curriculum. NMSA (2010) echoed Alexander (1968): "An integrative curriculum revolves around important questions students ask, rather than around a predetermined body of content" (p. 21). Learner-centered inquiry is advocated as a means of responding to young adolescent cognitive, moral, and socio-emotional developmental characteristics.

The distinction between adult-chosen curricular content and learner-centered inquiry mirrors the distinction between religion, as acceptance of and belief in specific doctrine, and spiritual development, as a process of evolving reflection about meaning. In that distinction—made by advocates of a domain of spiritual development—inquiry is one of the main features that sets spirituality apart from religiosity as scholarly constructs. Spiritual developmental processes of searching, posing questions, and making meaning sound very similar to the types of learner-centered inquiry activities recommended by middle grades advocates. Therefore, one conclusion I draw about the educational relevance is that there is theoretical potential for increased teacher knowledge of the domain of spiritual development to support design of classroom inquiry-based projects.

In addition to inquiry as a learning activity, inquiry is also privileged as a disposition. I refer to disposition in the same way that Dewey (1916) characterized disposition in a learning context[2]. Dewey wrote about dispositions as resources for adaption; learning is a change in disposition. Through "educative teaching" (p. 13), as opposed to mere training, a learner acquires certain mental-emotional dispositions. Held in highest regards of all, dispositions is "...a habit of learning. He learns to learn" (p. 45). In the findings from this study, the meta-paradigms of Ecological Epistemology and Holistic Ontology guide an educational approach that views learners as active agents in their own life-long learning who possess integrity and competence in their current stage of growth. The disposition of inquiry may be cultivated and stimulated in schools, but the purpose of education is not simply to train students to mimic questioning and curiosity in a classroom; the purpose of education is to develop full human potential, in all contexts, by nurturing the whole child/adolescent. This purpose is seen most explicitly in the following paradigm categories: *Empowering Education* (middle grades), *Aligning Heart and Will* (spiritual development), and *Re-Framing Accountability* (holistic education).

Through the shared commitment to the principles of constructivist learning theory, I see an opportunity for legitimizing teacher knowledge of adolescent spiritual developmental processes. An explicit description of what happens in the domain of spiritual development could deepen and expand a developmentally respon-

---

[2]   I am indebted to Webster (2013) for the idea to pair Dewey's definition of inquiry with spiritual developmental processes.

sive middle grades teacher's application of constructivist learning principles. For example, one of the processes of spiritual development is formulating an interpretive narrative as a source of making meaning and knowing purpose. An example of the language found in the spiritual development literature is "...spiritual development [is] a process of actively constructing a view of the self in the context of self-transcending myths and frames" (Benson, 2006, p. 489).

My conclusion, the implications of which I address in the next section, is that it is possible to extract characteristics of the processes of human growth categorized as spiritual development and apply them within the relational, constructivist-based framework of the middle grades concept. This opportunity is made possible by the paradigmatic level of shared commitment to a particular theory on human learning.

However, a related conclusion I draw from these results suggests a challenge to the integration of knowledge about the spiritual domain of development in public education in the United States today. The challenge comes from the dissonance between ideas about how learning happens, as expressed by the foundational literature of these three fields, and culturally dominant assumptions about how learning happens.

For example, one of the findings was a shared value for humanist perspectives on learning and development, as seen in the narratives on the paradigms Ecological Epistemology and Holistic Ontology. The humanist perspective views learners and developing subjects as active agents, not as passive recipients of transferable information. Expressed most clearly in the Holistic Education data set as the paradigm category *Beliefs About What it Means to be Human*, my finding was that a belief about the nature of being human that was radically different from the one held by proponents of public education in the U.S. was an energizing force within the field of holistic education. One of the ways in which holistic education is defined is in its critique of dominant epistemological values that are sustained through the practice of schooling.

The theme of cultural critique was found in the middle grades literature as well, through the paradigm categories *Separating and Re-Integrating* and *Empowering Education.* Within the spiritual development literature, *Legitimizing Spiritual Development* is a category I interpreted as sustained by defensive walls against dominant epistemological and ontological values in the field of developmental sciences.

The fields' embrace of constructivist learning theory is a clue to the challenges facing the incorporation of spiritual development theory in public education in the United States today. I perceive that, as a learning theory, constructivism and social constructivism have not fully penetrated models of teacher or student learning in public education. Because of this, developmental theories that rely on constructivist learning principles will be harder to address in meaningful ways in teacher/student education. So, taking the opportunity to use constructivist learning theory as a culturally acceptable bridge between the middle grades concept and adolescent spiritual development is limited by the dissonance between constructivist principles/assumptions/values and the technocratic epistemologies that support the factory and banking models of public education in the United States today.

However, this contrast between opportunity and challenge in regard to constructivist learning theory is related to my second conclusion: that I found evidence of a paradigm shift.

Cultural-Historical Relevance: Paradigm Shift

I conclude that the paradigm narratives and dynamic of paradox suggest a paradigm shift in the developmental and social sciences in the United States. This shift is most clearly illustrated by the field of spiritual development. In Kuhn's (1996) definition of a paradigm shift, the move occurs when new questions cannot be answered with old tools. Questions about meaning, purpose, connection, and transcendence are not new questions; placing them in a developmental framework is a new question.

The shared discursive interrelationship of a dynamic of paradox suggests a paradigm shift. Positivist principles are applied to make claims about the objective reality of young adolescent development, knowledge, and learning. But while the claims are grounded in positivist ontology, the grounding paradigms for the content of the claims—ecological epistemology and holistic ontology—challenge the dominant discourse on knowledge and learning as manifest in public school in the U.S.

The clearest illustration of a potential paradigm shift, or at least of the paradigm confusion that Kuhn (1996) postulated, is the findings from the paradigm category *Legitimizing Spiritual Development*. In my rendering of that paradigm's influence, I found that the advocates for a developmental categorization of spirituality affirmed the same empiricist principles that they also critique for excluding spirituality as a legitimate domain of human development. This irony suggests Kuhn's (1996) theory of scientific revolution, which he characterized as the result of a crisis of competing paradigms.

Kuhn used the analogy of a political revolution when describing his theory on scientific revolutions. One of the ways in which he found the two types of revolutions analogous is in the questioning of an established authority, as well as the institutions representing that authority. I think the findings from this study suggest a similarly foundational (paradigmatic) questioning of the authority represented in schools. The locus of learning and knowledge moves from external sources, such as organized disciplines of knowledge, teacher lectures, and implementation of state standards, to internal sources of authority. Examples of what I consider to be internal sources of authority are students' previous knowledge and cultural background, students sharing ideas collaboratively and problem-solving in authentic situations, and the middle grades concept of core, or integrative curriculum, which privilege student academic interests.

While my interpretation of the co-existence of dichotomous paradigms suggests a potential paradigm revolution, I also conclude that the shared pattern of discursive interrelationships between Positivist Ontology and Ecological Epistemology/Holistic Ontology has a variant that implies a difference in how far along the paradigm shift process the three fields are, compared with one another. The results from this study suggest that the field of middle grades education is at the edge of a paradigm shift, but is not as fully immersed in a paradigm shift as the field of spiritual developmental theory or holistic education.

The ecological epistemology and holistic ontology embraced by middle grades advocates does not extend its influence to allow for explicit inclusion of student spiritual development, despite the findings from this study which suggest the field's deep congruence with the same commitment to the inner life expressed in the (hi)stories of holistic education and spirituality as a developmental domain. Based on the results of this study, I conclude that the foundational literature of the middle grades concept lacks a critical (i.e., critical theory) pedagogical or theoretical perspective. I found that perspective in the foundational literature of the other two fields, holistic education and spirituality as a developmental domain (e.g., *Schooling for Cultural Consensus* and *Legitimizing Spiritual Development*). In those (hi)stories, there was a willingness to see the fields of developmental sciences and education as social constructions that replicated certain political and cultural values. The critical perspective opened up a conceptual space for re-evaluating the relevance of spiritual development in the developmental sciences and in education. Lacking the influence of a critical perspective, the field of middle grades education is not yet well-positioned to entertain the explicit inclusion of a developmental domain that is not seen as relevant by the dominant discourse of public education in the United States.

Methodological Relevance: On the Nature of Findings

The last conclusion I address relates to the research methodology that made these conclusions possible. Critical historiographical findings are distinct from traditional quantitative or qualitative findings in that the new knowledge generated comes from systematic conceptual analysis of extant texts. In this sense, critical historiography is more similar to philosophy, although hermeneutics can also be part of a qualitative study.

While the purpose of this text is not a deep exploration of the reasons critical historiography is an unconventional method in educational research, given its less visible presence in the field, I chose to address one specific challenge to its legitimacy as methodology. An explicit rebuttal to this challenge could help clarify the methodology for future researchers, and locate this study and its findings within the larger context of educational research

During the research design phase I was presented with several clarifying questions about the methodology of critical historiography: How are the findings of critical historiography substantially distinct from a well-conducted review of the related literature? What delineates historiography from a literature review, given the many similarities in terms of purpose, procedures, and results? In a critical historiographical study, what are the criteria for establishing that the results are sufficiently distinct from the conclusions reached from a review of the related literature?

To address these questions retrospectively, I compared conclusions that I reached as a result of the literature review with findings from the research that were related to the literature review conclusions. For example, one observation I made early on my review of the literature was that some phenomena, such as having a greater sense of purpose, were described in the middle grades literature as part of social and/or emotional development (e.g., Van Hoose, et al., 2001) whereas in the spiritual development and holistic education literature, the same phenomena were categorized as spiritual (e.g., Fowler, 1981; Kessler, 2000). This observation challenged my initial problem statement: that developmental needs related to the spiritual domain of human development were excluded from the middle grades concept. Perhaps those issues were being addressed in the foundational literature, but just under a different name in order to honor cultural and legal expectations in U.S. public education.

The findings from this research suggest that the prevalent paradigms influencing the middle grades concept are resonant with an explicit inclusion of spiritual developmental needs and interests. Also, the inter-textual pattern on 'the valuing of a person's inner life' shared by all three data sets affirms the hypothesis that whether or not the term *spiritual* is being used as a signifier, some developmental needs and interests—labeled as *spiritual* in holistic education—are being addressed in the foundational literature on the middle grades concept.

In this example, the initial conclusions drawn from a review of the literature are complementary to the findings from the research. For my research purposes, these findings are encouraging, in terms of establishing the educational relevance of spiritual development in middle grades education.

However, the presence of complementary conclusions does not confirm that there is no qualitative difference between a literature review and historiographical study. Based on the experience of conducting this research and its results, I conclude that the method of historiography is distinct from a literature review. The inter-textual and inter-discursive findings from this research were subjected to far more rigorous and lengthy processes of systematic analysis than the conclusions I reached from conducting a review of the related literature. In addition, the texts that I cited as foundational were only included in the data sets after a more substantive series of tests than any applied during the literature review (see Chapter Five).

An analogy to illustrate my claim is substituting the data sources in this study with human subjects. If I were investigating the educational relevance of the spiritual domain of development in middle grades education using middle grades teachers as sources of data, I might inform my research design and problem statement by having a series of conversations with licensed, experienced teachers. Conclusions drawn from these conversations, without applying an analytical heuristic—even if I strategically selected which teachers I was going to talk to—would be qualitatively distinct from conclusions drawn from a systematic and trustworthy analysis of written transcripts of interviews with participants who became part of the study after being subjected to a series of criteria for inclusion.

As I discuss in the next section, the results of a critical historiographical study have substantial implications for further field-based qualitative and quantitative research. Indeed, my hope in designing this research was that the results would not just inform, but provide a clarified theoretical foundation for further research on the relevance of spirituality in public education in the United States. Part of my rationale for conducting a study that would produce new knowledge came from my observation about the lack of definitional clarity around spiritual development within academic literature and educational practice. The findings from this study stand on their own as trustworthy, substantive, and of value in their own right.

Implications

In this section, I address implications for practice within the fields of middle grades education and educational research. In considering potential implications, I drew from my professional background as a middle and high school teacher in public and private schools as well as my service and teaching as an emerging scholar/teacher educator in higher education. The first two implications—leveraging spiritual development knowledge within the accountability-based framework and using empowering and clarifying language in spiritual development teacher education—are intended for a middle grades audience. I include in that audience classroom teachers, administrators, and university-level teacher educators. The last two implications are intended for a university-level audience, as they pertain to (a) recommendations for future research on how to integrate knowledge of adolescent spiritual development in middle grades curriculum and instruction and (b) the merits of critical historiography for research that influences educational policy.

Middle Grades Education

In considering educator implications of this research, I negotiated a tension: Is my goal to revolutionize middle grades education through a radical reconceptualization of what it means to be developmentally responsive? Or, is my goal to give teachers a conceptual and linguistic framework for tending to their students' spiritual development that does not jeopardize how they are perceived to be in compliance with the Establishment Clause (and potentially, their jobs)? In my discussion of implications for practice in middle grades education, I address both aspects of this tension.

Facilitating outcomes in an accountability-based system.
An entry point for legitimizing teacher knowledge of adolescent
spiritual development within the educational discourse is to position such knowledge as promoting academic achievement in the
middle grades. The conclusions I reached regarding the ways in
which spiritual developmental processes (i.e., awareness of interconnection) have the potential to enrich elements of the middle
grades concept (i.e., caring relationships) suggest that even within
the context of secularized discourse, teacher knowledge of spiritual
development can theoretically influence academic achievement. In
this section, I make the case that knowledge of two aspects of
spiritual development processes—reciprocity with other domains
of development and integration—can be drawn upon to facilitate
positive academic outcomes in today's accountability-based system
of public education.

The reality for most public educators at this time in the United
States is reliance upon a particular pedagogical model of accountability and outcomes. Therefore, a potentially realistic strategy for
integrating spiritual development in the middle grades concept is
to use the same behaviorist concepts that influence the accountability framework. This is a deeply ironic pairing, behaviorism
with spiritual development theory, as the former discounts the
significance of a person's inner life as it relates to changes in behavior (i.e., learning) and the latter prioritizes a person's inner
life. However, given my conclusion that a paradigm shift is only
suggested but not assured by the findings of this study, and that
such a revolution is hampered in the field of middle grades education by the lack of a demonstrated critical (theoretical) perspective,
imagining an implication that honors the current cultural-
historical consensus is strategic.

In the holistic education paradigm category *Re-Framing Accountability*, the influence of the behaviorist philosophy in the
dominant educational discourse is not challenged. What it means
to be accountable is reframed, but the underlying principle of accountability is not questioned. In a behaviorist model, education
has inputs and outputs, both of which can be measured and manipulated by the teacher (Skinner, 1987). This model has been
affirmed in the past 25 years in the United States through policies

such as state and local district establishment of learning outcomes and standards in the 1990s, the federal accountability policy NCLB in the 2000s, and nation-wide adoption of the Common Core State Standards in the 2010s. I suggest that teacher knowledge of adolescent spiritual development could be considered one input into curricular design and instructional strategies. I offer two suggestions for leveraging teacher knowledge of adolescent spiritual development as an input to improve academic outcomes.

First, the reciprocity amongst developmental domains is a way in which inclusion of knowledge about adolescent spiritual development fits within the accountability framework. In the results of this study, spiritual development is presented as a developmental process that involves multiple domains of human development, such as cognition and social/emotional development. For example, the shared meta-paradigm of Holistic Ontology came from several data that characterized the relationship between spiritual and cognitive growth as symbiotic. So, in an educational discourse that strongly privileges cognitive growth, what is good for the cognitive domain is relevant as an educational concern. Put more simply, if being responsive to adolescent spiritual development is good for adolescent cognitive development, then it is a legitimate component of middle grades education.

From my review of the literature on social-emotional education, this line of logic is used in that field as well. Durlak and associates (2011), who found statistically significant academic achievement gains for students receiving social-emotional educational programs, also situated the potential relevance of social-emotional education within an NCLB educational context.

From my historiographical analysis, as well as my initial review of the literature, I encountered a common challenge to any discussion of the relevance of affective qualities of students: Tending to the inner lives of students compromises the opportunities to engage in the *real work* of public education, i.e., academic achievement (Juvoven, 2007; Kessler, 2000; Woolley & Bowen, 2007). The present research suggests that teachers could be better equipped to engage in what the dominant educational discourse characterizes as the real work by leveraging knowledge of adolescent spiritual developmental processes. However, this research can only clarify the potential of incorporating knowledge about spiritual development; further work, similar in design to the research conducted on the correlation between social-emotional education programs and academic achievement (e.g., Durlak et al., 2011), is still necessary to provide evidence to support my claim.

A second strategy for leveraging knowledge of spiritual development to improve academic outcomes is the pairing of a main component of the middle grades concept with a central element of spiritual development: integration. One of the central tenets of the middle grades concept, as affirmed in this research, is school organization and learning activities that promote integration, of one's life in and out of school, of a sense of place in one's intellectual community, and of culturally sanctioned knowledge. As a developmentally appropriate principle of middle grades education, integration is promoted as a means of increasing academic achievement (e.g., NMSA, 2010). In the findings from this study, spiritual development is conceptualized as a process of integration; the meta-paradigms of Ecological Epistemology and Holistic Ontology privilege integration as a core principle. Teacher knowledge of what the process of integration looks like for 10- to 15-year-olds from the perspective of their spiritual development can be used to further inform the principle of integration as part of middle grades curriculum and instruction. Thus, this research implies that teacher knowledge of adolescent spiritual development could be considered an asset, not an intrusion, in the work of implementing a developmentally responsive education that promotes academic achievement in an accountability era.

In rendering these suggested implications, I have leaned more toward the pragmatist approach of offering strategies that do not jeopardize teachers' standing vis-à-vis dominant cultural and legal consensus about the educational relevance of spiritual development. Implicitly though, situating spiritual development as a means of promoting academic achievement opens the door to an explicit radical reconception of what it means to be developmentally responsive in middle grades education.

Unpacking the contents of spirituality. The results of this study affirm what I had learned from the literature review and through my personal communications over the past two years about the subject of my research: the power of the term *spirituality* when it is used as a descriptor for a domain of human development. For some, framing spirituality as a scientifically accepted domain of human development—that is, use of the phrase spiritual development—empowers teachers to include the inner lives of students when planning curriculum and instruction (e.g., DeBlasio, 2011). For others, the phrase immediately conjures up an intractable association with religion; this association, in the context of public education in the U.S., is an instant challenge to the legitimacy of leveraging knowledge of students' inner lives when planning curriculum and instruction.

Therefore, a strategy for incorporation of spiritual development in the middle grades concept is to articulate the contents of that domain using language that empowers and clarifies, rather than discourages and confuses. Empowering and clarifying language might look like this: Spiritual development is identified as a process of making meaning of one's life, experiencing connection with someone or something greater than oneself, constructing an interpretive framework or lens through which life experiences are unraveled, cultivating compassion and empathy, strengthening resilience, and making commitments to certain values and/or beliefs. An implication of this research is the addition of new knowledge with which to skillfully introduce constructs from spiritual development theory and research into the professional development of teachers and administrators who work in secular, public schools. In this way, the results of this research complement the scholarly leadership of de Souza (2006), who also advocated for a model inclusive of spiritual development when designing learning environments that meet the needs of all learners.

In addition to employing empowering and clarifying language, another implication of this research is the creation of professional development curriculum that teaches educators about young adolescent spiritual development which draws from multiple literatures. Informed by the critical historiographical findings from this research, such a professional development curriculum would utilize literature from holistic education and the developmental sciences, while staying firmly grounded in literature that describes the middle grades concept.

A source from the developmental sciences that could be useful is King and Roeser's (2009) chapter on adolescent spiritual development in *The Handbook of Adolescent Psychology*. Recall that King and Roeser (2009) reported six ways in which adolescent spiritual development was conceptualized: (a) as a relational system; (b) as a meaning system; (c) as the creation of cognitive-conceptual schema; (d) as an identity-motivation system; (e) as the experience of various states of transcendent awareness; and (f) as a "dynamic developmental systems perspective in which [spiritual development] is seen in relation to multiple contexts, people, symbol systems, and opportunities and risks" (p. 440). Their framework, rooted in the language and constructs from psychology, is useful for clarifying how spiritual development supports and is supported by other domains of human development within particular cultural contexts.

King and Roeser's (2009) work on adolescent spiritual development could be used in conjunction with my findings on the contents and processes of spiritual development from the paradigm category *Aligning Heart and Will*. For example, the developmental process of making commitments to certain values and/or beliefs could be explained within several of King and Roeser's (2009) frameworks: as a relational system, as a meaning system, and as an identity-motivation system. While I decided that King and Roeser's (2009) text did not fit within the parameters of this research, I do think that text is important for helping to transfer these findings into practice.

In an effort to use empowering and clarifying language that also utilized multiple fields of literature, researchers could conduct further content analysis of the data from the middle grades texts. The purpose of this analysis would be to interpret for recommendations that might correspond to aspects of young adolescent development as also characterized in the holistic education and spiritual development texts as elements of spiritual development. Also, it would honor the recommendations that already integrate developmental attributes directly related to the inner lives of middle grades students.

Finally, in contexts where use of the term *spiritual* was so untenable as to be disruptive rather than constructive, it would be possible to refer to spiritual developmental processes using less dissentious language. The term *inner lives* might capture and communicate similar human attributes as those from adolescent spiritual development without being too threatening to the assumptions and beliefs about the purpose of education in the United States. I recognize that even the limited acceptance of a relatively innocuous term like *inner lives* is an accomplishment given the dominance of technocratic and behaviorist influences on curriculum and instruction for most of the 20th century. However, I view this compromise as an imperfect solution at best, because it does not address the underlying relationship between power and knowledge that has deemed spirituality as not relevant to public education. Closely related to the implications identified in this section are those of the next section. Now, I turn to a more focused consideration of the implications of this research for the field of educational research, in the middle grades and at other levels.

Educational Research

I recommend two related areas for future research. The first focuses on how to integrate knowledge of adolescent spiritual development in public schools in the United States. The second concerns legitimizing historiography within the field of educational research, particularly for policy makers.

Stepping stone for future work on spiritual development. I intend for this work to be one small contribution to a much greater project of situating spiritual development within the middle grades concept to more fully realize the promise of developmentally responsive education. Instead of "making final pronouncements on the way things are," the findings from this research are part of "a larger interdisciplinary and intercultural conversation" (Kincheloe, 2008, p. 132). This research could be extended with field-based inquiry that compares and refines ideas about how middle grades teachers can leverage a more holistic knowledge of the development of young adolescents. For example, a potential future research question informed by the results of this research is: How do middle grades teachers perceive the educational relevance, if at all, of the inner lives of their students? As pointed out in the previous section, using the term *inner lives* could be initially strategic (in terms of an overall data collection strategy) during the shifting tide of a paradigm revolution that situates spirituality and spiritual development as legitimate educational concerns.

Drawing from the findings of the present research, I envision other researchers being better positioned to design quantitative or qualitative research with middle grades teachers as sources of data. For example, using the combined results from the prevalent paradigm narratives, a researcher could design a quasi-experimental study using a survey instrument that asks teacher participants to categorize adolescent developmental characteristics by domain. One group would receive a survey that offers spiritual as one domain category among the more typical options (e.g., cognitive, social); the other group would have the same domain options except for the spiritual category. Results would be analyzed for a comparison of developmental characteristics that are categorized as spiritual when offered the option and how those same characteristics are categorized when spiritual is not an option. These results could be combined with another study using qualitative coding techniques to conduct further analysis of extant texts. That study would focus on identifying recommendations from the literature on the middle grades concept that address aspects of young adolescent development characterized in other literature as spiritual development. That type of analysis was only begun here; it could be deepened to produce results more focused on translating theory into practice.

If the study described previously were conducted, the research purpose would shift away from generating new knowledge about the positionality of spirituality as a domain that has a legitimate place within middle grades education, which was the purpose of this critical historiographical research. The new research purpose would be to generate culturally respectful professional development curricula that deepens the holistic aspects of the middle grades concept and empowers middle grades teachers with the competencies and dispositions to leverage knowledge of adolescent spiritual development. This critical historiography would serve as a stepping stone for further research that is less centered on whether spiritual development is considered to be relevant in the U.S. system of middle grades education, and more focused on how to integrate knowledge of adolescent spiritual development in public schools in the United States.

Legitimizing historiography. The American Educational Research Association (AERA) dedicates a division to historiography and the history of education. However from my own experience in a doctoral program, as a faculty member in a teacher preparation program, and my reading of the educational research literature, my impression is that historiographical research is an outlier in educational research. Historiographical research uses techniques that are both quantitative and qualitative as an approach, but it doesn't fall neatly into either category of educational research. Given the supremacy of the two categories, a methodology that isn't easily packaged into one or the other is deemed suspect at worst, and impractical at best. Even forming my dissertation committee was challenging in terms of finding a tenure-track faculty member in my graduate school of education who has expertise with historiographical research. As Thayer-Bacon and Moyer (2006) found in their own work as philosophical/historiographical teacher-researchers in the field of education, "in the absence of more familiar and tangible products such as taped interviews, field sites, or chi-squares, alternative forms of research can appear abstract and disconnected from educational practice" (p. 139). Kincheloe (2001, 2005, 2008), whose work on critical constructivism shaped many of my ideas, also expressed this perspective. This challenge was a potential limitation to my selection of critical historiography as a method for dissertation research. However, after conducting this research, and becoming increasingly familiar with the literature on historiography in education, I am convinced of both its merits and applicability in the field of education.

As a method, critical historiography is especially applicable for my area of specialization, curriculum and instruction. The content of curriculum and the strategies of instruction are not neutral (Kincheloe, 2008). Educational historians Novoa and Mashal (2003) argued:

> The formation of educational knowledge—what is important to know and what should or should not be reflected in the study and practice of education—has historically been a consequence of social and political as well as academic developments. More than epistemological discussion, these developments entail a process that is historically contingent, vulnerable, and reflective of the political mood and intellectual space that they express. (p. 423)

Critical historiography reflects post-structural arguments against language as a "closed structure" (Bentley, 1999, p. 141). Through the hermeneutical approach of critical historiography, foundational texts are interpreted for the epistemological and ontological worldviews that influence the content. By shining a light on those worldviews, what is considered *legitimate educational knowledge* is seen as products of social and historical processes. Critical historiography is a research method that opens up space for alternative ways for middle grades teachers to consider the domain of spiritual development as they work with curricular content and select instructional strategies.

My research design was facilitated by a research methodology that emphasized written texts as data and a research paradigm, critical constructivism, that emphasized "the deep social assumptions and power relations embedded in everyday language....the ways unexamined language shapes education, the research about it and the narrative format that transmits it to the reader" (Kincheloe, 2008, p. 122). My purpose for doing this research was to bring more clarity to the developmental processes characterized as *spiritual* in the contemporary narrative in the U.S. and to be able to articulate how these processes could be considered relevant within a secular educational context. Critical historiography suited that purpose, as it allowed me to draw heavily upon the foundational literature that influences educational practice in the middle grades, while at the same time interrogating the tacit rules guiding those (hi)stories.

Finally, as Kaestle (1997) argued in his rationale for educational research that is historiographical, many of today's major decisions about practice and policy in public education are driven by a belief in how things have always been done. I do not propose that this is a phenomenon unique to education. However, if educators are going to draw from historical accounts for their decisions, a more nuanced understanding of the assumptions and agendas that are behind the foundational literature could better serve all students.

Hopefully, by nesting my conclusions regarding the educational relevance of spiritual development within their cultural-historical and methodological contexts, I have strengthened my vision of a new conceptual landscape of middle grades education in the United States. As I had suspected when I began this research project, issues of discourse and cultural context weigh heavily on any exploration of spirituality and public education. However, through these conceptual conclusions about the ways in which knowledge of spiritual development enriches the central tenets of the middle grades concept, I see great promise for increasing a sense of belonging for young adolescents in schools, empowering teachers who are inclined toward a holistic pedagogy, and positively influencing academic achievement.

Chapter Nine

A Discourse of Possibility

The Purpose and Promise of Education

IN my earlier explanation of how I use the term *relevance* in this research, I characterized relevance as a topic or idea that was germane to the context. Germane is an intentional word choice; its origins are the Latin *germanus*, which means genuine or having the same parents (*Oxford Dictionary of English*, 2010). Knowing its etymological origins led me to consider the parents of education, and I thought of the purpose of education. Relevance is connected to purpose, and so the absence of explicit consideration of the spiritual domain of human development could be related back to questions about the purpose of education in the United States.

If the purpose of education is limited to the transmission of certain knowledge or skills, I can see how the relevance of spiritual development might be called into question. As the findings and conclusions from this study show, spiritual development is conceived of as a process of *inquiry:* making personal meaning, being aware of interconnection, and exploring commitments to values and beliefs. The spiritual development processes are not consistent with an educational purpose focused on transmission of predetermined knowledge and skills. While participation in religious traditions may involve transmission of doctrine as knowledge, in the (hi)stories of spiritual development and holistic education, spiritual development is not synonymous with religiosity. Therefore, in educational endeavors with the purpose of knowledge transmission only, spiritual development is not relevant.

But what if the purpose of education is not only "to deliver the answers" but also to "enable students to live with...questions" (Webster, 2013, p. 70)? In that educational endeavor, teacher knowledge of adolescent spiritual developmental processes becomes highly relevant, given the primary traits of spiritual development: constructing an interpretive narrative, making meaning of one's purpose in life, connecting to something greater, and strengthening resilience.

And so, the questions I am left with are: What is the power of the term *spiritual* when used as a descriptor for human attributes or activities that could be categorized with other terms? Is there something to be gained in the field of education by integrating the term *spiritual* into our pedagogical lexicon? Or, is the purpose of public education in the United States too radically challenged by using the term *spiritual*? Are other terms, such as inner life, more palatable simply because they do not produce the same deep level of challenge to the adults who are more comfortable with a learning theory that privileges adult control and requires student submission in the classrooms? These questions reflect the ontological and epistemological levels of inquiry that characterizes this research in particular and the cultural depths of critical historiography in general.

This critical historiographical research offers direction for field-based methods to explore these final questions. It addresses a gap in the literature of the middle grades concept by providing a sound theoretical basis for pursuing a more holistic implementation of developmentally responsive education for young adolescents. It is hoped that this theoretical basis will guide and inspire middle grades educators and scholars who care about young adolescents.

What I conclude from this research is that there are deep, paradigmatic connections amongst the fields of the middle grades concept, spirituality as a developmental domain, and holistic education. These connections suggest that the foundation is there for integrating a more holistic middle grades concept, through the shared commitments to caring relations and constructivist learning theories. As an artifact of research informed by the critical constructivist perspective, this text offers a bridge between a (merely) theoretical justification for the legitimacy of spiritual development and the deployment of enactment tools for educators. In the next section, I offer a more specific vision for strengthening the bonds between theory and practice through a new pedagogical framework. As I asserted in the introductory chapter, one of the empowering aspects of critical constructivism—the researcher paradigm that guides critical historiography—is its commitment to theory explicitly situated in classroom practice.

Changing What One Knows: Spiritually Responsive Pedagogy

In describing one of the effects of conducting research guided by critical constructivism, Kincheloe (2008) submitted that "....critical constructivist research changes not only what one knows but who one actually is" (p. 132). His assertion proved true on both accounts in my experience designing and conducting a critical historiography.

On the one hand, Kincheloe describes a change in what one knows. With the findings of my research in hand, I call for the establishment of a new pedagogical framework: spiritually responsive pedagogy. This new framework empowers teachers to promote a sense of belonging for all students through skillful leveraging of their knowledge of spiritual development when planning curriculum and instruction. It is the "different image of the same landscape" I invoked at the beginning of this text: "A new image must be articulated or described so others can move within the landscape as they did in the past, but with greater freedom and new awareness of their choices and limitations" (Huebner, 1999, p. 404). In this section, I describe my vision for spiritually responsive pedagogy; in the concluding section of this chapter, I reflect on the second part of Kincheloe's submission—that the researcher's identity is changed as well.

During one recent autumn, I had the opportunity to be a guest speaker in a graduate learning theory class at a private, Catholic college in the Portland metropolitan area. I was asked to present my ideas on developmentally responsive instruction that include the domain of spiritual development. After presenting this work, the graduate students discussed the implications of it, as well as their own personal responses in the context of their work as educators at various stages of their career, in private and public secondary schools. I took notes on the conversation and analyzed them later for themes.

I noticed two patterns of responses to the topic of explicit inclusion of the term spiritual: one group of students expressed a sense of what I described as relief and empowerment. These students said they were grateful to be offered a language and framework for addressing the inner lives of their students, something they believed was relevant in a learning context. They perceived a person's inner life as a correlate to human spirituality and spiritual development. Another group of students expressed confusion and skepticism. Their skepticism was not in regard to the characteristics of adolescent spiritual development; they linked their skepticism and confusion to the application of the word spiritual as a descriptor. As one student said, "I was thrown off by the word spiritual because I immediately conjured up associations that did not seem legitimate for a public school."

I think the work presented in this text is for the teachers in the first group, who express a thirst for knowledge and tools that enable them to respectfully but intentionally tend to the spiritual needs, interests, and abilities of their students. These teachers see, as I do, spiritual development as a developmental resource for growth in all other domains of human development. They see, as I do, a relationship between learning and the spiritual resources of developing a personal interpretive narrative, experiencing a connection to transcendence, and cultivating resilience and hope. They see, as I do, the need for professional development curriculum that expands their knowledge of young adolescent development to increase their capacity for being developmentally responsive educators who empower all learners.

For these teachers, I propose a new framework: spiritually responsive pedagogy. Akin to the construct of culturally responsive pedagogy (Gay, 2010), a spiritually responsive pedagogical framework empowers educators committed to a vision of education that values the full development of human potential over technocratic proficiencies that alienate teachers and students. In this tentative introduction to a definition and description of spiritually responsive pedagogy, I borrow from Gay's (2002, 2010) central scaffolding linguistic devices, as I envision strategic advantages to emulating her design elements for culturally responsive pedagogy. Spiritually responsive pedagogy is defined as using the spiritual developmental characteristics, experiences, and perspectives of learners as conduits for educating them more effectively. This pedagogical framework is based on the assumption that when academic knowledge and skills are situated within the crucibles of spiritual development, they are more personally meaningful, have higher interest appeal, and are learned more easily and thoroughly[1]. The promise of this framework stands in the conviction that classrooms embracing spiritually responsive pedagogy will exhibit: (a) students who are more actively engaged participants in reciprocal teaching and learning; (b) academic relationships that are grounded in presence, creativity, and a shared sense of purpose and belonging; and (c) the increased application of democratic principles in educational experiences.

While more work is required to fully develop a comprehensive spiritually responsive pedagogy, to begin that work I suggest a set of four required elements: (a) a spiritual development knowledge base; (b) spiritually responsive curricula and instruction; (c) acknowledgment of the spiritual dimension of learning in schools; and (d) holistic accountability.

As with Gay's (2010) culturally responsive framework, a spiritually responsive framework would include specific recommendations for implementation. The first of these recommendations is filling in the gaps in teachers' knowledge base about academic constructs of spirituality and spiritual development. This new knowledge would be derived from multiple sources, such as theoretical claims, research studies, practical experiences, and personal stories. The new knowledge would be interdisciplinary: philosophy, history, sociology, cultural studies, psychology, and foundations of education, as well as the results of research conducted in the fields of applied developmental psychology, cultural anthropology, curriculum and instruction, assessment, and leadership and policy, are examples of academic disciplines from which a knowledge base would be created. Diverse types of research methodologies that contribute to the knowledge base for a spiritually

---

[1]   The language used in these sentences is similar to verbiage used by Gay (2002), p. 106.

responsive pedagogical framework would make manifest the critical constructivist principles of bricolage and multilogicality. Diverse methodologies would include action research, arts-based research, multiple case study, quasi-experimental study, grounded theory, and discourse analysis, among others. The content of the knowledge base would include theories about what develops in the spiritual domain and the processes of that development. The hybridity of stage-based and systems-based theories of human development would be addressed, as well as the reciprocity amongst different domains of development. Finally, the knowledge base would reflect culturally inclusive constructs of spiritual development.

The second element of spiritually responsive pedagogy is curricula and instruction that is spiritually responsive. This element would offer strategies for converting knowledge about spiritual development into curricular designs and instructional practices that tend to the needs, interests, and abilities of the learners vis-à-vis their spiritual development. Developmental characteristics from the spiritual domain would be important criteria or reference points for determining how curriculum and instruction should be modified for meeting the needs of the learners. Curriculum may include content that is spiritually responsive, such as a text or concept that helps students make meaning of their own experiences in relation to something larger than themselves. Spiritually responsive curriculum might also include a specific work of fiction in which central characters address their own spiritual questions, concerns, and insights. Learning activities that cultivate awareness of interconnections with others, facilitate opportunities to cultivate resilience, creativity, wonder, and awe (e.g., listening to music, artistic responses to algorithms), and use paradox as an instructional heuristic are all examples of instructional strategies that convert knowledge about spiritual development into classroom practices.

A third element of spiritually responsive pedagogy is an acknowledgment of the spiritual dimension of learning in schools. This is perhaps one of the most crucial elements, as it directly counters the historical pattern of spirituality's invisibility in schools (except for schools affiliated with a religious tradition or holistic philosophy, e.g., anthroposophy in the Waldorf tradition). It is potentially one of the most challenging elements, as it assumes the adoption of a humanistic perspective on human growth and learning; such a perspective is not necessarily the dominant guiding view for public education in U.S. schools today.

An acknowledgment of the spiritual dimension of learning requires an intentionally respectful negotiation of the distinctions between religiosity and spirituality. Kessler (2000) modeled this delicate negotiation effectively by seeking out dialogue with members of local religious communities in the schools she worked with, seeking their input and feedback on her programs that tended to the spiritual development of her public high school students. Acknowledging the spiritual dimension of learning would need to be accompanied by an honoring of the various expression of spiritual development by diverse learners. Teachers would demonstrate courage by naming the spiritual dimension, and claiming that language. This demonstration of courage, along with applying spiritually responsive pedagogy, could energize and enrich teacher relationships with families and students. An endorsement of the spiritual dimension of learning also acknowledges the significant role of the environment in cultivating healthy development, not just in the spiritual domain but in other domains as well.

The fourth and final element of spiritually responsive pedagogy is holistic accountability. Although the construct of accountability is somewhat flawed in its positivist implications, its utility as a term comes from its simplest implication in education: That teachers have a responsibility to serve all of their students by providing educational experiences that empower, nurture, and promote academic achievement. By adding the descriptor *holistic*, the criteria for what it means to be accountable as an educator or school system that applies spiritually responsive pedagogy are transformed. Holistic accountability implies an understanding of human growth and learning that is grounded in caring relationships. Holistic accountability occurs in schools that are conceived of as ecological, not industrial, systems. Teachers who manifest holistic accountability possess an engaged sensibility: an orientation of interconnectedness, as well as a deep sense of presence in their classroom and professional communities. Lastly, this element of spiritually responsive pedagogy reflects a shift in the sources of power in educational systems: This shift is away from policy-makers who may or may not be intimately connected to classroom realities toward teachers, students, and building level administrators whose authority is animated (and informed) by the generative nature of daily interactions and quality relationships.

For readers familiar with Gay's (2010) work on culturally responsive pedagogy, several parallels will emerge from this brief survey of the four elements of spiritually responsive pedagogy. First, in both spiritually responsive pedagogy and culturally responsive pedagogy, the teacher's disposition is one of responsiveness to the learners. It implies a posture of open-mindedness, curiosity, and willingness, as well as an abiding respect for human integrity. The onus is on the teacher, not the learner, for making appropriate adaptations to meet the needs of the educational context and circumstances. Second, spiritually responsive pedagogy, like culturally responsive pedagogy, reflects an epistemology that privileges social constructivist learning theory (Ernst, 1994) and transformative learning theory (Mezirow, 2000). Both learning theories are represented through the framework's emphasis on the role of the learning environment and the ways in which teachers, as applied developmentalists, experience an inter-subjective relationship between their own development and that of their students (Nakkula & Ravich, 1998).

Finally, like Gay's (2010) framework, spiritually responsive pedagogy is a call to action. Both pedagogical stances are founded on the belief that (good) education promotes liberation and agency, not compliance and alienation. A just and truly democratic society in which all participants are valued and cared for is the vision; spiritually responsive pedagogy is a bridge between theory and practice that teachers can use to embody that vision.

As a pedagogical framework, spiritually responsive pedagogy emanates from the critical constructivist worldview. Knowledge and perspectives from multiple academic fields are woven into a complex but forthright set of guiding principles with which to translate holistic theories about learning and human growth into curricular, instructional, assessment, and organizational practices designed to cultivate the phenomenon of belonging in a school context. Such a framework is also consistent with the position I have maintained throughout this research: I distinguish between teaching spirituality in schools and leveraging knowledge of spirituality in schools—I focus on the latter, not the former. The middle grades concept is not about teaching young adolescents about their developmental stage. It is about purposively teaching with those developmental traits in mind. What I call for is the explicit inclusion of the spiritual domain when teaching with the intent of being responsive to the learner's growth and development, a conviction I characterize as spiritually responsive pedagogy.

As Kincheloe (2008) recommends, critical constructivist research is part of an ongoing conversation, a transition point between past and future. His recommendation is similar to the perspective embraced by Fowler (1981): Our present reality has a magnificent quality of reflecting the source of our wisdom and the promise of more to come. My call for the development of a spiritually responsive pedagogy reflects a wisdom gratefully received from pioneer thinkers such as Kincheloe and Fowler, and offers hope for others who are as relieved and empowered as I am by the explicit inclusion of spirituality in our work as educators.

The creation of a new framework for teachers who perceive the need for a spiritually responsive pedagogy also reflects what Giroux (1981) characterized as a discourse of possibility. Criticality, one of the central principles of critical historiography, perceives historical discourses as socially constructed interactions between individuals and societal structures that are influenced by power and privilege. The critical perspective encourages the researcher to identify and interrogate the predominance of Western theoretical paradigms, creating a discourse of possibility. Criticality is manifested in a critical historiography by the technique of asking unique questions, allowing the researcher to draw from her imagination in order to articulate a novel theory, a discourse of possibility. New theoretical knowledge, in turn, becomes a resource for "critically engaging and mapping the crucial relations among language, texts, everyday life and structures of power as part of a broader effort to understand the conditions, contexts and strategies of struggle that will lead to social transformation" (Giroux, 2003, p. 97). The research presented in this text is important, therefore, not only as an example of the process of conducting an unconventional research methodology in the field of education, but also as an example of how theoretical work must simultaneously be connected to the macro context of a movement to demand emancipatory education for all students, and the micro context of practical application for classroom teachers.

Changing Who One Is: Integrating Political Identity With Spiritual Commitments

In addition to changing what one knows, Kincheloe argued that critical constructivist research changes who one is. His pairing of knowledge and identity as equally important aspects of the research act affirms Palmer's (1998) commitment to the person in the profession, Freire's (1993) construct of *humanization*, and the concept of researcher reflexivity in critical qualitative research (e.g., William-White, 2013).

My identity as a radical educator expanded to incorporate the principles of holistic education more explicitly as a result of conducting a critical historiography. My internal rearrangement reminds me of the transformation of Buddhist teacher Thich Nhat Hahn during the U.S. war in his homeland of Vietnam (Malkin, 2003). In his transformation, he integrated his deep spiritual practices with his political endeavors. Being a Buddhist political activist is challenging, given the Buddhist principle that human beings' rigid notions about institutions, identities, and relationships are delusions that mask a spacious, loving, and intelligent reality. Thich Nhat Hahn was compelled to address this challenge as he sat in the meditation hall while violence against his people raged outside. The integration of spiritual practice in the Buddhist context with social justice action is often described in Western culture as "Engaged Buddhism" (e.g., Macy, 1991).

In my transformation through this critical constructivist research, my rearrangement went in the opposite direction: I developed a deeper awareness of how to integrate my radical political pedagogy with my spiritual commitments. Although the work of bell hooks, who writes often of the spirituality of critical pedagogy, has been a powerful influence for the past 20 years, it was not until my work on this critical historiographical research that my conceptual comprehension of critical spiritual pedagogy became an embodied insight. Through my engagement with critical historiography, I found my own area of convergence between my political and spiritual commitments.

I was led to this transformation through my historiographical analysis of the foundational literature of holistic education. Advocates of holistic education make explicit the relationship between societal values and what types of knowledge and learning are privileged in public education in the United States. In the holistic framework, knowledge is viewed as a reflection of whose perspective is most valued and which conceptions of reality are considered to be legitimate. This strategy de-naturalizes a tacit understanding of knowledge as a neutral construct. In contemplating this finding, I saw the connection between the holistic strategy of challenging the inevitability of current practices and my own strategy for designing a critical historiographical research project. I chose a research design that would enable me to interrogate the ways in which power and knowledge played a role in the absence of the spiritual domain of development in the middle grades concept in the United States.

This connection between the perspective of holistic advocates and my research design led me to re-think how I describe my pedagogical stance as an educator. Although I have not previously self-identified as a holistic educator, I do now. The transformation was bound up with my pedagogical values not only as a professional educator, but also as a parent of two school-aged children.

During the process of conducting this research, I was often asked what I thought of my daughters' education in the public neighborhood school, especially when the person with whom I was speaking knew about my background in education. My children's school had an excellent reputation in the district. These types of exchanges—comparing and contrasting schools—are common as small talk amongst parents. Why wouldn't they be? We all care about the educational experiences of our children.

As it happened, during that time period I was not happy with their educational experiences—too many worksheets with a copyright of 1987 and too much sitting and listening as the primary learning activities. I typically expressed my dissatisfaction with a disclaimer, "But, I am a holistic educator," a response that I had *not* offered in previous years. But the words came out easily, with little forethought. I simply aligned my critique of the technocratic pedagogy I saw at my children's school with the field of holistic education. Before my work on this research project, I aligned such a critique only with the work of radical political educators such as hooks and Freire.

My pedagogical transformation, therefore, involved a deeper understanding of the principles of holistic education—which I had previously reduced to the spiritual emphasis—and how those principles are consistent with my identification as a radical political educator. I also came to a deeper place of appreciation of the spiritual underpinnings of the work of hooks and Freire.

The results of integrating my radical political pedagogy with my spirituality include a stronger sense of academic integrity as well as a clearer perspective on the problem of the absence of spiritual development from the middle grades concept. In exploring the relevance of spiritual development in middle grades education, I am convinced that the problem is rooted in the current dominant paradigms about learning, human development, and the purpose of education. In that consensus, learning is viewed as a passive activity, children and adolescents are believed to be immature and unreliable, and education is preparation for an industrial workforce. Within such a consensus, educational priorities are social control, adult domination, and a one-size-fits-all pedagogical model.

If we are—as has been suggested by this research project and affirmed by other scholars (e.g., Wilber, 2000)—on the precipice of an ecological revolution in U.S. society, then I feel hopeful about the likelihood of the field of middle grades education enriching their emphasis of caring relations and constructivist learning theory with explicit inclusion of adolescent spiritual developmental characteristics. But the field will first need to be willing to adopt a more critical stance on the implementation of public education in the U.S., to be willing to embrace the perspective that education is not neutral.

Appendices

Appendix A. Summary of Research Activities

Selection and preparation of data for specific analyses •   Potential texts identified from meta-analysis •   Criteria tests are administered for each potential datum •   Defense of data selections written
First Round of Data Analysis: Initial Coding • Initial Codes capture content of passages (datum) • Data interpreted for assumptions, values, and beliefs (BVA interpretations) • *In vivo* code names used (not exclusively) • Constant comparative method *within* each text • Each text coded independently from the other texts • Memo-writing • Product: Ten tables of Initial Codes that summarize and account for indirect evidence of paradigms for each text; quotations for each Initial Code; BVA interpretations for each Initial Code
Second Round of Data Analysis: Focused Coding • Constant comparative method *across* data within each data set using Initial Codes only • Memo-writing • Product: List of Focused Content Codes (FCCs) for each of the three data sets • Constant comparative method using FCCs and BVA interpretations; BVA categorized by FCC • Product: Tables of BVA by FCC • Memo-writing (analysis of BVA by FCC tables) • Product: List of Paradigm Codes for each of the three data sets (5 per data set) • Product: Written interpretive narratives of the paradigm categories for each of the three fields (3 data sets, 5 paradigm narratives per data set)
Third Round of Data Analysis: Contrapuntal Reading • Reading across the Paradigm Narratives contrapuntally • Interpreting for inter-textual and inter-discursive patterns between the paradigms of the three fields • Constant comparative analysis: returning to all previously rendered data analysis • Product: Written interpretive narrative of the three paradigm types and discursive inter-relationship between the paradigms in the conceptual nexus • Product: Conceptual diagram of the inter-discursive relationships between the paradigms of the three fields

Appendix B. Initial Coding Table Artifact

Excerpt from initial coding table: Lounsbury and Vars, 1978; Middle Grades Concept data set

Page in text	Initial Code	Quotation from coded passage	Researcher's interpretations of beliefs, values, and/or assumptions expressed directly or indirectly in the text
111–112	Curriculum development framed as curriculum leadership	"How do teachers, together with administrators, bring the proposed curriculum into being?" 111	*Value:* multiple participants in curriculum development *Belief:* curriculum development is a leadership issue *Assumption:* participants involved with curriculum leadership have the skills to collaborate
112–114	Change is about realizing your hopes, potential, best wishes for yourself and the students	"...the word 'change' is misleading...they [teachers] need to be 'released' rather than 'changed,' to be their best selves." 113	*Belief:* curriculum development is not about "getting better." It is an internal transformation yielding externalized benefits in the classroom
112–114	Collaboration	"Provide for collegial support and cooperative effort." 114	*Value:* curriculum improvement should be undertaken collaboratively, with open communication, explicit supports, and permission to experiment *Value:* collective wisdom/group wisdom

Appendix C. Focused Coding Table Artifact

Excerpt from the Middle Grades Concept data set
   BVAs categorized by FCCs

Focused Content Code: 'MG as critical period (for individuals, for society)'

Data Source	Alexander, 1968	Lounsbury & Vars, 1978	Carnegie, 1989	NMSA, 2010
Researcher's interpretation of beliefs, values, and assumptions expressed in the data	Assumption—that it is possible to determine what is best for all ya 10–12	Belief—ya is a crucial stage of life because the primary task is developing a sense of selfhood, while in community 3–4	Assumption—because of the changes in tech and media, things are harder for ya "today" 9	Belief—about who ya are and what they do Belief—about the long-term outcomes that are connected to ya 3
*Numeral refers to page in text	Belief—ya is a unique period in human life-span, characterized by variability 12–14	Belief—maturity happens earlier for ya than it has at any other point in history Assumption—possible to qualify the typical characteristics of ya 34–37	Belief—at risk students benefit more Value—to better serve at risk ya 9–10	Belief—there are things which threaten healthy dev that are particular to contemporary society Belief—ya a crucial period in terms of long term outcomes 6
	Belief—mge is a critical point in the long term capacities/success of a person 71–73	Belief—ya dev related to long term health of society 34–37	Value—economic rationale for transforming mge Assumption—capitalist model 70–77	Assumption—ya are not able to be critical consumers without guidance from teachers 8

Appendix D. Two Paradigm Narratives
With Extensive In-Text and Parenthetical Citations

A. From Middle Grades Concept data set:

Empowering education. The *Empowering Education* paradigm category encompasses teacher self-efficacy, learning theory, and the middle grades concept as educational reform. In this category, empowerment is both personal and collective, and occurs at classroom, school, and societal levels. This category and *Becoming Together* overlap: The strongest area of overlap is the function and value of teacher intrapersonal development. Seeing one's own humanity in order to see the humanity of others is emphasized in the 1968 and 1978 data as a necessary disposition or attitude (e.g., Alexander, 1968, pp. 87–88). In the 1989 and 2010 data, teacher intrapersonal development is characterized in terms of external, observable actions of caring and well-being (e.g., NMSA, 2010, p. 35 and p. 39). The middle grades teacher is valued as a core element of the middle grades concept; internal, personal transformation is believed to have external benefits for teaching and learning in schools (e.g., Lounsbury & Vars, 1978, pp. 112–114).

Teachers are empowered by middle grades advocates by being seen as the primary authorities on curriculum and instruction (e.g., Carnegie, 1989, pp. 54–58). In the data, testimonials from teachers were legitimized as evidence for the validity of the middle grades concept (e.g., Alexander, 1968, p. 70). Teacher authority was also reflected in specific recommendations of the middle grades concept. For example, in the Carnegie (1989) report, one of the recommendations is: "Decisions concerning the experiences of middle grades students should be made by adults who know them best" (p. 54). In my analysis, locating a source of authority within classroom teachers reflects an epistemological, and therefore paradigmatic, belief about whose knowledge counts when crafting curriculum practice and theory.

Another area of this paradigm category is learning theory. Subjectivist epistemologies dominate the data. Social constructivist and situated learning theories prevail. Learning happens when (a) the learner is an active participant in authentic learning contexts (e.g., Alexander, 1968, pp. 10–12; Carnegie, 1989, pp. 58–60); (b) when the learner is perceived by the teacher and by him/herself to have worthwhile assets (e.g., NMSA, 2010, pp. 24–26); and (c) learning occurs in and through community (e.g., Lounsbury & Vars, 1978, pp. 112–114). Beliefs and values about learning are also reflected by the learning activities that are considered legitimate. In the middle grades concept, academic curricula are not privileged over extracurricular activities: "considering, as we do, the total program of learning opportunities to be the curriculum, the term 'extracurricular' is not really an appropriate category for any learning opportunities" (Alexander, 1968, p. 65).

The middle grades are believed to be a potent site for reform of education in the United States, beyond just the middle grades. I interpreted a difference over time regarding the purpose of the reform. In the earlier two texts (i.e., Alexander, 1968; Lounsbury & Vars, 1978), the purpose of the middle grades concept as reform was to innovate education in the United States. In the latter two texts (i.e., Carnegie, 1989; NMSA, 2010), the purpose of the reform was to increase equity in education. For either purpose, I interpreted an explicit critique of the factory models of education in 21st century schools: "[Middle school] ought not to be an 'institution,' a teaching factory, but rather a center for learning and growing, a place especially designed for young adolescents where they are 'at home...'" (Lounsbury & Vars, 1978, p. xii).

B. From Spirituality as a Developmental Domain data set:

Seeing crucibles. Seeing Crucibles is closely related to, but distinct from, the use of paradox as a heuristic. The name of this paradigm category is *in vivo*, reflecting the authors' claims that spiritual development occurs within and as a result of interactions between separate entities. Captured in this category are ontological and epistemological perspectives that are subjectivist. The term crucible appeared in Benson (2006): "...it [spiritual development] also includes the myths learned on Grampa's or Grandma's lap and in the crucible of peer relationships, family, and community" (p. 490). Benson went on to claim that spiritual development occurs because of and is influenced by "...the ecologies one chooses to be the primary crucibles for development" (p. 490). In the field of chemistry, substances in a crucible are subjected to strong forces (e.g., high heat) resulting in the melting and re-forming process of alchemy. As a metaphorical term in the data and in this analysis, a crucible conceptually symbolizes the space of interaction between two or more forces in which the participating entities are irrevocably altered or transformed.

Crucibles are places of alchemy, a combination of the contents of the interaction and the resulting outcome(s) of the interaction. Throughout the data, the significance of a developing person's interaction with cultural and social context is explored in multiple ways. Crucibles are viewed as bidirectional influences (e.g., Benson, 2006, p. 490; Fowler, 1981, p. 100), adaptations (e.g., Oser, Scarlett, & Bucher, 2006, pp. 271–272), and "interplays" (Benson, 2006, p. 490). One datum refers to the bidirectional interplay between person and environment as a process of creating and inheriting: "the myths and narratives that organize and give direction to our lives involve a lifelong creative process in which persons actively create (whether the activity is conscious or not) a story, using source material that can come from many institutions and relationships" (Benson, 2006, p. 490). Oser, Scarlett, and Bucher (2006) referred to the crucible between parent and child as a process of "...co-constructing their spiritual identities" (p. 978). In these ways, spiritual development is framed as a type of social constructivist learning theory.

Another way in which spiritual development is seen as both a process and product of interactive transformation is in its relationship with other domains of human development. Human development is viewed as having separate domains whose growth and maturation are interrelated not only in terms of overlapping focus areas, but also in terms of stimulating further development. For example, all three data sources cite how shifts in cognitive capacities influence and are caused or accompanied by shifts in spiritual capacities (e.g., Benson, 2006, pp. 490–492; Fowler, 1981, pp. 149–150; Oser, Scarlett, & Bucher, 2006, pp. 972–976).

Other important though less frequent interactions that reflect the paradigm *Seeing Crucibles* are: (a) academics and practitioners in the field of spiritual development (e.g., Benson, 2006, p. 943); (b) structures and contents of spiritual development (e.g., Fowler, 1981, pp. 272–273; Oser, Scarlett, & Bucher, 2006, pp. 955–956); and (c) spiritual development theory and theories for other domains of human development (e.g., Fowler, 1981, pp. 275–276). For example, through intentionally created interactions between academics/researchers and practitioners/clinicians, a more useful theory for and applications of spiritual development can result (Benson, 2006).

In sum, this analytic category is intended to capture the conceptual tools employed by advocates of the field of spiritual development as a means of articulating the paradigm. *Seeing Crucibles* captures the fundamental valuing of interaction, the assumption that something of substance happens in the 'in-between' space, and the belief that human development occurs because of and within these crucibles.

Appendix E. Analytic Tool for Exploring Relationships Between Inter-Discursive and Inter-Textual Patterns

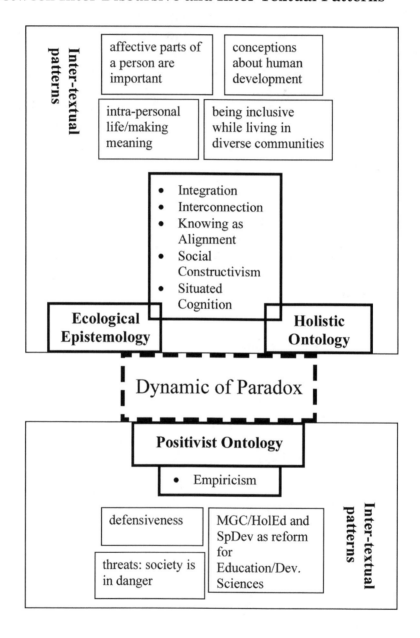

References

Alcalay, A. (1993). *After Jews and Arabs*. Minneapolis, MN: University of Minnesota Press.

Alexander, W. (1963, July). *The junior high school: A changing view*. Paper presented at the Tenth Annual Conference for School Administrators: A National Conference on the Junior High School, Ithaca, NY. In T. W. Smith, & C. K. McEwin (Eds.), *The legacy of middle school leaders: In their own words* (pp. 6–15). Charlotte, NC: Information Age.

Alexander, W. M., Williams, E. L., Compton, M., Hines, V. A., & Prescott, D. (1968). *The emergent middle school*. New York, NY: Holt, Rinehart, & Winston.

Balfanz, R. (2009). *Executive summary: Putting middle grades students on the graduation path*. Westerville, OH: National Middle School Association.

Bateson, G. (1972). *Steps to an ecology of the mind*. New York, NY: Ballantine Books.

Bateson, G. (1979). *Mind and nature: A necessary unity*. New York, NY: Dutton.

Bateson, M. C. (1994). *Peripheral visions: Learning along the way*. New York, NY: Harper Collins.

Beachum, F., Dentith, A., McCray, C., & Boyle, T. (2008). Havens of hope or the killing fields: The paradox of leadership, pedagogy, and relationships in an urban middle school. *Urban Education, 43*(2), 189–215.

Belousa, I. (2006). Defining spirituality in education: A post-Soviet perspective. In M. de Souza, G. Durka, K. Engebretson, R. Jackson, & A. McGrady (Eds.), *International handbook of the religious, moral and spiritual dimensions in education* (pp. 215–230). Dordrecht, The Netherlands: Springer.

Benami, A. (2006). *The spiritual dimension of education*. (Doctoral dissertation). Retrieved from ProQuest. (AAT 3211000)

Benson, P. L. (2004). Emerging themes in research on adolescent spiritual and religious development. *Applied Developmental Science, 8*(1), 47–50.

Benson, P. L. (2006). The science of child and adolescent spiritual development: Definitional, theoretical, and field-building challenges. In E. C. Roehlkepartain, P. E. King, L. Wagener, & P. L. Benson (Eds.), *Handbook of spiritual development in childhood and adolescence* (pp. 484–497). Thousand Oaks, CA: Sage.

Benson, P. L., Roehlkepartain, E. C., & Rude, S. P. (2003). Spiritual development in childhood and adolescence: Toward a field of inquiry. *Applied Developmental Science, 7*(3), 205–213.

Bentley, M. (1999). *Modern historiography*. New York, NY: Routledge.

Bondy, E., & Ross, D. (2008). The teacher as warm demander. *Educational Leadership, 66*(1), 54–58.

Borgman, D. (2006). Bridging the gap: From social science to congregations, researchers to practitioners. In E. C. Roehlkepartain, P. E. King, L. Wagener, & P. L. Benson (Eds.), *Handbook of spiritual development in childhood and adolescence* (pp. 435–444). Thousand Oaks, CA: Sage.

Bradley, C. (2011). *An inquiry into the relationships between spirituality and language pedagogy.* (Unpublished doctoral dissertation). Temple University, Philadelphia, PA.

Bruce, M. A., & Cockerham, D. (2004). Enhancing the spiritual development of adolescent girls. *Professional School Counseling, 7,* 334–342.

Brown, D. F., & Leaman, H. L. (2007). Recognizing and responding to young adolescents' ethnic identity development. In S. B. Mertens, V. A. Anfara, Jr., & M.M. Caskey, (Eds.), *The young adolescent and the middle school* (pp. 219–236). Westerville, OH & Charlotte, NC: National Middle School Association and Information Age.

Buchanan, I. (2010). "historiography". *A Dictionary of Critical Theory.* Oxford Reference Online. Oxford University Press. Retrieved from: http://www.oxfordreference.com/views/ENTRY.html?subview=Main&entry=t306.e324

Burke, P. (2001). Overture. The new history: Its past and its future. In P. Burke (Ed.), *New perspectives on historical writing* (2nd ed., pp. 1–24). University Park, PA: The Pennsylvania State University Press.

Cajete, G. (1994). *Look to the mountain: An ecology of indigenous education.* Durango, CO: Kivaki Press.

Carnegie Council on Adolescent Development's Task Force on Education of Young Adolescents. (1989). *Turning points: Preparing American youth for the 21st Century.* Washington, DC: Carnegie Council on Adolescent Development.

Carney, S., & Bista, M. B. (2009). Community schooling in Nepal: A genealogy of education reform since 1990. *Comparative Education Review, 53*(2), 189–211.

Caskey, M. M. (2003). Preparing middle level teachers in field based cohorts. In P. G. Andrews & V. A. Anfara (Eds.), *Leaders for a movement: Professional preparation and development of middle level teachers and administrators* (pp. 53–76). Greenwich, CT: Information Age.

Caskey, M. M., & Anfara, V. A., Jr. (2007). Research summary: Young adolescents' developmental characteristics. In M. M. Caskey (Ed.), *Middle level education: Research annual* (pp. 1–5). Westerville, OH: National Middle School Association.

Charmaz, K. (2006). *Constructing grounded theory: A practical guide through qualitative anaylsis.* Thousand Oaks, CA: Sage.

Claiborne, L. B. (2007). Beyond readiness: New questions about cultural understandings and developmental appropriateness. In J. L. Kincheloe & R. A. Horn, Jr. (Eds.), *The praeger handbook of education and psychology* (pp. 428–438). Westport, CT: Praeger.

Cohen, J. (2008). Social, emotional, ethical, and academic education: Creating a climate for learning, participation in democracy, and well-being. *Harvard Educational Review, 76*(2), 201–237.

Cohen, R. (2005). Journal writing in mathematics education: Communicating the affective dimensions of mathematics learning. In J. P. Miller, S. Karsten, D. Denton, D. Orr, & I. Colalillo Kates (Eds.), *Holistic learning and spirituality in education* (pp. 145-152). Albany, NY: SUNY Press.

Colalillo Kates, I. (2005). The creative journey: Personal creativity as soul work. In J. P. Miller, S. Karsten, D. Denton, D. Orr, & I. Colalillo Kates (Eds.), *Holistic learning and spirituality on education* (pp. 193–205). Albany, NY: SUNY Press.

Cottingham, M. (2005). Developing spirituality through the use of literature in history education. *International Journal of Children's Spirituality, 10*(1), 45–60.

Creswell, J. W. (2007). *Qualitative inquiry and research design: Choosing among five approaches.* Thousand Oaks, CA: Sage.

da Conceição Azevedo, M., & Gil da Costa, H. G. (2006). Creative and spiritual education through the human development process. In M. de Souza, G. Durka, K. Engebretson, R. Jackson, & A. McGrady (Eds.), *International handbook of the religious, moral and spiritual dimensions in education* (pp. 1321–1341). Dordrecht, The Netherlands: Springer.

Daniels, E. (2005). On the minds of middle schoolers. *Educational Leadership, 62*(7), 52–54.

Deakin Crick, R., & Jelfs, H. (2011). Spirituality, learning, and personalization: Exploring the relationship between spiritual development and learning to learn in a faith-based secondary school. *International Journal of Children's Spirituality, 16*(3), 197–217.

DeBlasio, G. (2011). The effect of spiritual intelligence in the classroom: God only knows. *International Journal of Children's Spirituality, 16*(2), 143–150.

de Jager Meezenbroek, E., Garssen, B., van den Berg, M., Tuytel, G., van Dierendonck, D., Visser, A., & Schaufeli, W. B. (2012). Measuring spirituality as a universal human experience: Development of the spiritual attitude and involvement list (SAIL). *Journal of Psychosocial Oncology, 30* (2). 141–167.

Delpit, L. (2006). *Other people's children: Cultural conflict in the classroom.* New York, NY: The New Press.

de Souza, M. (2006). Rediscovering the spiritual dimension in education: Promoting a sense of self and place, meaning and purpose in learning. In M. de Souza, G. Durka, K. Engebretson, R. Jackson, & A. McGrady (Eds.) *International handbook of the religious, moral and spiritual dimensions in education* (pp. 1127–1139). New York: Springer.

de Souza, M. (2012). Connectedness and *connectedness*: The dark side of spirituality—implications for education. *International Journal of Children's Spirituality, 17*(4), 291–303.

Dewey, J. (1902). *The child and the curriculum.* Chicago, IL: The University of Chicago Press.

Dewey, J. (1916). *Democracy and education.* New York, NY: The Free Press.

Doda, N., & Knowles, T. (2008). Listening to the voices of young adolescents. *Middle School Journal, 39*(3), 26–33.

Durlak, J. A., Weissberg, R. P., Dymnicki, A. B., Taylor, R. D., & Schellinger, K. B. (2011). The impact of enhancing students' social and emotional learning: A meta-analysis of school-based universal interventions. *Child Development, 82*(1), 405–432.

Eccles, J. S., & Midgley, C. (1989). Stage–environment fit: Developmentally appropriate classrooms for young adolescents. In C. Ames & R. Ames (Eds.), *Research on motivation in education: Vol. 3. Goals and cognitions* (pp. 13–44). New York, NY: Academic Press.

Eccles, J. S., Midgley, C., Wigfield, A., Buchanan, C. M., Reuman, D., Flanagan, C., & MacIver, D. (1993). Development during adolescence: The impact of stage–environment fit on adolescents' experiences in schools and families. *American Psychologist, 48*(2), 90–101.

Eccles, J., & Roeser, R. (2009). Schools, academic motivation, and stage-environment fit. In R. M. Lerner & L. Steinberg (Eds.), *Handbook of adolescent psychology* (3rd ed.; pp. 404–434). Hoboken, NJ: Wiley.

Erb, T. O. (2000). Do middle school reforms really make a difference? *The Clearing House, 73*(4), 194–200.

Erb, T. O. (2006). Middle school models are working in many grade configurations to boost student performance. *American Secondary Education, 34*(3), 4–13.

Erikson, E. H. (1968). *Identity: Youth and crisis.* New York, NY: Norton.

Ernst, P. (1994). Varieties of constructivism. *Hiroshima Journal of Mathematics Education, 2,* 1–14.

Everson v. Board of Education. 330 U.S. 1 (1947).

Feldman, D. H. (2008). The role of developmental change in spiritual development. In R. M. Lerner, R. W. Roeser, & E. Phelps (Eds.), *Positive youth development and spirituality* (pp. 167–198). West Conshohocken, PA: Templeton Foundation Press.

Felner, R. D., Seitsinger, A., Brand, S., Burns, A., & Bolton, N. (2007). Creating small learning communities: Lessons from the project on high-performing learning communities about "what works" in creating productive, developmentally enhancing, learning contexts. *Educational Psychologist, 42*(4), 209–221.

Foucault, M. (1973). *The order of things: An archaeology of the human sciences.* New York, NY: Vintage.

Fowler, J. (1981). *Stages of faith: The psychology of human development and the quest for meaning.* New York, NY: Harper.

Fowler, J. W., & Dell, M. L. (2006). Stages of faith from infancy through adolescence: Reflections on three decades of faith development theory. In E. C. Roehlkepartain, P. E. King, L. Wagener, & P. L. Benson (Eds.), *Handbook of spiritual development in childhood and adolescence* (pp. 34–45). Thousand Oaks, CA: Sage.

Fraser, D. (2007). State education, spirituality, and culture: Teachers' personal and professional stories of negotiating the nexus. *International Journal of Children□s Spirituality, 12*(3), 289–305.

Freire, P. (1993). *Pedagogy of the oppressed.* (M. Bergman Ramos, Trans.). New York, NY: Continuum. (Original work published in 1970).

Gandhi, M. K. (1953). *Towards new education.* Ahmedabad, India: Navijivan.

Gatto, J. T. (1999). Education and the Western spiritual tradition. In S. Glazer (Ed.), *The heart of learning: Spirituality in education* (pp. 151–172). New York, NY: Penguin Putnam.

Gay, G. (2002). Preparing for culturally responsive teaching. *Journal of Teacher Education, 53* (2), 106–116.

Gay, G. (2010). *Culturally responsive teaching: Theory, research, and practice.* New York, NY: Teachers College Press.

Gentilucci, J., & Muto, C. (2007). Principals' influence on academic achievement: The student perspective. *NASSP Bulletin, 91*(3), 219–236.

George, P. (2009). Renewing the middle school: The early success of middle school education. *Middle School Journal, 41*(1), 4–9.

Germane. (2010). In A. Stevenson (Ed.), *Oxford Dictionary of English.* Retrieved from http://www.oxfordreference.com/view/10.1093/acref/9780199571123.001.0001/m_en_gb0333000

Giroux, H. A. (1981). *Ideology, culture, and the process of schooling.* Philadelphia, PA: Temple University Press.

Giroux, H. A. (2003). Utopia thinking under the sign of neoliberalism: Toward a critical pedagogy of educated hope. *Democracy & Nature, 9*(1), 91–105.

Good, M., & Willoughby, T. (2008). Adolescence as a sensitive period for spiritual development. *Child Development Perspectives, 2*(1), 32–37.

Greenblatt, S. (1998). Culture. In D. Keesey (Ed.), *Contexts for criticism* (3rd ed.). Mountain View, CA: Mayfield.

Greene, W. L., Musser, P. M., Casbon, J., Caskey, M. M., Samek, L. L., & Olson, M. (2008). Caught in the middle again: Accountability and the changing practice of middle school teachers. *Middle Grades Research Journal, 3*(4), 41–72.

Guba, E. G. (1990). The alternative paradigm dialog. In E. G. Guba (Ed.), *The paradigm dialog* (pp. 17–27). Newbury Park, CA: Sage.

Guba, E. G., & Lincoln, Y. S. (2005). Paradigmatic controversies, contradictions, and emerging confluences. In N. K. Denzin & Y. S. Lincoln (Eds.), *The Sage handbook of qualitative research* (pp. 191–215). Thousand Oaks, CA: Sage.

Gutman, L. M., & Eccles, J. S. (2007). Stage—environment fit during adolescence: Trajectories of family relations and adolescent outcomes. *Developmental Psychology, 43*(2), 522–537.

Hall, G. S. (1904). *Adolescence: Its psychology and its relations to physiology, anthropology, sociology, sex, crime, religion and education.* New York, NY: D. Appleton and Company.

Hamilton, D. M., & Jackson, M. H. (1998). Spiritual development: Paths and processes. *Journal of Instructional Psychology, 25*(4), 262–271.

Hamm, J. V., Farmer, T. W., Robertson, D., Dadisman, K. A., Murray, A., Meece, J. L., & Song, S. Y. (2010). Effects of a developmentally based intervention with teachers on Native American and White early adolescents' schooling adjustment in rural settings. *The Journal of Experimental Education, 78*(3), 343–377.

Hart, T. (2004). Opening the contemplative mind in the classroom. *Journal of Transformative Education, 2*(1), 28–46.

Hay, D., & Nye, R. (2006). *The spirit of the child.* Philadelphia, PA: Jessica Kingsley Publishers.

Hay, D., Reich, K. H., & Utsch, M. (2006). Spiritual development: Intersections and divergence with religious development. In E. C. Roehlkepartain, P. E. King, L. Wagener, & P. L. Benson (Eds.), *Handbook of spiritual development in childhood and adolescence* (pp. 46–59). Thousand Oaks, CA: Sage.

Henry, A. (2006). Historical studies: Groups/Institutions. In J. L. Greene, G. Camilli, & P. B. Elmore (Eds.), *Handbook of complementary methods in educational research* (pp. 333–355). Mahwah, NJ: Erlbaum.

Hill, P., Jr. (1991). *Coming of age: African-American male rites-of-passage.* Chicago, IL: African American Images.

"historiography". (2011). *Oxford Dictionary of English.* A. Stevenson (Ed.). Oxford Reference Online. Oxford University Press. Retrieved from: http://www.oxfordreference.com/views/ENTRY.html?subview=Main&entry=t 140.e0380360

hooks, b. (1994). *Teaching to transgress: Education as the practice of freedom.* New York, NY: Routledge.

hooks, b. (2003). *Teaching community: A pedagogy of hope.* New York, NY: Routledge.

Huebner, D. E. (1985). Spirituality and knowing. In E. Eisner (Ed.), *Learning and teaching the ways of knowing* (pp. 159–173). Chicago, IL: University of Chicago Press.

Huebner, D. E. (1999). Education and spirituality. In V. Hillis & W. Pinar (Eds.), *The lure of the transcendent: Collected essays by Dwayne E. Huebner* (pp. 401–416). Mahwah, NJ: Erlbaum.

Hunter, J., & Solomon, J. (2002). A psychological view of spirituality and leadership: Finding meaning through Howard Gardner's notion of existential intelligence. *School Administrator, 59*(8), 38–41.

Husen, T. (1999). Research paradigms in education. In J. P. Keeves & G. Lakomski (Eds.), *Issues in educational research* (pp. 31–39). New York, NY: Pergamon.

Jackson, A., & Davis, G. (2000). *Turning Points 2000: Educating adolescents in the 21ˢᵗ century.* New York, NY: Teachers College Press.

Janesick, V. J. (2011). *"Stretching" exercises for qualitative researchers.* Los Angeles, CA: Sage.

Jewett, S. (2009). "You feel like you're in your second family": Spinning a relational web in middle school. *Urban Review, 41*(3), 201–221.

Johnson, C. N. (2008). The spirit of spiritual development. In R. M. Lerner, R. W. Roeser, & E. Phelps (Eds.), *Positive youth development and spirituality* (pp. 25–41). West Conshohocken, PA: Templeton Foundation Press.

Juang, L., & Syed, M. (2008). Ethnic identity and spirituality. In R. M. Lerner, R. W. Roeser, & E. Phelps (Eds.), *Positive youth development and spirituality* (pp. 262–284). West Conshohocken, PA: Templeton Foundation Press.

Juvoven, J. (2007). Reforming middle schools: Focus on continuity, social connectedness, and engagement. *Educational Psychologist, 42*(4), 197–208.

Kaestle, C. F. (1997). Historical methods in education. In J. P. Keeves (Ed.), *Educational research, methodology and measurement: An international handbook* (2nd ed.; pp. 75–81). New York, NY: Pergamon.

Kessler, R. (2000). *The soul of education: Helping students find connection, compassion, and character at school.* Alexandria, VA: Association for Supervision and Curriculum Development.

Kincheloe, J. L. (2001). Describing the bricolage: Conceptualizing a new rigor in qualitative research. *Qualitative Inquiry, 7*(6), 679–692.

Kincheloe, J. L. (2005). On to the next level: Continuing the conceptualization of the bricolage. *Qualitative Inquiry, 11*(3), 323–350.

Kincheloe, J. L. (2008). *Critical constructivism.* New York, NY: Peter Lang.

King, P. E., & Benson, P. L. (2006) Spiritual development and adolescent well-being and thriving. In E. C. Roehlkepartain, P. E. King, L. Wagener, & P. L. Benson (Eds.), *Handbook of spiritual development in childhood and adolescence* (pp. 384–398). Thousand Oaks, CA: Sage.

King, P. E., & Roeser, R. W. (2009). Religion and spirituality in adolescent development. In R. M. Lerner & L. Steinberg (Eds.), *Handbook of adolescent psychology* (3rd ed.; pp. 435–478). Hoboken, NJ: Wiley.

Knobel, M. (1999). *Everyday literacies: Students, discourse, and social practice.* New York, NY: Peter Lang.

Koenig, H. G., McCullough, M. E., & Larson, D. B. (2001). *Handbook of religion and health.* New York, NY: Oxford University Press.

Kohlberg, L. (1981). *Essays on moral development.* San Francisco, CA: Harper & Row.

Kuhn, T. S. (1996). *The structure of scientific revolutions* (3rd ed.). Chicago, IL: The University of Chicago Press.

Kuhn, T., Conant, J., & Haugeland, J. (2000). *The road since* Structure. Chicago, IL: University of Chicago Press.

Leavy, P. (2009). *Method meets art: Arts-based research practice.* New York, NY: Guilford Press.

Lee, V., & Smith, J. (1993). Effects of school restructuring on the achievement and engagement of middle-grade students. *Sociology of Education, 66*(3), 164–187.

Leithwood, K., Louis, K. S., Anderson, S., & Wahlstrom, K. (2004). *Executive summary: How leadership influences student learning*. Minneapolis, MN: University of Minnesota, Center for Applied Research and Educational Improvement.

Leopold, D., & Juniu, S. (2008). Incorporating a spiritual component into the health education aspects of a physical (activity) education program. *Physical Educator, 65*(4), 208–221.

Lerner, R. M. (2006). Developmental science, developmental systems, and contemporary theories of human development. In W. Damon (Series Ed.) & R. M. Lerner (Vol. Ed.), *Handbook of child psychology: Vol. 1. Theoretical Models of Human Development* (6th ed.; pp. 1–17). Hoboken, NJ: Wiley.

Lerner, R. M., Roeser, R. W., Phelps, E. (2008). Positive development, spirituality, and generosity in youth. In R. M. Lerner, R. W. Roeser, & E. Phelps (Eds.), *Positive youth development and spirituality* (pp. 3–24). West Conshohocken, PA: Templeton Foundation Press.

Lippman, L. H., & Keith, J. D. (2006). The demographics of spirituality among youth: International perspectives. In E. C. Roehlkepartain, P. E. King, L. Wagener, & P. L. Benson (Eds.), *Handbook of spiritual development in childhood and adolescence* (pp. 137–149). Thousand Oaks, CA: Sage.

Lohani, S., Singh, R. B., & Lohani, J. (2010). Universal primary education in Nepal: Fulfilling the right to education. *Prospects, 40*(3), 355–374.

Long, L. (2008). Narrative autoethnography and the promotion of spiritual well-being in teacher research and practice. *Pastoral Care in Education, 26*(3), 187–196.

Loukas, A., & Murphy, J. L. (2007). Middle school student perceptions of school climate: Examining protective functions on subsequent adjustment problems. *Journal of School Psychology, 45*(3), 293–309.

Lounsbury, J. H., & Vars, G. (1978). *A curriculum for the middle school years*. New York, NY: Harper & Row.

Lounsbury, J. H., & Vars, G. (2003). The future of middle level education: Optimistic and pessimistic views. *Middle School Journal, 35*(2), 6–14.

Maclean, M. J. (1982). Johann Gustav Droysen and the development of historical hermeneutics. *History and Theory, 21*(3), 347–365.

Macy, J. (1991). *Mutual causality in Buddhism and general systems theory: The dharma of natural systems*. Albany, NY: State University of New York Press.

Magnusson, D., & Cairns, R. B. (1996). Developmental science: Toward a unified framework. In R. B. Cairns, G. H. Elder, Jr., E. J. Costello, E. Jane (Eds.), *Developmental science: Cambridge studies in social and emotional development* (pp. 7–30). New York, NY: Cambridge University Press.

Malkin, J. (2003). In engaged Buddhism, peace begins with you. *Shambhala Sun*. Retrieved from: http://www.shambhalasun.com/index.php?option=content&task=view&id=1579.

Masterman, M. (1970). The nature of a paradigm. In I. Lakatos & A. Musgrave (Eds.), *Criticism and the growth of knowledge* (pp. 59–89). Cambridge, UK: Cambridge University Press.

Mattis, J. S., Ahluwalia, M. K., Cowie, S. E., & Kirkland-Harris, A. M. (2006). Ethnicity, culture, and spiritual development. In E. C. Roehlkepartain, P. E. King, L. Wagener, & P. L. Benson (Eds.), *Handbook of spiritual development in childhood and adolescence* (pp. 283–296). Thousand Oaks, CA: Sage.

McCullom v. Board of Education. 333 U.S. 203 (1948).

McEwin, C. K. (2013). Certification/licensure by state. In *Association of Middle Level Education: Professional Preparation.* Retrieved from: http://www.amle.org/AboutAMLE/ProfessionalPreparation/Certification-LicensurebyState.aspx

McLaren, P. (2009). Critical pedagogy: A look at the major concepts. In A. Darder, M. P. Baltodano, & R. Torres (Eds.), *The critical pedagogy reader* (pp. 61–83). New York, NY: Routledge.

Mertens, S. B., & Flowers, N. (2003). Middle school practices improve student achievement in high poverty schools. *Middle School Journal, 35*(1), 33–43.

Mezirow, J. (2000). *Learning as transformation.* San Francisco, CA: Jossey-Bass.

Miller, J. P. (2005). Introduction: Holistic learning. In J. P. Miller, S. Karsten, D. Denton, D. Orr, & I. Colalillo Kates (Eds.), *Holistic learning and spirituality on education* (pp. 1–6). Albany, NY: SUNY Press.

Miller, J. P. (2007). *The holistic curriculum* (2nd ed.). Toronto, ON: University of Toronto Press.

Miller, R. (1997). *What are schools for: Holistic education in American culture.* Brandon, VT: Holistic Education Press.

Miller, R. (1999). Holistic education for an emerging culture. In S. Glazer (Ed.), *The heart of learning: Spirituality in education* (pp. 189–202). New York, NY: Penguin Putnam.

Milojevic, I. (2005). Critical spirituality as a resource for fostering critical pedagogy. *Journal of Future Studies, 9*(3), 1–16.

Muijs, D. (2011). *Doing quantitative research in education with SPSS.* Los Angeles, CA: Sage.

Mulhall, P. F. (2007). Health promoting, high performing middle level schools: The interrelationships and integration of health and education for young adolescent success and well-being. In S. B. Mertens, V. A. Anfara, Jr., & M.M. Caskey, (Eds.), *The young adolescent and the middle school* (pp. 1–26). Westerville, OH & Charlotte, NC: National Middle School Association and Information Age.

Nakagawa, Y. (2000). *Education for awakening: An eastern approach to holistic education.* Volume Two of the Foundations of Holistic Education Series. Brandon, VT: Foundation for Educational Renewal.

Nakkula, M. J., & Ravich, S. M. (1998). *Matters of interpretation: Reciprocal transformation in therapeutic and developmental relationships with youth.* San Francisco, CA: Jossey-Bass.

Nakkula, M. J., & Toshalis, E. (2006). *Understanding youth: Adolescent development for educators.* Cambridge, MA: Harvard Education Press.

National Association of Secondary School Principals. (2006). *Breaking ranks in the middle: Strategies for leading middle level reform.* Reston, VA: Author.

National Forum to Accelerate Middle Grades Reform. (n.d.). Vision and mission. Retrieved from: http://www.middlegradesforum.org/index.php/about/vision-mission.

National Middle School Association. (2010). *This we believe: Keys to educating young adolescents.* Westerville, OH. Author.

Nicholas, G., & DeSilva, A. M. (2008). Application of the ecological model: Spirituality research with ethnically diverse youth. In R. M. Lerner, R. W. Roeser, & E. Phelps (Eds.), *Positive youth development and spirituality* (pp. 305–321). West Conshohocken, PA: Templeton Foundation Press.

Nichols, S. (2008). An exploration of students' belongingness beliefs in one middle school. *The Journal of Experimental Education, 76*(2), 145–169.

Niederman, R. (1999). *The conceptualization of a model of spirituality.* (Unpublished doctoral dissertation). University of Georgia, Athens, GA.

Noddings, N. (1988). *An ethics of caring and its implications for instructional arrangements.* Stanford, CA: CERAS, School of Education, Stanford University Press.

Noddings, N. (2005). *The challenge to care in schools: An alternative approach to education.* New York, NY: Teachers College Press.

Novoa, A., & Yariv-Mashal, T. (2003). Comparative research in education: A mode of governance or a historical journey? *Comparative Education, 39*(4), 423–438.

Orr, D. W. (1990). The liberal arts, the campus, and the biosphere. *Harvard Education Review, 60*(2), 205–216.

Orr, D. W. (1992). *Ecological literacy: Education and the transition to the postmodern world.* Albany, NY: State University of New York Press.

Orr, D. J. (2005). Minding the soul in education: Conceptualizing and teaching the whole person. In J. P. Miller, S. Karsten, D. Denton, D. Orr, & I. Colalillo Kates (Eds.), *Holistic learning and spirituality on education* (pp. 87–99). Albany, NY: SUNY Press.

Oser, F. (1991). The development of religious judgment. In F. K. Oser & W. G. Scarlett (Eds.), *Religious development in childhood and adolescence* (pp. 5–25). San Francisco, CA: Jossey-Bass.

Oser, F. W., Scarlett, W. G., & Bucher, A. (2006). Religion and spiritual development throughout the lifespan. In W. Damon & R. M. Lerner (Series Eds.) & R. M. Lerner (Volume Ed.), *Handbook of child psychology*, vol. 1: *Theoretical models of human development* (6th ed.; pp. 942–998). Hoboken, NJ: Wiley.

Osterman, K. F. (2000). Students' need for belonging in the school community. *Review of Educational Research, 70*, 323–367.

Owen Wilson, L. (2005). Listening to ancient voices: Reaching hearts and souls through benchmarks and rites of passage experiences in schools. In J. P.

Miller, S. Karsten, D. Denton, D. Orr, & I. Colalillo Kates (Eds.), *Holistic learning and spirituality on education* (pp. 167–177). Albany, NY: SUNY Press.

Palmer, P. (1997). The grace of great things: Reclaiming the sacred in knowing, teaching, and learning. In S. Glazer (Ed.), *The heart of learning: Spirituality in education* (pp. 15–32). New York, NY: Penguin Putnam.

Palmer, P. (1998). *Courage to teach: Exploring the inner lives of teachers.* San Francisco, CA: Jossey Bass.

Parker, A., Allen, D., Alvarez McHatton, P., & Rosa, L. (2010). Dance lessons: Preparing preservice teachers for coteaching partnerships. *Action in Teacher Education, 32*(1), 26–38.

Pearmain, R. (2005). Transformational experiences in young people: The meaning of a safe haven. *International Journal of Children's Spirituality, 10*(3), 277–290.

Pew Forum on Religion and Public Life. (2008). *U.S. religious landscape survey.* Washington, DC: Pew Research Center.

Piaget, J. (1967). *Six psychological studies.* New York, NY: Random House.

Popkewitz, T. (1991). *A political sociology of educational reform: Power/knowledge in teaching, teacher education, and research.* New York, NY: Teachers College Press.

Popkewitz, T. S. (1997). A changing terrain of knowledge and power: A social epistemology of educational research. *Educational Researcher, 26*(9), 18–29.

Popkewitz, T. S., & Brennan, M. (1998). Restructuring of social and political theory in education: Foucault and a social epistemology of school practices. In T. S. Popkewitz & M. Brennan (Eds.), *Foucault's challenge: Discourse, knowledge, and power in education* (pp. 3–35). New York, NY: Teachers College Press.

Purpel, D. E. (1999). Moral outrage and education. In T. Kane (Ed.), *Education, transformation, and transformation* (pp. 57–75). Columbus, OH: Merrill.

Revell, L. (2008). Spiritual development in public and religious schools: A case study. *Religious Education, 103*(1), 102–118.

Roehlkepartain, E. C., Benson, P. L., King, P. E., & Wagener, L. (2006). Spiritual development in childhood and adolescence: Moving to the scientific mainstream. In E. C. Roehlkepartain, P. E. King, L. Wagener, & P. L. Benson (Eds.), *Handbook of spiritual development in childhood and adolescence* (pp. 1–15). Thousand Oaks, CA: Sage.

Roeser, R., Eccles, J., & Sameroff, A. (2000). School as a context of early adolescents' academic and socio-emotional development: A summary of research findings. *The Elementary School Journal, 100*(5), 443–471.

Roney, K., Coleman, H., & Schlichting, K. (2007). Linking the organizational health of middle grades schools to student achievement. *NASSP Bulletin, 91*(4), 289–321.

Rury, J. L. (2006). Historical research in education. In J. L. Greene, G. Camilli, & P. B. Elmore (Eds.), *Handbook of complementary methods in educational research* (pp. 323–332). Mahwah, NJ: Erlbaum.

Ryoo, J. J., Crawford, J., Moreno, D., & McLaren P. (2009). Critical spiritual pedagogy: Reclaiming humanity through a pedagogy of integrity, community, and love. *Power and Education, 1*(1), 132–146.

Sadowski, M. (2008). *Adolescents at school: Perspectives on youth, identity, and education.* Cambridge, MA: Harvard Education Press.

Said, E. (1993). *Culture and imperialism.* New York, NY: Knopf.

Sallquist, J., Eisenberg, N., French, D. C., Purwono, U., & Suryanti, T. A. (2010). Indonesian adolescents' spiritual and religious experiences and their longitudinal relations with socioemotional functioning. *Developmental Psychology, 46*(3), 699–716.

Sarason, S. B. (1982). *The culture of school and the problem of change* (2nd ed.). Boston, MA: Allyn and Bacon.

Scales, P., Benson, P. L., Leffert, N., & Blyth, D. A. (2000). The contribution of developmental assets to the prediction of thriving among adolescents. *Applied Developmental Science, 4*(1), 27–46.

Schoonmaker, F. (2009). Only those who see take off their shoes: Seeing the classroom as a spiritual space. *Teachers College Record, 111*(12), 2713–2731.

Scott, D. G. (2006). Spirituality and identity within/without religion. In M. de Souza, G. Durka, K. Engebretson, R. Jackson, & A. McGrady (Eds.), *International handbook of the religious, moral and spiritual dimensions in education* (pp. 1111–1125). Dordrecht, The Netherlands: Springer.

Scott, J., & Marshall, G. (2009). "historiography" A Dictionary of Sociology. Oxford Reference Online. Oxford University Press. Retrieved from: http://www.oxfordreference.com/views/ENTRY.html?subview=Main&entry=t88.e1015

Search Institute. (2011a). Engaging international advisors in creating a shared understanding of spiritual development. Retrieved from: http://www.search-institute.org/csd/major-projects/definition-update

Search Institute. (2011b). What are developmental assets? Retrieved from: http://www.search-institute.org/content/what-are-developmental-assets

Sherrod, L. R., & Spiewak, G. S. (2008). Possible interrelationships between civic engagement, positive youth development, and spirituality/religiosity. In R. M. Lerner, R. W. Roeser, & E. Phelps (Eds.), *Positive youth development and spirituality* (pp. 322–338). West Conshohocken, PA: Templeton Foundation Press.

Simmer-Brown, J. (1999). Commitment and openness: A contemplative approach to pluralism. In S. Glazer (Ed.), *The heart of learning: Spirituality in education* (pp. 97–112). New York, NY: Penguin Putnam.

Skinner, B. F. (1987). *Upon further reflection.* Englewood Cliffs, NJ: Prentice-Hall.

Smith, A. (2003). Historiography. In G. Campbell (Ed.), *The Oxford Encyclopedia of Food and Drink in America*. Oxford University Press. Retrieved from http://www.oxfordreference.com/views/ENTRY.html?subview=Main&entry=t 170.e0397

Smith, T. W., & McEwin, C. K. (2011). *The legacy of middle school leaders: In their own words*. Charlotte, NC: Information Age.

Stoyles, G. J., Stanford, B., Caputi, P., Keating, A., & Hyde, B. (2012). A measure of spiritual sensitivity for children. *International Journal of Children's Spirituality, 17*(3), 203–215.

Strauss, A., & Corbin, J. (1998). *Basics of qualitative research*. Thousand Oaks, CA: Sage.

Tacey, D. (2006). Spirituality as a bridge to religion and faith. In M. de Souza, G. Durka, K. Engebretson, R. Jackson, & A. McGrady (Eds.), *International handbook of the religious, moral and spiritual dimensions in education* (pp. 201–213). Dordrecht, The Netherlands: Springer.

Tart, C. (1986). *Waking up: The obstacles to human potential*. Boston, MA: New Science Library.

Thayer-Bacon, B., & Moyer, D. (2006). Philosophical and historical research. In K. Tobin & J. L. Kincheloe (Eds.), *Doing educational research* (pp. 139–156). Rotterdam, The Netherlands: Sense.

Toepfer, C. F. (2011). Conrad F. Toepfer, Jr. In T. W. Smith & C. K. McEwin (Eds.), *The legacy of middle school leaders: In their own words* (pp. 53–69). Charlotte, NC: Information Age.

Vagle, M. D. (2012). *Not a stage: A critical re-conception of young adolescent education*. New York, NY: Peter Lang.

Van Hoose, J., Strahan, D., & L'Esperance, M. (2001). *Promoting harmony: Young adolescent development and school practices*. Westerville, OH: National Middle School Association.

Van Rooyen, B. M. (2007). *Spiritual well-being in a group of South African adolescents*. (Unpublished doctoral dissertation). University of the Free State, Bloemfontein, South Africa.

Villaverde, L., Kincheloe, J. L., & Helyar, F. (2006). Historical research in education. In K. Tobin & J. L. Kincheloe (Eds.), *Doing educational research.* (pp. 311–345). Rotterdam, The Netherlands: Sense.

Walker, A., & Shuangye, C. (2007). Leader authenticity in intercultural school contexts. *Educational Management Administration and Leadership, 35*(2), 185–204.

Warren, A. E. A., Lerner, R., & Phelps, E. (2012). *Thriving and spirituality among youth: Research perspectives and future possibilities*. Hoboken, NJ: Wiley.

Webster, R. S. (2013). Healing the physical/spiritual divide through a holistic and hermeneutic approach to education. *International Journal of Children's Spirituality, 17*(1), 1–12.

Wilber, K. (2000). *A theory of everything: An integral vision for business, politics, science, and spirituality*. Boston, MA: Shambhala.

William-White, L. (2013). Introduction: The current historic moment. In L. William-White, D. Muccular, G. Muccular, & A. F. Brown, (Eds.), *Critical consciousness in curricular research: Evidence from the field* (pp. 2-11). New York, NY: Peter Lang.

Wintersgill, B. (2008). Teenagers' perceptions of spirituality—A research report. *International Journal of Children's Spirituality, 13*(4), 371–378.

Wolcott, H. F. (2001). *Writing up qualitative research* (2nd ed.). Thousands Oaks, CA: Sage.

Wolcott, H. F. (2008). *Ethnography: A way of seeing*. Lanham, MD: Altamira Press.

Woolley, M., & Bowen, G. (2007, January). In the context of risk: Supportive adults and the school engagement of middle school students. *Family Relations, 56*(1), 92–104.

Yin, R. K. (2009). *Case study research: Design and methods*. Thousand Oaks, CA: Sage.

Zeichner, K. (1999). The new scholarship in teacher education. *Educational Researcher, 28*(9), 4–15.

critical qualitative research

Shirley R. Steinberg & Gaile S. Cannella, *General Editors*

The Critical Qualitative Research series examines societal structures that oppress and exclude so that transformative actions can be generated. This transformed research is activist in orientation. Because the perspective accepts the notion that nothing is apolitical, research projects themselves are critically examined for power orientations, even as they are used to address curricular, educational, or societal issues.

This methodological work challenges modernist orientations and universalist impositions, asking critical questions like: Who/what is heard? Who/what is silenced? Who is privileged? Who is disqualified? How are forms of inclusion and exclusion being created? How are power relations constructed and managed? How do different forms of privilege and oppression intersect to affect educational, societal, and life possibilities for various individuals and groups?

We are particularly interested in manuscripts that offer critical examinations of curriculum, policy, public communities, and the ways in which language, discourse practices, and power relations prevent more just transformations.

For additional information about this series or for the submission of manuscripts, please contact:
Shirley R. Steinberg and Gaile S. Cannella
msgramsci@aol.com | Gaile.Cannella@unt.edu

To order other books in this series, please contact our Customer Service Department:
(800) 770-LANG (within the U.S.)
(212) 647-7706 (outside the U.S.)
(212) 647-7707 FAX

Or browse online by series:
www.peterlang.com